ACT AND IMAGE

HOW DID HUMANS DEVELOP THE CAPACITY FOR SYMBOL IMAGINATION?

In this groundbreaking book, **Warren Colman** provides a reformulation of archetypal symbols as emergent from humans' engagement with their social and material environment. This view is rooted in a phenomenological perspective that sees psychic life as emergent from embodied action in the world. How then might humans first have developed the capacity for symbolic imagination, epitomised by the oldest known figurative image in the world, the 40,000 year old Lion Man of Hohlenstein-Stadel in Germany? Colman traces the emergence of symbolic imagination through the origins of language, the growth of human sociality and cooperation, and the creative use of material objects from the earliest use of stone tools through the first flowering of figurative imagery in the cave paintings and figurines of Upper Paleolithic Europe. Drawing on recent developments in cognitive archaeology, he argues that the social use of material objects play an active role in the constitution of symbols which enact a distinctively human imaginal mind. This leads to a consideration of how the imaginal world of the spirit may have come into being, not as separate from the material world but through active participation within a world that is alive with meaning. Thus, the psychic, social, and physical aspects of our being are all part of one world which, for humans, is always a symbolic world.

PRAISE FOR *ACT AND IMAGE*

As recent editor of the *Journal of Analytical Psychology*, Colman is well qualified to write such a book. He starts with the relatively modest aim of critically exploring Jung's theory of archetypes, but in doing so he persuasively sets out the theoretical foundations of depth psychology. Integrating research and thinking from neighboring fields, including developmental psychology, neuroscience, linguistics, and social anthropology, he effectively brings the fundamentals of analytical psychology up to date. Colman's book reminds me of the pioneering writings in the traditions known as phenomenology and philosophical anthropology, but it is rare for a book to be philosophically rigorous and at the same time accessible, clear, and empirically grounded. I hope that this book will have the influence it deserves.

—**Roger Brooke**, Professor of Psychology, Duquesne University, and author of *Jung and Phenomenology*

With characteristic lucidity, Warren Colman's *Act and Image* draws together a wealth of material from psychology, philosophy, and anthropology to both challenge and enlarge our understanding of the basic elements of C. G. Jung's system. His discussion of the central role of affective response to the symbolic is grounded in a thorough and wide-ranging command of sources rarely encountered in the psychoanalytic or Jungian literature. Colman's book will be essential reading for anyone venturing into the ongoing discussion of the theory of archetypes, the collective unconscious, and the nature of symbolism in analytical psychology.

—**George B. Hogenson**, Ph.D., LCSW, Jungian analyst and author of *Jung's Struggle with Freud*

Drawing on ideas from an impressively wide range of disciplines, Colman questions established ways of envisioning the collective unconscious, and re-visions it as emerging from our species' evolved capacity for symbolic thinking. As part of this re-visioning, Colman deconstructs the Cartesian, archetypal, and hierarchical view of the psyche, and instead sees the psyche as developing out of our embodied, relational and cultural nature. Colman's argument is audacious, layered, complex, and thought-provoking; it is a quest to understand the human psyche within a more modern framework and challenges readers to see themselves through fresh eyes.

—**Daniela F. Sieff**, D. Phil, and author of *Understanding and Healing Emotional Trauma: Conversations with Pioneering Clinicians and Researchers*

Act and Image is a rich and vital addition to the Jungian literature. Colman guides the reader through a sophisticated and in-depth reappraisal of several central Jungian concepts—archetype, image, symbol, and imagination. Drawing from philosophy, phenomenology, archaeology, and anthropology, he invites the reader to critically reflect on commonly held assumptions regarding the relationship between the mind, archetypes, symbols, and imagination. *Act and Image* is an intellectual tour de force which will reverberate throughout the field of Analytical Psychology. Highly recommended!

Mark Winborn, Ph.D., Jungian psychoanalyst, clinical psychologist, and author of *Deep Blues: Human Soundscapes for the Archetypal Journey* and *Shared Realities: Participation Mystique and Beyond*

First published 2016 by Spring Journal Books

Published 2020 by Routledge
2 Park Square, Milton Park, Abingdon, Oxon OX14 4RN
52 Vanderbilt Avenue, New York, NY 10017

Routledge is an imprint of the Taylor & Francis Group, an informa business

British Library Cataloguing-in-Publication Data
A catalogue record for this book is available from the British Library

Library of Congress Cataloging-in-Publication Data
A catalog record has been requested for this book

ISBN: 978-0-367-86267-1 (hbk)
ISBN: 978-0-367-86268-8 (pbk)
ISBN: 978-1-003-01805-6 (ebk)

Technical Assistance Provided by:
Erica Mattingly
eemattingly@gmail.com
Northern Graphic Design & Publishing
info@ncarto.com

Cover Image: "Lion Man" statuette carved of mammoth-tusk, ivory, height 311 mm, maximum width 73 mm. Discovered at the site of Hohlenstein-Stadel-cave, township Asselfingen, district Alb-Donau, Baden-Wuerttemberg, Germany. Upper Paleolithic period (Aurignacien), approximately 40000–35000 BP. Photographic credits:Yvonne Mühleis, © 2016, Ulmer Museum/ Landesamt für Denkmalpflege Baden-Württemberg. Used with permission.

*To my Jewish ancestors
God rest their dear souls*

ACT AND IMAGE

THE EMERGENCE OF
SYMBOLIC IMAGINATION

WARREN COLMAN

Routledge
Taylor & Francis Group

LONDON AND NEW YORK

TABLE OF CONTENTS

ACKNOWLEDGEMENTS

When Murray Stein asked me if I would like to write a book, he was making me an offer I couldn't refuse. I had been talking about writing a book for so long I'd almost given up believing it would ever happen. I have never been able to motivate myself to carve out the time required for writing without an externally imposed deadline, so everything I have written and published has been produced for a lecture, a conference, or a chapter in someone else's book. Murray's invitation for me to be the speaker in the Zürich Lecture Series in 2104 with a book deal tie-in offered by Spring Publications was therefore a tailor-made opportunity. Without Murray and Nancy Cater, the Editor of Spring, this book would never have happened.

The other person who made this book possible is Sue Colman. She, and the rest of my family, have willingly and uncomplainingly put up with me being continually unavailable at weekends for well over a year, with nothing but encouragement and support. To cap it all, she proofread the entire manuscript, picking up my haphazard punctuation and pointing out several unwieldy sentences where my enthusiasm for just one more clause had got the better of me.

Although most authors seem to discuss their work with many colleagues, I generally prefer to work alone until I have my ideas reasonably well-sorted out. I am grateful, though, to those who have read some of the draft chapters, particularly Jean Knox, George Hogenson, and Richard Carvalho who spared me the mortification of having misrepresented their work and ideas. Any remaining errors are, of course, my own responsibility. Jan Wiener and Isabel de Salis also read draft chapters and made helpful suggestions, the latter on the basis of no more personal acquaintance than a very enjoyable lunch after I gave a paper based on the book in Bristol in December 2014. So, thanks to Jen Madden for inviting me.

Elizabeth Urban spent an evening with me, discussing her extensive knowledge of the development of symbolic thinking in early childhood for what I had expected to be the second half of the book but which never materialized. Her interest in my work and generosity in sharing her own was nevertheless much appreciated. Peter Amman offered encouragement in Zürich and gave me a copy of his film, *The Spirit of the Rocks*, which enhanced my understanding of the world of those who created South African Rock Art. Steve Slann and Annushka Shani have also proved stimulating interlocutors who really seemed to get what I was trying to say.

Of course many people's ideas contribute to the development of one's own, but two colleagues further afield have been particularly influential: Roger Brooke and Joe Cambray. Roger Brooke's work on phenomenology laid the ground for much of my own approach over twenty years before I belatedly stumbled into phenomenology and realized it was what I had been looking for all along. My dialogue with Joe Cambray following a conference at which we both spoke about synchronicity opened my eyes to the way I was still caught in a Cartesian mind-set that divided mind from world. I think where I have ended up is different from where Joe is coming from but I might not have got there without him.

On a less personal note, the research for this book would have been impossible without the amazing possibilities of the Internet. As an independent scholar without access to the resources of an online library, I have had to rely on what I can download for free— it turned out to be far more than I could have expected or hoped for. Google Books also provided access to books I only wanted to browse and then, when I needed more, I joined the British Library where I spent a few blissful days in their Social Science Reading Room, feeling like a real scholar.

Finally, I would like to thank those academics and researchers whom I have never met but who have been my intellectual companions, guides, and inspirational heroes over the past couple of years of thinking and writing. Colin Renfrew's book *Prehistory: The Making of the Human Mind* kick-started the whole journey when I read it on a plane to Moscow in 2011. His work on cognitive archaeology took me to Lambros Malafouris and John Searle. I then discovered Michael Tomasello's book *Origins of Human Communication* and was convinced by his elegant and scientifically rigorous arguments for the origin of language. More recently, I came across Tim Ingold who opened up the world-view of hunter-gatherers and spoke to my own questionings about the Cartesian mind-set. All these and many more bear out the contention of this book that we are all enmeshed in a web of world-wide social-symbolic communication that now includes but goes far beyond the technological capacities of our computers.

INTRODUCTION

This book may surprise those readers who know my previous work which has mainly been concerned with the clinical practice of analysis. Here I branch out far beyond clinical work into an investigation of the origins of the human capacity for symbolic thinking, making very few references to psychotherapy and even less to child development. The reason for this is that what I naively expected to take up only the first half of the book, in fact, turned out to fill an entire book and, even then, to have only scratched the surface of the wide-ranging areas in which I became embroiled, including the philosophy of mind, phenomenology, archaeology, and anthropology.

As a non-professional in all these fields, I have sometimes felt that the task I have set before myself is wildly over-ambitious. I have tried to deal with this by providing accurate and accessible accounts of the many theories I have drawn on which I hope will demonstrate why I think they are important to the way we think about the mind. I hope too that I will have succeeded in conveying my own fascination for the many aspects of the emergence of the human species in a way that will interest and engage my readers as much as they have engaged and interested me. My conclusions are inevitably tentative and provisional due to the vast complexity of the subject matter, the limitations of my own knowledge, and, in relation to the archaeological material, the patchiness of the available evidence.

Of course, there is an obvious precedent for a Jungian analyst to range across so many other disciplines in the quest for psyche; it is the precedent set by Jung himself. Like many others, it was just this breadth of vision in Jung's work that attracted me to analytical psychology in the first place in preference to Freudian psychoanalysis. As much as I admire Freud and use psychoanalytic ideas in my work, I resonate with Jung's description of its constricting atmosphere and narrow outlook.[1] Freud's theoretical model has proved much more dynamic and flexible than Jung's and has led to far greater theoretical diversity and development. Yet there is a sense that most psychoanalysts rarely stray far from home when they attempt to address the larger questions posed by the psychoanalytic theory of the mind but tend to draw everything else into the psychoanalytic net. Where Freud deploys his considerable rhetorical skills to assure his readers that no conclusion other than his own is really possible, Jung is far more open, his work a sprawling, disorganized canvas recording his many forays into areas as diverse as anthropology, theology, alchemy, Gnosticism, quantum physics, and astrology.

We now know that Jung made many errors in his use of other disciplines, although I am inclined to see the liberties he took with his sources as more akin to art than science. Like an artist, Jung uses the work of others as material to construct his own grand vision. If this was his greatness, I am far from claiming to emulate him in following up some of the areas in which he was interested. Rather I am drawn to a cast of mind that seeks to explore widely and think deeply about the "big questions" of life, such as "Where do we come from?" and "What sort of thing is the mind?" no matter how modest the results of my own questionings.

Being a "Jungian" in this sense does not mean slavishly going over the same ground that Jung opened up. That way lie only stagnation, starvation, and death as the world moves on around us and we paddle further and further up a backwater of academic discourse becoming increasingly cut off from our erstwhile neighbors. Jung drew on the ideas of his time and as time goes on, these ideas become increasingly outdated. So rather than attempting to shore up Jung's original theories by cherry-picking anything that looks vaguely familiar (innate modules, Chomsky's grammar, etc.), a more radical way of following Jung is to pursue his areas of interest in a modern context. With the exception of my discussion of nineteenth century anthropology in Chapters 7 and 8, none of the theories on which I draw were extant during Jung's lifetime and, even in the course of my own career, once familiar ideas such as "libido" and "instinct," to say nothing of the now entirely discredited notion of "the primitive," have become increasingly antiquated. So my aim is to open avenues of research that might throw light on the kinds of things that led Jung to formulate the idea of archetypes in the first place. The question of "where symbols come from" must certainly be a key aspect of that enquiry.

When I gave the Zürich Lectures on which this book is based, I was surprised to discover that my audience seemed relatively unconcerned by this question. They seemed to more or less take the existence of archetypes for granted and to use them as heuristic and teleological devices without necessarily being concerned as to their origins one way or another. My impression was that, for those living and working in what is still the spiritual ancestral home of Jungian psychology, archetypes are not so much a hypothesis as a living reality that provides orientation and meaning for the practice of psychotherapy and living in general. To my mind, this illustrates the function of symbols; rather than archetypes being a hypothesis *about* the origin of symbols, they have become symbolic images in themselves. This is an example of what I discuss in Chapter 5 as constitutive symbols and which, in Chapter 8, I link with Lévy-Bruhl's use of Durkheim's notion of collective representations.

The encounter with the classical archetypal perspective in Zürich also made me aware of my own perspective as a developmentalist. Even though there is virtually nothing in this book about developmental psychology in the way it is usually understood, the developmental perspective shapes and informs the way I approach psychology and the kinds of questions I ask. It seems natural to me to ask "Where did it come from and how did it develop?" as a way of understanding something. My audience in Zürich, who do not share this perspective, was able to provide one of those valuable, yet all too rare experiences in which we are able to see our own assumptions from the outside. Normally, we are all ensconced within our own way of seeing things which becomes "natural" and taken for granted. Reality is always elusive and at best partial. This, too, I would understand in terms of collective representations. Since we cannot think without a system of collective symbolic representations to think with, no mode of thought can be separated from the sociological context in which it occurs.

This last point touches on another perspective which informs my thinking: a longstanding interest in the relation between psyche and society. As an undergraduate, I was interested in psychology and philosophy but, in English universities at that time, both disciplines were dominated by positivist assumptions which meant that they deliberately ignored the things that really mattered to me such as the nature of consciousness, what made people the way they were and what, after all, was the meaning and purpose of it all? So I got my psychology (and my interest in symbols) from studying English and my philosophy from studying Sociology which gave me an abiding perspective on how people are shaped by social factors as well as psychological ones. But how do the two relate and intertwine? Where does psyche end and society begin? Forty years later, I feel I have at last been able to make some inroads into this problem by taking up a phenomenological approach that breaks down the Cartesian divide between the mind and the world. In particular, in Chapter 3, I arrive at the conclusion that psychic facts are social facts since we are all continually immersed in social being and cannot exist as psychological individuals except in and through our participation in a social and material world. Throughout the book, my approach is informed by this implicitly sociological perspective; I see human consciousness and symbolic imagination as emergent from the social organization and material engagement of early hominins which have "scaffolded" the imaginative possibilities that fill our mental worlds today, from the great creations of art, religion, and science to the innermost recesses of our most private dreaming.

I begin the book with the oldest figurative image in the world—the Lion Man of Hohlenstein-Stadel, now thought to be in the region of 40,000 years old. In the prologue I show how the Lion Man might be understood within Jung's proposition of a collective unconscious and how this has been thrown into question by the reconfiguration of archetypes as emergent rather than pre-existent. This issue is explored in detail in Chapter 1, where I discuss the various theoretical problems and contradictions in archetype theory that have been pointed out by numerous commentators before me. Over the past fifteen years or so, archetype theory has been reconfigured in terms of emergence theories, notably by Jean Knox and George Hogenson. In view of this, I argue that the notion of archetype has become redundant since emergent forms cannot properly be described with a term that, by definition, refers to pre-existent forms.

Hogenson's work becomes the starting point for the exploration of a radically expanded view of the mind in Chapter 2. I begin by placing this in the context of the philosophical debates between idealism and materialism subsequent to Descartes and go on to describe a range of approaches that aim to break down the Cartesian divide between mind and matter, most of which situate mind in the context of action within a species-specific environment which, for humans, is primarily the symbolic environment of culture. This is one reason for the book's title: *Act and Image*. Images emerge in and through action in the world.

Chapters 3 and 4 trace the possible evolutionary trajectories for the emergence of symbolic thought and action from our common ancestor with chimpanzees, our closest living relative on the hominid family tree.[2] Chapter 3 looks at the origins of language, fantasy, and sociality through studies of what chimpanzees (and bonobos) can and cannot do. I am particularly interested in the work of Michael Tomasello who roots the origins of language in the development of "shared intentionality" creating a social basis for what Stephen Levinson calls "the human interaction engine."[3] This approach emphasizes the social nature of symbolic communication which resonates with the notion of an extended mind developed in Chapter 2. In Chapter 4, I turn to archaeology and paleontology and describe current understandings of the evolution of the human species from the earliest use of stone tools 2.5 million years ago to the use of symbolic objects in the form of shell bead necklaces and other forms of personal ornamentation from around 100,000 years ago. Where Chapter 3 is focused on sociality, Chapter 4 is focused on the role of material engagement in shaping the mind, drawing on the relatively new discipline of cognitive archaeology.

Chapter 5 is perhaps the centre-point of the work since it is here that I propose an alternative to archetypes as an explanatory theory, drawing on John Searle's work on the construction of social reality through the use of constitutive symbols. The idea that symbols constitute the realities they represent underscores the basic theme of the book—that the mind is constituted in and through social living in a symbolically-enriched cultural environment. Crucially, the way that constitutive symbols work also offers a means of underpinning the reality of psyche without needing to posit an "objective psyche," thus breaking through the subjective-objective barrier, rooting psyche in the social and material world, and allowing for different perspectives on the world which may be equally real.

By this point, I am ready to return to the apparent explosion of figurative creativity in the first *Homo sapiens* to settle in Europe in the period known as the Upper Paleolithic, beginning around 40,000 years ago. This is the starting point for Chapter 6, but it was here that the book really began to take off in a direction I had not expected. I found myself drawn deeper into anthropological studies due to the fact that the nearest comparison we have available today is the world of hunter-gatherers. What became immediately apparent is that peoples living in oral nomadic cultures have very different ways of thinking, feeling, and being in the world: for them the world is alive with a quality that in our literate, urbanized world has come to be known as "spirit." So here I found myself returning to one of Jung's abiding concerns—the alienation of modern Western society from a sense of spiritual rootedness in the world. Having rejected the notion of universal pre-existing archetypes "in the mind" as the explanation for the ubiquity of spiritual symbolism, Chapter 6 suggests an alternative explanation that develops the idea of *extended mind as extended affectivity*. I contend that symbolic imagination is an expression of the way in which we formulate our emotional connection to those aspects of the living world that have the most importance to us. This occurs through the means of constitutive symbols emergent from shared activity in the context of collective intentionality.

In the course of this investigation, I became immersed in the various ways that imaginal thinking differs from rational thinking. Chapter 7 looks at the various ways these two kinds of thinking have been elaborated in psychoanalytic theory, starting with Jung's own contrast between directed and non-directed thinking in his 1912 work *The Psychology of the Unconscious*. In the final chapter (Chapter 8) I turn to an unlikely source for my own theoretical model: Lévy-Bruhl's often discredited and misunderstood notion of *participation mystique*. I argue that Jung lost the most valuable aspect of Lévy-Bruhl by "psychologizing" his idea, thereby making it a purely internal process "inside" the mind of the individual. Properly understood, and shorn of its evolutionist assumptions about the "primitive," *participation mystique* offers a powerful model for a non-Cartesian way of being in a world that is enlivened and enlivening through our material and social engagements within it.

Finally, a note on the bibliography: When references are given in footnotes, it can be hard to find the original citation for a subsequent occurrence of the same reference. In order to make this easier, I have included a bibliography that includes all citations that occur in more than one place in the book.

PROLOGUE

Sometime in the past 100,000 years or so our early modern human ancestors began to use their increasingly sophisticated grasp of tool-making to fashion objects with no immediate practical purpose in terms of subsistence survival. These objects were made of shells, and must have been used for body decoration since they are all perforated with a punched hole. Together with the use of red ochre, probably for a similar purpose, they are amongst the earliest indications of the use of material objects for symbolic purposes. Such discoveries in the Blombos caves in South Africa and the Skhul and Qafzeh caves in Israel have pushed back the time-scale for the emergence of fully modern human behavior by some 50,000 years or so. Until quite recently, it was believed that modern human behavior first occurred in the "creative explosion" associated with the arrival of Cro-Magnons into Europe around 40,000 years ago. The spectacular discoveries of cave art at Lascaux, Altamira, and Chauvet—the latter discovered as recently as 1994—appeared to provide ample evidence for this view.

Yet, although they can no longer be regarded as the earliest fully modern humans, the Aurignacian peoples who made the cave paintings at Chauvet are still the first humans known to have made figurative representations of animals and humans. Currently, the oldest of these are small figurines carved from mammoth tusks discovered in the Swabian caves of Hohle Fels and Hohlenstein-Stadel in Germany. The so-called Venus of Hohle Fels is the oldest known representation of a human figure to date. Discovered in 2009, it is thought to be almost 40,000 years old. With its huge breasts, enlarged buttocks, and prominent vulva, this is certainly not a direct representation of a human body. It does not have a head but instead features a carefully carved ring above its shoulders suggesting that it was worn as a pendant. Whatever its meaning and purpose, its non-representational form indicates that amongst the many newly emerging skills and abilities of these peoples was a capacity for imagination—the transformation of what is given, present, and visible into a new form shaped by the activity of the human mind. Whether we should call this "art" is another matter since it is unlikely that our modern notion of "art" bears much relation to the actions and purposes of these ancient human societies.

An even more conclusive example of the transformative activity of imagination is to be found in the famous lion-headed statuette of a human figure found in the same area at the Hohlenstein Stadel cave. This too has recently been dated to 40,000 years old.[1] The Lion Man, or, to give its German name, *der Löwenmensch*, was painstakingly reconstructed from fragments of mammoth ivory tusk that had been gathered up by Robert Wetzel just before the outbreak of World War II.[2] Due to the intervention of the war they were not worked on until over thirty years later when Dr. Joachim Hahn succeeded in putting together over 200 of the fragments to reconstruct the standing figure of a human with an animal head. Only in 1989 did the discovery of further fragments show that the head was that of a lion. In her book *Ice Age Art* written to accompany a British Museum exhibition of 2013, Jill Cook writes that the Lion Man is

> indicative of a mind capable of imaging new concepts rather than simply reproducing real forms. ... [S]uch a mind must indicate the activity of a complex super-brain like our own, with a well-developed pre-frontal cortex powering the capacity to communicate ideas in speech and art.[3]

Nor was this the work of some idle caveman whittling away a tusk in his spare time. The positioning of the figure within the tusk shows that "the maker deliberately selected a portion of tusk suitable for a preconceived work."[4] A reconstruction of the figure using the kind of stone tools available to the original maker showed that the total time required to create the original might be almost 400 hours. So it is likely that the maker lived in a community with enough division of labor to provide him or her with subsistence while making it which, in turn, would imply that the making of such an object was a socially valued activity, almost certainly with great symbolic importance.

What then might that symbolic significance be? What meaning does this remarkable image send down to us across the millennia? Unfortunately, we can never know because the social context in which the symbolic meaning of this image was constructed and embedded is entirely lost to us. Yet the image remains powerfully alive and tantalizing in its enigmatic significance, as if it speaks to us in a language we cannot understand but to which we still have an affective response. As Jill Cook says, "We cannot read the language in which the Lion Man was made although our fascination with such a remarkable object inevitably tempts us to try."[5]

One possible approach might be to compare this lion-man with other symbolic images that combine human and animal form. We might, for example, consider the significance of spirit animals in shamanic practices that still exist in some parts of the world where a shaman may become identified with a spirit animal and take on its qualities and attributes. For example, the bear has great spiritual significance in many indigenous Northern cultures in America and Siberia and there are examples of shamans who wear the skin of a bear, including the head, thus making themselves into a "bear-man" in a similar fashion to the image of the Lion Man.

We might make a further link with shamanism via the association between the sculptures of the Swabian caves and the paintings made at Chauvet. Both belong to the Aurignacian culture and, at Chauvet, there are several paintings of lions, albeit these date from several thousand years later (approximately 32,000–30,000 years ago). David Lewis-Williams has undertaken an extensive comparison between cave paintings and the use of rock art in South Africa, Australia, and North America and has concluded that the cave paintings of the Paleolithic period are a record of the shamanic visions in which the contours of the cave were seen as an entrance to the spirit world from which the painted images were emerging.[6]

We might also consider the qualities that might be associated with lions and which, therefore, the symbol of a lion-man might be thought to represent. Here we would be drawing not only on our own contemporary culture but on the symbolic significance of lions throughout recorded history. We would then find many examples of lions being used as symbols of power and royalty (the king of beasts) as well as associations with courage, strength, physical prowess, power, violence, aggression, devouring. We might conclude that even if the Aurignacians were not always hunting lions they may have wished to identify themselves with or even worship the image of a being who combined these symbolic elements with human ones. And we might also be impressed by the extraordinary longevity of this symbolic image, even if the most notable examples of it in recent years have been utilized to advertise Lee jeans (in the 1970s) and bottled water

for the 2012 Olympics. Or, there are the closely related images of
Christ as a lion in the figure of Aslan in C. S. Lewis' *Narnia* tales as
well as the popular film and musical of *The Lion King*.

Most striking of all, especially for those with an interest in Jung, is
the parallel with the lion-headed God Aion of the Mithraic cults with
whom Jung became identified in one of his visions in December 1913,
recorded in *Liber Primus* of *The Red Book*. During his encounter with
Salome, Jung has a vision of himself as the crucified Christ with a
black serpent wound around his body and his countenance becomes
that of a lion. Shamdasani notes that in the 1925 seminars, Jung
commented that the animal face into which he felt his transformed
was "the famous *[Deus] Leontocephalus* of the Mithraic mysteries"
and he later used this image as the frontispiece of *Aion*.[7]

In fact, the image of a lion-headed god has quite a history. It
seems to have first appeared in Nubia as Apedemak perhaps as long as
4,000 years ago and this may have been the origin of Maahes, a minor
Egyptian god of the New Kingdom, around 3,500 years ago. Maahes
was a solar war god, often depicted wielding a knife and known as
"The Lord of the Slaughter" although his name means something
like "one who can see in front." This might suggest an intriguing
association with the lion-headed god of Mithraism who may (or may
not) have been identical with Aion, the god of Time. Perhaps "seeing
in front" is a reference to the future? Whether this was the case or
not, the lion-headed god appears to have been linked with time and
seasonal change.[8]

Despite the antiquity of these figures in the scheme of recorded
history, their age pales in comparison with the far greater antiquity of
the Aurignacian lion-man. While we are separated from the Egyptian
gods by 4,000 years at most, we are separated from the Aurignacian
era by 40,000 years; there is a gap of over 30,000 years between the
image from the Upper Paleolithic era and that belonging to the earliest
historical era of Egyptian civilization. So it would be quite a stretch
to assume that we could make direct connections between all these
images despite the tantalizing and fascinating sense of familiarity.

Yet this is just what Jung did with his daring hypothesis of a
collective unconscious in which he proposed that there is a collective
layer to the psyche that is shared by all of humanity throughout time
and space. Jung was deeply impressed by the occurrence of the same
themes and motifs throughout the world's mythology and believed that

these commonalities could not be accounted for by any kind of cultural transmission. Hence he proposed that the collective psyche is shaped by an (unspecified) number of archetypes that he regarded as "the *a priori* determinants of all psychic processes."[9] Elsewhere he writes,

> Now the archetypes do not represent anything external, non-psychic, although they do of course owe the concreteness of their imagery to impressions received from without. Rather, independently of, and sometimes in direct contrast to, the outward forms they may take, they represent the life and essence of a non-individual psyche. Although this psyche is innate in every individual, it can neither be modified nor possessed by him personally. It is the same in the individual as in the crowd and ultimately in everybody. It is the precondition of each individual psyche, just as the sea is the carrier of the individual wave.[10]

So whatever its specific cultural meaning and significance, a Jungian view of the Aurignacian Lion Man would see it as a manifestation of an innate, universal, and non-individual psyche whose existence provides evidence of the activity of the collective unconscious going right back to the dawn of European civilization and the earliest emergence of figurative symbolic representation. Murray Stein suggests that, from a classical Jungian perspective, the Lion Man could be seen as a symbol of the birth of consciousness out of the unconscious self. (personal communication, October 3, 2014) Drawing on the symbolic analogies between the self, the lion, and the sun he elaborates this view:

> The sun represents the self, the source, and ultimate power. The lion and the sun are identical in meaning in this [symbolic] vocabulary. So the lion-headed figure symbolizes a central power in the collective psyche (the group), a leader, the bright light, and highest value and strength of the group's consciousness. He/she is a light-bringer or Light-maker, certainly a ruling principle. The self is emerging as the centre of the group's consciousness. (personal communication, October 14, 2014)

This compelling symbolic exegesis may go some way to explaining why Jung seems to have had little interest in tracing the actual historical origin of the archetypes of the collective unconscious. Since he assumed that the archetypes were the same everywhere, and this provided him with a means of interpretation that could be universally applied, the question of origins may have seemed

unimportant or even missing the point that the psyche is not bound
in time but is eternal. So Jung contented himself with rather vague
references to the "archaic" and "primordial," seeing the unconscious
as "the totality of all archetypes ... the deposit of all human experience
right back to its remotest beginnings."[11] Or he used the evocative but
equally vague image of the "two million-year-old man:"

> Together the patient and I address ourselves to the "'two
> million-year-old man'" that is in all of us. ... In the last
> analysis, most of our difficulties come from losing contact
> with our instincts, with the age-old unforgotten wisdom
> stored up in us.[12]

Now it is significant that Jung is referring to his clinical work here
since, in the clinical setting, even the most scientifically attested facts
are likely to take on a metaphorical form.[13] Here Jung is clearly using
the idea of the "two million-year-old man" primarily as a symbolic
image whose purpose is to help patients make a more meaningful
emotional contact with their "instincts" and their "inner wisdom"
sometimes referred to as the wisdom of the body. Asking patients
to consider what their inner "two million-year-old man" might think
and feel is a rather different matter from a scientific enquiry into the
prehistory of the mind on the basis of archaeological data. So we might
wonder what conception Jung actually had of the last two million years
of human evolution beyond his wry remark in the same passage that
"in the 2,000,000 years we have existed on earth we have developed
a chin and a decent sort of brain."[14] Although he claimed to "try to
trace the strata of the human mind from its earliest beginnings, just as
a geologist might study the stratification of the earth,"[15] his method of
doing so was not through the study of the mind's earliest beginnings
but through what he took to be its archaic layers in the minds of his
patients and, to some extent, the so-called "primitives" of colonized
indigenous peoples. There are no references in Jung's collected works
to the search for human origins that had been going on since the latter
part of the nineteenth century.

The Search for Human Origins

Archaeologists had been searching for early human remains since
the publication of Darwin's *Origin of Species* in 1859 and *The Descent
of Man* in 1871. There had been a number of fossils discovered in
Europe since the skeleton discovered in the Neander Valley in

Germany in 1856 gave its name to the species *Homo neanderthalensis*, and, in the latter part of the nineteenth century, there was considerable speculation about a variety of possible precursors to *Homo sapiens*. The first discovery of a truly primitive human skull was made in Java in 1891 by Eugene Dubois who named it *Pithecanthropus erectus*, a member of the species we now know as *Homo erectus*.[16] There were further discoveries in the 1920s, notably a much older fossil discovered in South Africa by Raymond Dart in 1924 of a skull that looked like that of a young ape but showed a number of human-like features which he named *Australopithecus africanus*. His claims that it might be a potential human ancestor were treated with great skepticism at the time, although the australopithecines are now recognized as an important link in human evolution between our common ancestor with chimpanzees around six million years ago and the emergence of *Homo erectus* around 1.8 million years ago. In the 1920s, though, Dart's find was thought to be only 500,000 years old and therefore too recent to be a genuine human ancestor.[17]

It was not until the development of physical dating methods using the decay of elements such as potassium and carbon that reliable methods of dating ancient fossils became available. Frequently, the use of such methods dramatically increases the expected age of fossils—in one of the first applications of potassium-argon dating in 1960, for example, fossils and artifacts from the Olduvai Gorge in Tanzania (which include some of the earliest known stone tools used by humans) were found to be 1.8 million years old, doubling previous estimates of their age.[18] So Jung could not have had anything but a rough estimate of the time-scale of human evolution and he may have suggested two million years as a reasonable guestimate of when humans began to evolve. In one sense, he turned out to be quite accurate since *Homo erectus*, whose first appearance is now dated to approximately two million years ago, is sometimes regarded as the first "true" human.[19] Although earlier hominin species exist such as *Homo habilis* who, between 2 million and 2.5 million years ago, were the likely makers of the "Oldowan" stone tools, it is only with *Homo erectus* that the carefully crafted "teardrop-shaped" Acheulean hand-axes begin to appear, and it was probably during this period that the first dramatic increase in hominin brain size begins to appear in the fossil record. Even so, this is a far cry from any evidence of a human consciousness capable of formulating any kind of symbolic belief system or indeed any but the most rudimentary form of symbolic communication.[20] So Jung's main evidence for the existence of archetypes—the universal occurrence of similar themes in the mythologies of the world—must certainly be considerably more recent than the "two million-year-old man."

This does not necessarily mean that some kind of archetypal heritage could not be older than modern humanity since our biological heritage is deeply rooted in our animal ancestry and there is much that we retain from our primate and mammalian origins. Notably, some form of attachment behavior is evident in all species of mammals and perhaps in birds too, albeit not necessarily in the highly developed form in which we recognize it in humans where it occurs in conjunction with intersubjectivity.[21] Jung does make a suggestion of this kind when he proposes that the collective unconscious as the ancestral heritage of possibilities of representation may be common not only to all men but "perhaps even to all animals." He goes on to speculate that the "psychic organism," through its correspondence to the body

> in its development and structure ... still preserves elements that connect it with the invertebrates and ultimately with the protozoa. Theoretically it should be possible to "peel" the collective unconscious, layer by layer, until we came to the psychology of the worm and even of the amoeba.[22]

He gives no indication, however, of how mythological motifs of the collective unconscious may actually correspond to or arise from processes of physical evolution of this kind, so it is really little more than a nod in the direction of Darwinian evolutionary theory.

A second approach would identify the collective unconscious with the emergence of modern humanity, suggesting that this represents the neurological programming of the specifically-human brain. Jung certainly links the collective unconscious with the structure of the brain in many of his references to the subject. In perhaps the first of these, written in 1916, he writes,

> Every man is born with a brain that is highly differentiated. This makes him capable of a wide range of mental functions, which are neither ontogenetically developed nor acquired. ... This explains, for example, the interesting fact that the most widely separated peoples and races show a quite remarkable correspondence, which displays itself, among other things, in the extraordinary but well documented analogies between the forms and motifs of autochthonous

> myths. The universal similarity of human brains leads to
> the universal possibility of a uniform mental functioning.
> This functioning is the *collective psyche*.[23]

Both of these lines of enquiry have been pursued by Anthony Stevens who took Jung's reference to the "two million-year-old man" as the title of his Fay Lectures in 1993.[24] Stevens suggested that the image of the "two million-year-old man" was a kind of personalisation of "the archetypal units of which the phylogenetic (biologically evolved) psyche is composed" and, as such, constituted "the phenomenological embodiment of our evolutionary inheritance."[25] Stevens deserves great credit for taking seriously the biological aspect of archetypes and working strenuously to put analytical psychology on a scientific footing by linking it with ethology and evolutionary psychology. In recent years, though, his work has tended to fall out of favor amongst those interested in linking Jungian thought with modern scientific currents.[26] In particular Jean Knox has argued against the biological inheritance model of archetypes while George Hogenson has criticized the theoretical foundations of evolutionary psychology on which much of Stevens' work relied. These debates are reviewed in the next chapter.

In this book, I want to argue from a related but somewhat different perspective that emphasizes the role of the social and material environment in the construction of symbolic thought and imagination. In so doing, my aim is to cut across the traditional arguments between "cultural" and "biological" origins of archetypes by showing that this kind of dispute, like the "nature vs. nurture" dispute with which it is linked, is based on a misapprehension of human nature for which culture *is* biological. More broadly, these debates are rooted in a fundamentally Cartesian misapprehension about the nature of mind which separates the mind from the world in which it is realized. In this broader view, mind is an emergent phenomenon of human social being. That is, our human nature has evolved through the development of sociality and sociality is the essential medium for the development of mind. While the imagination seems to be *par excellence*, that aspect of mind which does not depend on the facticity of the material world, I want to argue that it could not have come into existence except through the long evolution of human sociality rooted in material engagement with objects, skills, and cooperative social practices. In terms of Jungian thought my ultimate aim is to turn archetype theory on its head; rather than seeing archetypal images as being derivative of the structure of a collective psyche composed of the fundamental forms of "archetypes in themselves," I want to argue that any kind of form or structure is secondary to the process whereby archetypal images are created through the activity of symbolic imagination. That is, symbolic imagination is not shaped by pre-existing psychic forms so much as being the means by which it is possible to conceive of such forms in the first place. Ontologically, the image is primary and the abstract forms represent further levels of symbolic thought being *constituted by* rather than *constitutive of* symbolic imagination.

Although this leads to a rejection of Jung's hypothesis of a collective unconscious of archetypal forms, this does not mean a rejection of Jung's work *per se.* Following Shamdasani's illuminating insight, this view sees Jung as more of a psychological essayist than a theorist.[27] Hence Jung's work does not depend on its supposed central plank of the collective unconscious with which he has been so often identified. Rather, what we see in Jung is a life-long fascination with the working-out of symbolic imagination throughout human history and culture. The more arcane and esoteric the forms taken by imagination (notably alchemy), the greater Jung's interest since, by his own account, he was looking for parallels to his own extraordinary visions of 1913–1916. Jung knew first-hand just how remarkable the products of symbolic imagination could be. In my view, his hypothesis as to the explanation for these occurrences was secondary and ultimately was just that—a hypothesis, not a theory. It is a fascinating hypothesis and despite my skepticism about much of the theorizing on which it is based, I find myself repeatedly coming back to it. This is, in my view, because Jung asked the right question, and it is the question which is ultimately of more enduring interest than the answer.

So the way I want to formulate Jung's question about the world-wide commonalities in symbolic imagery is this: what is the origin and nature of symbolic imagination? I hope to show that this leads to a somewhat different answer than if the answer is assumed to be "the archetypes" or even the more neutral "the unconscious," not least because these beg the question of whether the origin is psychological, let alone whether the psyche can be separated out from the material and social world. By focusing on the symbolic image rather than the archetype in itself, I hope to be able to open up avenues for further exploration towards closing the Cartesian gap between mind and world and dissolving the conflict between psyche and society as the determining contexts of human consciousness. Firstly, though, I want to look in more detail at the archetypal hypothesis, and discuss some of the problematic inconsistencies and difficulties with Jung's formulation and the controversies that have arisen over the past fifteen or twenty years with the reformulation of archetypes as emergent rather than pre-existent forms.

CHAPTER ONE

THE ARCHETYPAL HYPOTHESIS

Where Do Archetypes Come From?

One of the key tenets of Jung's archetypal hypothesis is that of the "inborn image." By this, he did not mean an actual image but "a possibility of representation," a necessary caveat to distinguish the archetype from any proposal of "inherited ideas." To clarify this he later introduced the distinction between the archetypal image and the archetype in itself although he was notoriously inconsistent about this and habitually referred to images as archetypes.[1] Nevertheless, it is clear that he identified the source of these "inborn images" with the structure of the human brain, as previously quoted.[2] Similarly, in another reference to the "two-million-year old man" he says,

> All men were born with a brain ready-made. It took millions of years to build the brain and the body we now have. Your brain embodies all the experience of life. The psyche, which may be called the life of the brain, existed before consciousness existed in the little child.[3]

This is clearly a very innatist view of the psyche, especially the notion that the brain is "ready-made." This links with two further ideas that crop up repeatedly in Jung's discussion of archetypes—the notion that they are "*a priori*" and that they are linked with instincts. These themes occur in Jung's first use of the term *archetype* in his 1919 paper *Instinct and the Unconscious*, where he says,

> In this deeper stratum [of the unconscious] we also find the *a priori* inborn forms of "intuition" namely the archetypes of perception and apprehension which are the necessary *a priori* determinants of all psychic processes.

> Just as his instincts compel man to a specifically human
> mode of existence, so the archetypes force his ways of
> perception and apprehension into specifically human
> patterns. The instincts and the archetypes together form
> the collective unconscious.[4]

Jung continued to refer to the connection between instinct and archetype throughout his writings but it remains uncertain whether he regarded archetypes *as* instincts or as analogous to instinct.[5] So, for example, he would describe the archetype as "the instinct's perception of itself" or "the forms that the instincts assume"[6] but at the same time would differentiate between "the instinctual forces of the psyche and of the forms or categories that regulate them, namely the archetypes."[7]

In his later work, especially his 1947 essay *On The Nature of the Psyche*, he seems to distinguish between the "instinctual" pole of the psyche which he connects with body, nature, and matter and the "spiritual" pole which he connects with the archetype, albeit he uses the image of the spectrum to suggest that they are different forms of the same thing with balances of energy flowing between them. For example, he says, "in spite or perhaps because of its affinity with instinct, the archetype represents the authentic element of spirit."[8] At this time, Jung seemed to be redefining his view of archetypes away from his previous reliance on some form of biological inheritance and more towards a metaphysical or transcendent view of archetypes as being somehow inherent in the nature of the world as a whole. So we now see caveats such as "This is not to say that the psyche derives exclusively from the instinctual sphere and hence from its organic substrate."[9] Furthermore, the archetype needs to be liberated not only from its physiological (instinctual) origins but even from the psyche.

> The archetype, describes a field which exhibits none of
> the peculiarities of the physiological and yet, in the last
> analysis, can no longer be regarded as psychic, although
> it manifests itself psychically … there is probably no
> alternative now but to describe their nature, in accordance
> with their chiefest effect, as 'spirit.'[10]

Perhaps the clearest evidence of the shift in Jung's views away from a biological inheritance model of archetypes comes in his discussion of synchronicity, which provided much of the stimulus for this reconsideration. There he writes "the archetypes are not found exclusively in the psychic sphere but can occur just as much in circumstances that are not psychic."[11]

The other key element in this rethinking was Jung's collaboration with Pauli, which offered him the possibility of grounding his theory of archetypes in physics rather than biology, using the analogy of the atom rather than instinct. Keen as he was in exploring this link, he was scrupulous enough to end his complicated and often downright obscure 1947 essay with the caveat (perhaps prompted by Pauli?) that "we are concerned first and foremost to establish certain analogies, and no more than that; the existence of such analogies does not entitle us to conclude that connection is already proven."[12]

Jung's strenuous efforts to link archetypes with atomic physics reveals two things. Firstly, it shows how important it was to him that his theories should have some basis in empirical science. Secondly, it shows that he must have felt that the biological model of inheritance via the "two million-year-old man" of the ready-made brain did not fully encompass what he had in mind and what he believed the nature of archetypes to be.

I think this uncertainty goes back to Jung's original formulation in 1919 which had its roots as much in Platonic philosophy as biological inheritance. Having spent the first half of his discussion on the analogy between instinct and archetypes ("inborn forms of intuition"), he suddenly shifts his frame of reference from biology to philosophy and refers to the archetypes in Plato (as "metaphysical ideas") and in Augustine "from whom," he says, "I have borrowed the idea of the archetype." [13] He then traces the "deterioration" of the metaphysical value of the idea through Descartes, Spinoza, Kant, and Schopenhauer. Ignoring the complex philosophical differences between all these thinkers he concludes, "We can see once again that same psychological process at work which disguises the instincts under the cloak of rational motivations and transforms the archetype into rational concepts."[14]

This conclusion begs the question, to say the least. At a stroke, Jung has claimed philosophical authority for the archetype as a metaphysical conception while reducing philosophy to a rational disguise for his own formulation of instinctual intuition. He has assumed that the philosophical idea of the archetype is itself an archetype which, like mythological motifs, can be traced through philosophical history and reduced back to its putative instinctual origin. This technique, which Jung shares with Freud, uses the notion of the unconscious as a form of superior knowledge and claims to offer more encompassing or "real" explanations for other forms of discourse by tracing them back to their supposed roots in the unconscious. This is an example of "behindology"—the notion that behind the apparent motives, meanings, and rationale of people's actions, thoughts and behavior are their "real" unconscious motivations which can only be revealed through the particular beliefs about the unconscious that the author happens to hold. These interpretations are then taken as explanatory justification or even proof of the author's formulation.

Behindology

Psychoanalysis is not alone in its deployment of behindology which, to some extent, is an element of any theory that seeks to discover the underlying structures behind the surface, especially when those surfaces are regarded as mere appearances which belie the underlying reality. The term *behindology* is derived from the Italian *dietrologia*, originally referring to the suspicion in Italian political life that the surface or official explanation for something can rarely be the real one, not surprising given the prominence of the Mafia in Italian political life. More broadly, it has become a byword for conspiracy theories and the culture of suspicion that surrounds them. Ironically, as one sociologist of conspiracy theory has pointed out, sociology itself frequently invokes behindology—the attempt to uncover the "real" social forces or structures behind social activity: "Dietrologic has no faith in surfaces and always assumes that the interesting things are happening behind the skin of the world."[15] The same ploy turns up in neuroscience when claims are made that certain perceptions merely "seem" to be the case while their neural correlates are taken to be what is "really" going on. For example, Daniel Dennett uses research that shows that the brain perceives much less of a perceptual object than is apparent to consciousness. He concludes that consciousness *seems* continuous but *really* it is full of gaps.[16] Here, the materiality of the brain is assumed to be the real reality behind the apparent reality of consciousness, which merely *seems*.[17] Such assumptions are challenged both by phenomenological approaches and emergence theories—the former is precisely interested in the surface "skin of the world" while the latter argues that emergent forms are not reducible to the sum of their parts.[18] Critiques of Jung's structural approach to the archetypes have come from both directions but it is worth pointing out that Jung himself was quite capable of taking a phenomenological approach, such as his insistence that the dream was not a disguise, his well-known recommendation to "stick to the image," and his Goethe-inspired emphasis on allowing Nature to speak out of her own fullness.[19] The bewildering shifts in Jung's discourse are well brought out by Hobson.

> Sometimes he claims to use objective observation and classification in accordance with traditional scientific method. At other times his language is very similar to that of those phenomenological psychologists who have been influenced by Husserl. ... Yet he also insists that the theory of the archetypes is an explanatory concept similar to that of botanical families—a method of thought quite foreign to phenomenology.[20]

Knox's Four Core Themes

These inconsistent formulations and discourses make the archetype a notoriously difficult concept to pin down. One of the most comprehensive efforts to do so is Jean Knox's identification of the following four core themes or models that repeatedly emerge in the debate about archetypes.[21]

- Biological entities in the form of information which is hard-wired in the genes, providing a set of instruction to the mind as well as the body
- Organizing mental frameworks of an abstract nature, a set of rules or instructions but with no symbolic or representational content, so that they are never directly experienced
- Core meanings which do contain representational content and which therefore provide a central symbolic significance to our experience
- Metaphysical entities which are eternal and are therefore independent of the body

Now, with the foregoing discussion in mind, I think it is possible to reconfigure this excellent summary into just two major themes: the first and the last. From the start, I suggest, Jung saw archetypes as both biological and metaphysical, a combination of instinctual intuition and Platonic Idea. He attempts to merge both of these disparate intellectual traditions in his main definition which is the second of Knox's models—i.e., abstract mental frameworks with no representational content. This is the definition of archetypes as "the possibility of ideas" or "the archetype as such" which can be derived from or explained by either the biology of the evolved "ready-made brain" or the later, more metaphysical version of the psychoid archetype which exists as a kind of transcendent eternal truth, inherent in the structure of the universe itself as the "principle of meaning" of the *unus mundus* and, therefore, also inherent in living matter.[22] This is also the definition that Knox herself chooses, albeit she gives it an entirely different derivation. She identifies organizing mental frameworks with primitive "image schemas" rooted in sensory-motor experiences of bodily action and spatial orientation. Her ingenious reformulation of archetypes as emergent properties of early psychic development is considered later in this chapter.

As for the third definition, referring to core meanings, this is mainly due to the oscillation in Jung's discourse noted by Hobson and Fordham between a phenomenological, experiential discourse and a more "scientific" theoretical one.[23] As Hobson puts it, it is

> the difference between defining the word in terms of phenomena which it signifies and the direct personal experience of those phenomena. He is not content to describe or point to an event or object so that it can be recognized intellectually, but seeks for a language which will express an experience with its associated affect.[24]

The "two million-year-old man" is an example of this kind of discourse. When Jung describes this archetypal inheritance as "the Great Old Man" he is, as Stevens points out, using a personification which he considers to be the typical way in which archetypal ideas express themselves, that is, the way archetypal predispositions (the "organizing mental frameworks") present themselves to the conscious mind in dreams and myths.[25] So Jung considers that in order for the abstract principles to do their work as guiding the way we live and giving life a deeper meaning, it is necessary for them to be "incarnated" as symbolic representations but insists that these core meanings are only potentials and possibilities, dependent on culturally available means of representation for their realization.

Knox argues, however, that, in practice, it is not possible to distinguish abstract organising frameworks from core representational meanings, partly because of the way the biological aspect of archetypes is merged with the incompatible notion of Platonic ideas which certainly do imply core meanings such as the idea of the good. The problem here is that either the abstract possibility of an idea cannot be kept sufficiently distinct from the actual examples (archetypal images) to which it gives rise or else there is such a gap between the two that it proves impossible to say what the nature of this "possibility of an idea" or "archetype in itself" is supposed to be or where the boundary is between the contentless archetypal pattern and the manifest content. For example, Knox takes Stevens to task for illustrating the archetype as such with the mother-child infant system, most of which is realized in actual experience and is therefore content rather than potential for content (pattern of behavior, possibility of ideas, etc.).[26] Knox is not saying that there is nothing innate about infant attachment but rather that the innate elements can only be simple non-representational mechanisms, not complex elaborations of perception and behavior that give infants an "idea" of what they can expect to find in a mother.

What Do Archetypes Explain?

One possible explanation for the shifting sands of Jung's discourse and the wide range of sources on which he draws is the tentative hypothetical nature of his enquiry. Hobson, while warning against the "pseudo-problems" created by mixing incompatible languages, reminds us that "Jung has repeatedly emphasized that his general formulations are very tentative, and that he is concerned mainly with disclosing a wide field of obscure and unexplored experience."[27] More recently, Shamdasani's portrayal of Jung as a psychological essayist makes a similar point, suggesting that Jung was less concerned with formulating a systematic theory than with addressing matters that interested him from a wide variety of directions which may not necessarily cohere into any unified whole. Shamdasani's claim is supported by Jung's declaration that, in his clinical practice, he was "unsystematic very much by intention." Not only does he eschew adherence to one particular method, he goes on to say that it was the need to understand psychotic symbolism that led him to study mythology.[28] So it seems likely that the same eschewal of a single approach may have carried over into the latter area of study as well. Hence Jung is likely to have regarded the absence of any fixed or final view about the archetypes and the collective unconscious as a positive virtue, a sign of his attempt to "guard against theoretical assumptions."[29] While he never wavers in his belief in the existence of archetypes, he also never rests in seeking out one after another possible sources in which he might find an explanatory grounding. Nevertheless, his unsystematic inconsistency has left a problematic legacy. It is no use relying on Jung as the authority for his own concepts since, to do so, simply imports the inconsistencies without the effort to seek more satisfactory explanations. I take the latter to be a more valuable bequest from Jung than the former. In this section, I will make a start by outlining some of the problematic aspects of Jung's arguments for the explanatory value of archetype theory.

Firstly, Jung begins with images and mythological motifs and then attempts to abstract these into classificatory schemas that are intended to act as general formulae. But he then seems to go further, implying that these classifications provide *explanations* for the phenomena in question. This is a bit like saying plants grow in the way they do because they belong to a particular genus or species. The classification does no more than pose the deeper question of what the mechanisms are that generate species and their divergence—the question addressed by Wallace and Darwin to which the theory of evolution was their answer. Jung never seems to ask the question "why are there archetypes and where do they come from"; they seem to be put forward as either biologically "inborn" or metaphysically *a priori*.

Secondly, it is inevitable that the abstract "archetype-in-itself" will bear the residue of the images (or pattern of behavior) from which it has been derived since the purported universality of the images provides the schema for the archetype in the first place. It is not merely that we can only *recognize* archetypes in their phenomenal form and that they are ultimately unknowable, but that the concept has little meaning without the phenomena to which it purportedly gives rise. This is true not only of examples which are identified with their phenomenal imagery such as the archetype of the snake or the trickster but also to more abstract archetypes such as the anima, the self, or the archetype of meaning. If, to take one of Jung's analogies, archetypes are like the axial structure of a crystal, how is that to be demonstrated other than by the resulting forms, especially if (as in the later "transcendent" version) the purported structural element is designated as an "unknowable" thing-in-itself? That is, what evidence is there for a structural element *behind* the phenomena beyond the occurrence of the phenomena themselves?

Thirdly, there are two problems associated with the notion of universality. Firstly, Jung relies on the comparative method, derived from nineteenth-century anthropology, according to which phenomena occurring in different cultures or historical eras could be compared with each other to discover common themes. This was already being challenged by Franz Boas in 1896 and was certainly known to Jung by 1909 since Boas was one of the speakers at the famous Clark University conference when Freud and Jung made their first visit to America.[30] Boas argued that the comparison of similar phenomena from different cultures in terms of a given theory was an invalid scientific procedure since it ignored the specific circumstances in which particular adaptations may have been made. Similar effects may be due to different causes and so each phenomenon or artefact had to be considered within its own surroundings. Jung's use of the comparative method was particularly loose in this respect since it frequently relied on using the metaphorical mode of imaginal thinking. For example, he argues that the concept of energy as used in modern physics is based on a primitive intuition of a primordial image on the basis of its analogical similarity with the affectively based experience of *mana* in Polynesian religion.[31] Here he takes analogy as identity and yokes together two very disparate modes of thought without regard for their differences. This is more than a confusion of phenomenological description and explanatory theorising: it is the use of fantasy thinking, which specializes in metaphor and symbol, as a purported scientific explanation in the realm of directed logical thinking. That is, a legitimate analogy for, say, working with a dream-image is here presented as if it constitutes a scientific argument.

The second problem associated with universality is more pronounced in some of Jung's followers than in Jung himself. As I have said, the purported universality of mythological motifs was the starting point for Jung's enquiries. Whether or not it was a valid assertion, it was still the *explicandum* (that which is to be explained) rather than the *explicans* (the proposed explanation). Yet, frequently, Jungians attempt to justify or even prove the existence of archetypes on the basis of the universality of certain phenomena, leading to heated debates about whether such universals exist, such as typical gender attributes for example. This is a mistaken use of inductive reasoning. Induction proceeds from an initial argument about some observation to its confirmation by collecting further empirical examples.[32] But the argument in question here would be the proposition that images or patterns of behavior are universal, not the hypothesis that they can be explained by archetypes. Suppose, for example, that all known societies practice some form of initiation ritual. It might then be reasonable to argue that initiation rituals are universal, even if, in practice, this required yoking together some very different activities carried out in very different contexts.[33] Even so, this would provide no justification for explaining this universality on the basis of an archetype of initiation prompting individuals and societies to behave in pre-specified ways at pre-specified times. At best, the proposed explanation is a hypothesis that cannot be demonstrated by the phenomena themselves, no matter how universal they are. At worst, it would be an example of a *dormitive principle*, a term referring to Moliere's satire of the physician who claims that opium induces sleep because it contains a sleep-inducing factor (*virtus dormitiva*). In this case, the "dormitive" explanation of initiation would be that it is an expression of an initiation archetype. In sum, the point is that even if universals *do* exist, that does not prove anything about archetypes since the theory of archetypes is supposed to be the *explanation* of universals. Universals are the *explicandum*, not the *explicans*.

In this respect, the theory of archetypes is more like the theory of phlogiston. Throughout the eighteenth century it was widely accepted that all flammable materials contained a substance named phlogiston which was released when they were burned. At the time, this was a perfectly respectable and reasonable theory, but subsequent observations raised a number of difficulties. Initially, apparent contradictions, such as the fact that metals were heavier after burning rather than lighter as they should have been if their phlogiston had been liberated, were dealt with by presuming that phlogiston was a principle rather than a substance. Eventually, though, the theory was disproved by Lavoisier's discovery of an element in the air—oxygen— that combined with burned substances to form oxides. Interestingly, when Lavoisier set out to show that phlogiston was imaginary, he called it "a veritable Proteus that changes its form every instant," a rather apt description for the multi-faceted notion of archetypes.

The real point here, though, is not whether Jung was wrong but that the archetype was a *hypothesis* and therefore one that requires testing and revision in the light of subsequent findings. For Jung, the only alternative to his proposal of archetypes as the underlying principle responsible for the universality of mythological motifs was the possibly of cultural diffusion (of which cryptomnesia would be a special example), so he directed his arguments to disproving such possibilities. It would no more have occurred to him that such motifs could be repeatedly and reliably emergent without requiring an underlying principle than it would have occurred to eighteenth-century chemists that flammable materials did not release something but combined with something as yet unknown in the make-up of air.

Teleology and Meaning

One way around this difficulty is to downplay the substantive term "archetype" and refer merely to factors which are "archetypal." Hence it might be said that initiation is "archetypal" without claiming the existence of an initiation archetype. This implies that initiation occurs so frequently because it is inherently important for human ways of living, without claiming that it is driven by an archetype. It indicates the *purposive* aspect of such (more or less) universally occurring phenomena. Raya Jones argues that this was where Jung's real interest lay. "The causal question was secondary and relatively trivial for Jung. His researches and clinical work concern primarily the teleological 'what for' of phenomena such as mythological fantasies."[34]

When Jung refers to "the symbol creating function," Jones thinks he has rather more in mind than a dormitive principle:

> To say that symbols are 'caused' by a symbol-creating function would be as pointless as saying that someone crossed the road because the body has a 'walking function' and it's not what Jung is saying about symbols. He consistently locates symbols in the eye of the beholder, *and explores their functions for psychological transformations.*[35] [italics added]

Similarly, Murray Stein points to the teleological aspect of archetypal explanations which "have to do with emergence of archetypal forces that have a purpose or telos—the creation of human wholeness. ... The evolution of cultures and human history is driven by archetypal forces that have a teleological thrust."[36]

This approach to archetypes or archetypal forces has an implicitly ethical and spiritual imperative. If there are teleological forces at work in the human psyche, aligning ourselves with them can offer us a purposive goal in life, providing meaning in an otherwise meaningless universe. It may be dangerous to ignore these forces since, if they are not aligned with consciousness, they may become destructive as in the case of psychotic possession.

For those who take this approach, neither the role of archetypes as a scientific explanatory hypothesis nor their ontological provenance are particularly important. These can be dispensed with while retaining their heuristic value as purposive-guiding principles for a way of life in tune with our deepest nature. It was this that Jung personified in the "two million-year-old man," regardless of anything that actually happened or not in the evolutionary past of human prehistory. As Jones suggests, this approach utilizes symbols as functions for psychological transformation. Archetypes are employed as a symbolic language to describe these teleological psychological forces. They are not intended to *explain* symbols (the "causal" view, as Jung sometimes called it) but are a means of interpreting the meaning, purpose, and function of symbols in terms of a particular ethical-spiritual psychological philosophy of life (the "final" view). As such, they express a belief system and an orientation to living that might loosely be called a Jungian mythology. Effectively, they *are* symbols since the terms now function in the same way as the symbols they were originally intended to explain—as psychic organizers making sense of experience, functioning as the facilitators of psychological transformation. The language of archetypes has become a mythological language in its own right, subject to the same protean transformations and dream-like fantasy logic that so exasperates the logically minded. Perhaps the only way to interpret a symbol is by means of another symbol. Anything else will destroy its meaning in the attempt to reveal it for the very reason that Jung says that symbols are irreducible carriers of essentially unknown meaning.[37]

"The Frustration of Archetypal Intent"

The ethical aspect of archetypes as a guide to right ways of living provides a further reason why many Jungians wish to hold on to them and seem to feel threatened by emergence theories. This has to do with the mistaken belief that if there are no archetypes, there are no universals, and, therefore, the only alternative is the idea that the human mind is a *tabula rasa* on which culture and society can write whatever it likes. This seems to open a Pandora's box of "anything goes" relativism, the idea that human culture is infinitely malleable with no fixed points at all. This concern is apparent in those Jungians who have sought to align archetype theory with evolutionary psychology, most notably, Anthony Stevens and, latterly, Erik Goodwyn. For Stevens especially, the aim of putting Jungian theory on a scientific footing that takes seriously the biological aspect of archetypes as a form of evolutionary adaptedness goes hand in hand with a strong opposition to the moral (or rather, immoral) implications of relativism.

One of Stevens' most passionate concerns is with "the frustration of archetypal intent." This idea is based on a central tenet of evolutionary psychology that the human species evolved for a particular way of living that existed in the Paleolithic era. This idea is used to provide explanations for most of the way we behave today and Stevens also uses it to argue that many of our present woes are the result of attempting to live in ways that do not suit our species-specific way of life, a view that seems to imply a paradoxical mixture of freedom and determinism redolent of the Christian doctrine of original sin. Apparently, we are free to choose our way of life but will be in trouble if we do not choose what God ("the archetypes") wants. Stevens joins forces with anthropologists such as Robin Fox to insist on universal characteristics of the human species that we neglect at our peril. There is a strong socio-political agenda here that Stevens makes quite explicit in terms of an extended and repeated attack on environmentalists who deny the role of the innate in the service of human malleability.

This debate frequently invokes relativism as its target of opposition. For example, Jerry Fodor, who first put forward the idea of a mind composed of specific modules pre-adapted for particular functions, has said that he was motivated by his hatred of relativism.

> I hate relativism more than I hate anything else except, maybe, fibreglass power boats. What it overlooks, to put it briefly and crudely, is the fixed structure of human nature. … If there are faculties and modules, then not everything affects everything else; not everything is plastic.[38]

This seems to be related to a rather extreme version of relativism that became dominant in academic life in the 1970s, particularly in America, that rejected any innate limits to human (or animal) nature on the basis that such views were reactionary, biased towards the maintenance of a social status quo, and, therefore, politically oppressive of disadvantaged groups. Debate on these matters was particularly heated in the area of gender differences since the belief that men and women are essentially different ("essentialism") was strongly opposed by feminists arguing for equal opportunities in areas held to be innately masculine. Here, Jung is staunchly in the essentialist camp, his views of anima and animus being one of his most uncompromising statements about the innateness of archetypal potentials.

> Every man carries within him the eternal image of woman, not the image of this or that particular woman, but a definite feminine image. This image is fundamentally unconscious, an hereditary factor of primordial origin engraved in the living organic system of the man, an imprint or 'archetype' of all the ancestral experiences of the female, a deposit, as it were, of all the impressions ever made by woman—in short, an inherited system of psychic adaptation. *Even if no women existed, it would still be possible, at any given time, to deduce from this unconscious image exactly how a woman would have to be constituted psychically.*[39] [italics added]

Note that Jung does not merely refer to an archetypal *idea* of women held by men, but that the archetype, like Adam's rib, provides a blueprint in the male psyche for the reconstruction of exactly how a woman should be. It's hardly surprising that women might object to this sort of thing since Jung is effectively saying that women should conform to male fantasies!

Leaving aside its unfortunate socio-cultural implications, Jung is at least being consistent here in regarding the archetype not only as an image but also as a pattern of behavior. It is this which is most enthusiastically taken up by Stevens. Early in his career, he was struck by the similarity between the work of the ethologists, such as Tinbergen and Lorenz, and Jung's view of archetypes, particularly his analogy between archetypes and the behavior of yucca moths, leaf-cutting ants, and so forth. This aspect of Jung's thinking is summed up in a well-known quotation that Stevens references several times in his work.[40]

> [The term archetype] is not meant to denote an inherited idea, but rather an inherited mode of functioning, corresponding to the inborn way in which the chick emerges from the egg, the bird builds its nest, a certain kind of wasp stings the motor ganglion of the caterpillar, and eels find their way to the Bermudas. In other words, it is a 'pattern of behaviour.' This aspect of the archetype, the purely biological one, is the proper concern of scientific psychology.[41]

Stevens interest in this "purely biological" aspect of archetypes has led him to pay considerable attention to how archetypes might be instantiated in the brain and the role they might have played in evolution in the past as well as providing guides for what might be "natural" behavior today. In *The Two Million-Year-Old Self* Stevens draws extensively on Robin Fox's book *The Search for Society*, one of whose main themes is to establish a "natural morality" as an evolutionary imperative of human society. Judging by the tone of Fox's attack on the idea that "everything is cultural," it would seem that he hates the idea of the *tabula rasa* even more than Fodor hates fibreglass power boats.

> All in all, for a variety of ideological reasons, anthropology along with psychology and sociology kept the world safe for humanity by refusing to allow that anything about culture could be 'reduced' to biology. ... The human infant was a *tabula rasa* on which culture imprinted itself and the subsequent behaviour of the infant was therefore wholly a matter of which particular culture had been imprinted on it.[42]

Naturally, such a view is anathema to an attempt to establish a biological and therefore universal and absolute base for how people should live.

> If man accepts that all behaviour is culturally learned and that he can learn anything, he can invent any kind of society and culture for himself. If he believes that he has a species-specific repertoire of behaviour that can be combined successfully only in certain ways, then there are definite limits to what this animal can do, to the kinds of societies he can operate, to the kinds of cultures he can live with.[43]

The woeful implications of a belief in unlimited cultural learning are spelled out by Stevens:

> In the last few decades we have turned our society into an anarchic laboratory, where the archetypal structures involved in pair-boding, child-care, and social regulation are being tested to breaking point. Our civilization is contravening archetypal imperatives on an unprecedented scale.[44]

In order to establish the reality of these "archetypal imperatives" Stevens quotes an impressive list of features derived from anthropologists such as Fox, Murdock, and Brown which are displayed by all human cultures and can therefore be regarded as universal.

> According to these anthropologists, no human culture
> is known that lacks laws about property, procedures for
> settling disputes, rules governing courtship, marriage,
> and adultery, taboos relating to food and incest, rules
> of etiquette prescribing forms of greeting and modes
> of address, the manufacture of tools and weapons,
> cooperative labour, visiting, feasting, hospitality, gift-
> giving, the performance of funeral rites, belief in the
> supernatural, religious rituals, the recital of myths and
> legends, dancing, mental illness, faith healing, dream
> interpretation, and so on.[45]

Like the evolutionary psychologists, Fox and Stevens argue that
the basis of these universal features of human society lies in the kind
of environment and socio-technical requirements for which humans
originally evolved—the Savannah lifestyle of the Paleolithic era.
This then becomes a kind of "golden age" reference point: since
we evolved to live in that way, our social and psychological well-
being is likely to become disturbed if we depart too far from it. Fox
is unequivocal that our environment of evolutionary adaptedness is to
be found in the Late Paleolithic, some fifteen to forty thousand years
ago. Then, he believes "it all began to go wrong."[46] One of the key
elements of this belief lies in the innatist notion of "the ready-made
brain." For, according to this view, it is the brain that cannot cope
with what Stevens calls "the frustration of archetypal intent."

> The brain ... is still the primate brain ... geared for a
> particular range of adaptive responses. Force it to try to
> work outside that range for long enough, and it will react—
> it will rebel. It will regress to those pristine behaviours
> (including the very necessary aggressive ones) surrounding
> its primary functions, survival and reproduction.[47]

Sociobiology and Its Critics

There are several assumptions on which this view rests, many
of which turn on its reliance on the modular theory of evolutionary
psychology which is under increasing pressure from a range
of alternative approaches in disciplines such as developmental
psychology, neuroscience, linguistics, complex systems theory, and
theoretical robotics, all of which involve models of emergence and
self-organization rather than "hard-wired" innatism.[48] The force and
significance of these criticisms were first introduced into the Jungian

community by George Hogenson in his debate with Anthony Stevens at the IAAP Cambridge Congress in 2001.As Hogenson has described it more recently,

> My contention was that the ground had shifted so irrevocably under the evolutionary model of the archetypes as specifically proposed by Stevens that his position was no longer sustainable. Needless to say he saw the matter differently and, in one form or another the debate has continued ever since.[49]

This debate seems to have become extremely heated and I have been struck by the tenacity of the proponents of innatism and the way they repeatedly return to the straw man criticism that the emergence model implies a "tabula rasa."[50] If innatist views represent a kind of moral compass or a possibility of reliable certainty in a world of bewildering change and apparent social decay, then it is not so surprising that many would wish to cling on to Jung's proposal of an archetypal basis to our lives rooted in a deep continuity with our evolutionary past. The debate then becomes unnecessarily polarized between what (mistakenly) appears to be a limitless cultural relativism and a fealty to some kind of biological imperative.

Although the "tabula rasa" idea that human nature depends on "nurture" rather than "nature" goes back to Aristotle, it was articulated explicitly by John Locke for whom it underpinned a belief in humans being free to make their own character and become the authors of their own souls. Hence it has become associated with social and political views concerned with promoting social change—views that the anti-relativists make clear they detest, though not necessarily all for the same reasons. Nevertheless, the political aspect of Stevens' attack on those who believe that social and political change can bring about changes in human character is apparent in the intemperate sarcasm with which he attacks Marxists. He claims,

> When confronted with evidence which suggests that archetypal structures function as the basis of human experience, [Marxist psychologists and sociologists] block up their ears and drum their heels, insisting that human nature cannot exist and that it is no fit subject for empirical inquiry.[51]

No doubt there is a grain of truth in this and there have been some unpleasant examples of academics, such as the founder of sociobiology, E. O. Wilson, being accused of being racists, fascists, sexists, and the like because of their views that some of the more unpleasant aspects of human behavior are inherent in human nature.[52] Pots-calling-kettles-black comes to mind or, in more theoretical terms, a possible case of projective identification. But it is important to recognize that the sociological critique of sociobiology and, latterly, evolutionary psychology is not simply political but is based on firm theoretical foundations.

Ideology, Science, and Cultural Politics

The narrow version of this concerns the ideological influences on any cultural endeavour in the sciences, arts, or religion. The broader version is concerned with the embeddedness of all human activity and thought within a cultural context, by which I mean a system of symbolic references and meanings. Both factors are addressed by the British neuroscientist and critic of evolutionary psychology Steven Rose, in relation to the external framing of scientific ideas.

> [External framing] includes the economic and political logic which drives society to fund some types of research and not others, and more subtly it includes the cultural and social forces which shape our metaphors, constrain our analogies, and provide the foundations for our theories and hypothesis-making.[53]

So it is not entirely surprising that a model which, by definition, rejects this embeddedness or, at best, regards it as less significant than evolutionary imperatives would also not recognize its own ideological influences.

In this respect, sociobiology and evolutionary psychology can easily become expressions of a conservative ideology which legitimizes the status quo by arguing that things are the way they are due to biological imperatives and claims the authority of science in doing so. The amount of space that so many writers in the field seem to give to challenging Marxist and feminist critiques makes it difficult to believe that they themselves are devoid of any political agenda. Steven Pinker wrote an entire book, *The Blank Slate*, in defence of the existence of "human nature" taking up such hot topics as gender differences, child-rearing practices, and the inherence of violence in human nature, a topic he has followed up subsequently in *The Better Angels of Our Nature*.[54] He argues that those who are ranged against the views of evolutionary psychology (such as neurobiologist Steven Rose, paleontologist Stephen Jay Gould, and geneticist Richard Lewontin) have an ideological bias that distorts and misrepresents the arguments of their opponents to such an extent that any attempt at rational discussion becomes "a politicized minefield" that creates "an atmosphere of intimidation."[55] Given this context, evolutionary psychologists can hardly claim to be unaffected by the social, cultural, and political climate in which they write or that their own scientific work is "above" such matters.

It is notable that many of the topics chosen for research by evolutionary psychologists are precisely those which would challenge radical views of the family and sexual politics—e.g., Buss' work on mate selection, Daly and Wilson's arguments for why step-parents are more likely to kill their step-children but show solicitude for their own offspring, and Thornhill and Palmer's especially controversial argument that rape is an evolutionary strategy for reproductive success.[56] Whether intentional or not, these topics are certainly "consistent with a backlash against a socially and economically successful feminist movement,"[57] and the fact that researchers choose to research a topic like rape in terms of evolutionary adaptation from the distant past rather than sexual power relations in social groups in the present reveals a particular way of seeing the world.

Such perspectives tend to screen out the moral and social conflicts involved by an appeal to the authority of "objective" science, itself a key feature of the ideology of an increasingly technocratic world of global capitalism. Indeed, the basic presupposition of evolutionary psychology is that social behavior is driven by biological imperatives and is therefore (relatively) independent of social and cultural influences. Archetype theory shares similar assumptions so it is no wonder that those who favour the biological view of archetypes should be attracted to evolutionary psychology as offering support for at least one version of Jung's views. It is also not surprising that theories of this kind will tend to support conservative socio-political viewpoints since the focus will be on "what has always been" rather than "what might be"—that is, "what has always been" is equated with what is "natural."[58]

Cultural Embeddedness:
The Power of Symbols to Shape Our World

Social attitudes inevitably influence how social and psychological phenomena are construed and this in turn challenges the notion that it is possible to reliably assert what is "universal" and what is not. Relativism, let alone the *tabula rasa*, is tangential to this issue. It is more a matter of recognising that we all exist within a particular socio-cultural world whose atmosphere we live and breathe and whose presuppositions about the world inevitably shape our outlooks, beliefs, interests, values, and intellectual preoccupations. Most of this is implicit or, in psychological language, unconscious. It is instantiated in the way our language is structured, in the values and assumptions of the family, and in the way we are introduced to the world around us, especially through the culturally embedded symbolic systems of language, thought, and imagery. As Lakoff and Johnson have shown, metaphors have the power to define reality.

> They do this through a coherent network of entailments
> that highlight some features of reality and hide others. The
> acceptance of the metaphor, which forces us to focus *only*
> on those aspects of our experience that it highlights, leads
> us to see the entailments of the metaphor as being *true*.[59]
> [italics in the original]

Writing in the late 1970s, they give an example of President Carter declaring the energy crisis as "the moral equivalent of war," thus giving rise to a series of entailments about how to think about the energy crisis in terms of the "war" metaphor. The post-9/11 "war on terror" takes this further; an actual war is conducted on the basis of a metaphorical equation—an emotional state (*terror*) becomes a metaphorical "enemy," giving rise to a series of entailments with impossible end-points. How can an emotional state (*terror*) be defeated on the battlefield?

Cultural symbols, as well as being shaped by the view of the world (ideology) in which they arise, also have the power to reinforce that world view. For example, in the England of the 1950s, where I grew up, it seemed quite normal that the trademark logo of the most popular jam-makers, Robertson's, was a little black golliwog. I would never have consciously connected this symbol for jam with actual people, and growing up in a middle class suburb of London, I rarely saw any black people anyway. So I would not have realized how offensive it was to black people; nor, without the active campaigning and "consciousness raising" of the anti-racist movement since the late 1970s, would I have recognized how it implicitly influenced my attitude towards them. Astonishingly, this symbol was not removed by Robertson's until 2001, but, by 2013, it was possible for a chef who referred to the Robertson's image in the presence of a black colleague to be found guilty of racism by a British Court of Appeal.[60] Even now some people might see this as "political correctness" rather than a recognition of the power of symbols to shape how we see the world.

The golliwog is not a fully fledged symbol in Jung's sense of being a representation of unknown meaning. Although it is emergent from a particular cultural context, it is not irreducible to the sum of its parts and therefore not an emergent phenomenon in the technical sense. Nevertheless, it is much more than a sign or an icon since it operates as a representational node in a network of complex and indeterminate social and psychological elements, containing within itself radically opposed meanings for widely separated social groups. So the ongoing conflicts about its use and meaning continue to represent that social conflict in symbolic form. I suggest it is best regarded as an example of Durkheim's notion of a "collective representation"—a socially generated phenomenon that not only represents an aspect of society but also subtly and subliminally shapes perceptions and organizes emotional responses. It is not merely what it does—legitimizes an infantilized caricature of black people—but *how* it does it that is most relevant to the theme of this book. The symbol does not create meaning out of nothing but organizes social and emotional elements into a representational form that generates further levels of emergent meaning which are anchored by the symbol. It will be my contention that such processes of symbol formation not only do not need an archetype behind them but that the meanings encapsulated by the abstract notion of archetype are sufficiently explained by the emergent features of symbols themselves. Put simply, symbols create archetypes rather than archetypes creating symbols.

The rather commonplace, even hackneyed example of the golliwog illustrates a larger theme: the way that symbolic meanings change over time as a result of social and political factors. The experience of "waking up" out of meanings that had previously been unquestioned, implicit, and taken for granted has convinced me of the power of symbolic systems of thought to virtually create the reality in which we live. Ironically, symbols not only promote consciousness, but can also obscure consciousness so that we need to "wake up" from the assumptions of their metaphorical entailments in order to become conscious of them. Thus, symbols can create a view of the world that we cannot escape because it is so taken for granted. In that sense, we are like the people of Plato's cave who take their views of the world to be the world itself with the rather important difference that instead of there being some "real" reality outside the cave, there are simply other views and other caves. It is only by recognising that whatever our view of the world, it is inevitably shaped by an invisible cultural web through which it arises and through which it continues to exist that we can be alert to the need to critique our perspective as much as we can, for example, by travelling to other caves and seeing how differently things may be there. Far from this leading to a groundless "anything is possible" kind of relativism, it actually uses relativism as a means of establishing a deeper grasp of reality through having a more extensive experience of it. In that respect, universalist viewpoints tend to *limit* the way we see the world because the normative convictions of the world-view within which they are propounded then become built-in and more difficult to scrutinize.

It is not only our ways of seeing the world that are influenced by social and environmental factors, but also our ways of living. Contrary to the "frustration of archetypal intent" idea, the very fact that we *can* choose to live in such a variety of different ways indicates the flexibility of human nature as well as its biological consistency. Humans are astonishingly adaptable, not only to different physical environments but also different socio-cultural ones, albeit not without considerable dislocation and disorientation. It seems unlikely that even Robin Fox with his glorifications of the "Paleoterrific" would be able to fit right in to living in an Aurignacian community of 35,000 years ago.[61] On the other hand, in the last decade or so, millions of Chinese have been making the transition from age-old traditional rural communities to modern city life with surprising success.[62] If ways of living are so affected by changing socio-cultural circumstances, it seems obvious that these must constitute active factors in shaping those ways of living. This does not mean that culture can write what it likes on an infinitely malleable human nature but that there is something wrong with the way culture and nature are being opposed in this debate. For humans, culture *is* our nature and we could not live without it. It is because cultures are so variable that we are able to adapt to such a variety of environmental circumstances. Increasingly, too, human environments have become cultural environments, further eroding the division between "nature" and "culture." We are in fact cultural animals with a cultural nature.

This does not necessarily deny the universality of those aspects of human culture cited by Fox and Stevens.[63] It does, however, challenge the notion that this can only be explained by reference to archetypes as biological universals located in the structure of the brain. Fox's argument for this involves an interesting thought-experiment in which if a new Adam and Eve could grow up, survive, and breed in total isolation from any existing human culture, they would recreate all the universal features of culture within a few generations.[64] But of course, this is entirely impossible since it is obvious even to Fox that no human infant could possibly survive without parental care and this is the very medium by which the newborn is introduced to culture. Just as there can be no brain without a body, so there can be no human being without a long history of evolution that creates a socio-cultural, as well as material, environment. So cultural reproduction is just as assured and inevitable as biological reproduction and does not need to be carried in the brain since it is reliably and necessarily carried (however imperfectly and variably) by human mothers. There is simply no need to require that cultural expectations are programmed into the brain and it would place a wholly unnecessary burden on the brain to do so. Why would evolution go to the trouble of allocating resources to the brain for "how to do social living" when they can be carried within the social milieu itself? Once culture develops, it becomes an inherent aspect of the biological medium in which we are all reared from the get-go. As the evolutionary anthropologist and developmental psychologist, Michael Tomasello puts it, "fish are born expecting water and humans are born expecting culture."[65] We simply cannot live without culture so we could no more re-create it *ab novo* than the fish could create the water in which it needs to be immersed. Human beings cannot be recreated without a pre-existing culture because human beings are cultural animals. Without it, they simply would not be able to become human.

Emergence Theories: Knox and Hogenson

To understand human nature, then, we need to understand how we are engaged with culture in a reciprocal dynamic interaction. It is to these issues that the emergence theories of Knox and Hogenson have addressed themselves in somewhat different ways.

Image Schemas (Knox)

Knox points out that core symbolic meanings cannot possibly be inherited because the human genome has turned out to be far too limited to carry such complex information.[66] She therefore espouses a third way between those viewpoints which assume a high level of innate "programs," "modules," and "algorithms" and those which reject any form of innate structure and argue from a purely environmental or constructivist view.

Knox's third way is derived from a developmental approach to learning which recognizes the limitations of what can be encoded in genetic information while acknowledging that innate mechanisms provide the basis for learning processes to be kick-started through "initial predispositions and attention biases which activate learning."[67] The extensive research on which she draws demonstrates that rather than being pre-given (cf., Jung's "ready-made brain"), psychic structures are *emergent* through the interaction of very simple innate responses with the environment. Even the structures that reliably emerge are much more simple than Jung's model of archetypes and, as I shall show, a large gap remains between these "image schemas" and the much more elaborated symbolic themes that constitute archetypal imagery.

Knox takes the idea of image schemas from Jean Mandler's work on the processes by which infants begin to form concepts.[68] Many of these early image schemas are organized around those features of bodily spatial organization identified by Lakoff and Johnson as the core metaphors to be found at the root of language such as "containment," "path of travel," "link," and "up/down." These originally physical images are later applied to more abstract realms, enabling the development of more complex meanings by a process of metaphorical extension. Since image schemas are the basis from which all later symbolic imagery is derived, Knox proposes that they constitute the archetype as-such which

> is never experienced directly but acts as a foundation or ground plan. ... This provides the invisible scaffolding for a whole range of metaphorical extensions that can be expressed in conscious imagery and language and that would therefore seem to correspond to the archetypal image.[69]

In this way she refashions Jung's definition of archetypes as "the possibility of ideas" in developmental terms. While rejecting their claim to be innate structures, she preserves the fundamental idea of archetypes as abstract organising frameworks combined with core meanings, albeit as much simpler structures than those proposed by Jung. She argues that their apparent universality is due to the commonalities of human experience.

This is an elegant solution to the problem of how core meanings can emerge if they are not innate, firmly based on current empirical research in developmental psychology. Unfortunately, Knox's formulation is fundamentally different from whatever Jung meant by archetypes. This turns on the distinction between the archetype as a source of mental imagery, metaphor, and conceptual organization and the archetype as "a pattern of behavior." For Jung this meant far more than the simple sensory-motor behaviors that are organized into image schemas; it referred to archetypes as the fundamental drivers of *all* human behavior and especially the more complex behaviors that are symbolized in mythology, religion, and other collective narrative such as fairy tales. Whether or not his claim is valid, Jung argued that archetypes were the drivers of our deepest strivings as human beings and are therefore powerful sources of emotional experience. So, for instance, he suggests that there is an archetype of "meaning" because the need for meaning is such a fundamental aspect of human motivations and gives rise, for example, to religion and mythology— that is, not merely the *imagery* of religion and mythology but the need to create that imagery and those religious practices in the first place.

Image schemas may form the archetypes of symbolic imagery insofar as they provide the source domains for more complex abstract metaphors and symbols but they do not constitute the archetypes of the patterns of action to which those metaphors and symbols refer. So they tell us very little about the behaviors and emotional experiences that generate symbols, nor what those symbols might mean. To be clear, image schemas do show how it is possible to form symbols by means of metaphorical extensions and they are firmly rooted in embodied action, but Knox's project, especially in her more recent work, is concerned with how infants develop from relating through action to a capacity for self-reflection. She turns to neuroscience for an explanation of the "move from motor activity to the most primitive concepts (image schemas) and to more complex conceptual and symbolic representation."[70] As a developmental psychologist concerned with linking developmental processes with their neuroscientific correlates, her interests lie far from Jung's concern with the great symbolic systems of world religion and mythology and the patterns of collective human behavior he believed them to represent. So one might say that image schemas are patterns *of* simple basic embodied action-schemas but they are not patterns *for* action in the sense of being schemas for, say, loving one's mother or pursuing a heroic goal, let alone the formation of a god-image. By contrast, however muddled and contradictory Jung's account of archetypes may be, they are intended not only as models for how we formulate symbols but also for what those more complex symbols are about.

This is what can make Knox's image schemas seem like bloodless abstractions remote from the affectively charged imagery of Jung's work. She has provided an intellectually consistent and justifiable case for archetypes but at the price of removing from them most of what they are aim to describe and explain. While these basic schemas may be required for the later formation of symbols, they are not themselves symbolic—they are neither signifiers nor what is signified but simply the basis *for* signification. Gallese and Lakoff make it clear that image schemas refer to the formation of concepts but concepts are not symbols.[71] For example, many animals will have image-action schemas that provide them with a basic conceptual orientation to their species-specific milieu. And this is particularly true of those animals with advanced problem-solving and tool-using skills, notably corvids (crows) and great apes. But only humans use symbols. This point is often confused because the term *symbol* is used in cognitive science to refer to formal, disembodied representations that are purported to exist in the mind as "copies" of sensory perceptions. The phenomenologically informed, enactive approach which is one of the main influences in Lakoff and Johnson's work explicitly eschews this notion as I discuss further in the next chapter. The sense in which only humans use symbols refers to their use as a particular form of *communication* that is unique to humans, notably (but not exclusively) language. Image schemas, which are implicit non-conscious structures, can have no communicative meaning in themselves albeit they lend meaning to symbolic communication by means of action-based metaphors that derive from them. The meaning is emergent from the relation between source and target domains. For example, the physical action of grasping provides the meaning (conceptualization) for what it means to grasp a point but only the latter usage constitutes a symbol.

A further point concerns the potential slippage between brain and mind. Gallese and Lakoff discuss these early concepts in terms of the activity of functional clusters of neurons in the brain. They stress that "[t]his does *not* mean that we take functional clusters themselves to be symbolic. The symbols are only *our names* for functional clusters, which, as we have seen, function from a computational point of view as neurally realised units."[72] So while the word *grasp* could not have a meaning without an image schema of grasping, the word does not refer to the abstract non-experienceable image schema but to the physical action of grasping itself. Thus, image schemas cannot be signified by symbols any more than they can act as signifiers. What they can do is act as a means of conceptual orientation and as the source domain of metaphors, but that is a different matter entirely.

Thus, it is quite clear that image schemas do not refer to what symbols represent but merely provide the basic possibilities for how symbols may be constructed. As soon as they become metaphorically extended, they have become symbolic images, rather than the core meanings that Knox, like Jung, proposes to separate from their manifestations as "archetypal images." An example of this is Knox's argument that "there may be no such thing as an archetypal mother but instead there is an image schema of containment."[73] Here the original image schema of *containment* in the (literal) sense that Lakoff and Johnson refer to it has been metaphorically enriched by extension to the target domain of mother-infant interaction. Once again, we couldn't think these thoughts without image schemas but the thoughts cannot be directly derived from the schema. Image schemas are necessary but not sufficient for symbolic thought.

So we are still left with the problem of how to derive a system of complex signifiers and what they signify from the simple, core meanings from which Knox claims they can emerge. If what we are trying to demonstrate and explain is the universality of complex patterns of symbolic imagery and meaning together with the typical forms of human behavior they represent, we will need to look elsewhere.

Patterns of Action: Emergence in Complex Dynamic Systems (Hogenson)

Where Knox focuses on image as embodied concept, George Hogenson shows how the pattern of behavior is embedded in a complex, dynamic system that extends beyond the individual brain or mind and includes the environmental context.[74] Hogenson points out that in his later work, Jung's account of the pattern of behavior in a leaf-cutting act has subtly shifted from the notion of an internal image being triggered off by an external situation to a more holistic view in which the image is a function of the dynamic system formed by the creature and its environment:

> The instinct of the leaf-cutting ant fulfils the image of ant, tree, leaf, cutting, transport, and little ant-garden of fungi. If any one of these conditions is lacking, the instinct does not function, because it cannot exist without its total pattern, without its image.[75]

Hogenson argues that "Jung takes very seriously the notion that the archetypal is always embedded in a context, and that the context is equally as important as any structure that may be provided by the archetypes."[76]

In subsequent papers, Hogenson cites two illuminating examples of the way infants are boot-strapped into social and intentional behavior through the mother's pre-socialized response to very simple reflex behaviors, resulting in the emergence of more complex behaviors that do not need to be pre-specified in innate "modules." The first of these concerns Thelen and Smith's demonstration that there is no innate form of proto-grasping.[77] While grasping has a regularity amongst adults there is no such regularity amongst infants. The only common feature in infants is that their caregivers all think their infants are trying to grasp something. So, concludes Hogenson, "grasping is an emergent pattern of action that derives from complex interactions between an infant and adult who themselves have come to view inchoate patterns of action as purposeful."[78] The second example is the burst-pause pattern of nursing demonstrated by Kaye and Wells.[79]

> This nursing pattern is universal among human infants, and also unique to human infants. No other mammal displays this particular pattern, which is tightly structured in time. The pattern is, therefore, universal and innate, and

> clearly the product of human evolution. The presence of
> this pattern of nursing also entrains a highly predictable
> response pattern on the part of the mother; the infant's pause
> invariably results in an attempt on the part of the mother to
> encourage the infant to resume nursing, usually by jiggling
> the infant. ... But the burst-pause-burst pattern has nothing
> intrinsically to do with successful nursing. Rather the
> contrary. This leads Kaye to suggest that the nursing pattern
> is the first step in the development of another universal
> pattern of human action, turn taking in conversation.[80]

So the emergence of the distinctly human form of interaction ("conversation") can only emerge when the infant's innately evolved pattern of action that, on its own has no intentional content, is met by the social and cultural expectations of a mother who "has a complex, culturally determined, symbolic, interpretative strategy that begins, importantly, with the notion that all action is meaningful, i.e., intentional."[81] And such interpretation is itself embedded in highly variable personal and cultural meanings so, as Hogenson points out, "the actual outcomes of the negotiation between mother and infant can be quite idiosyncratic given differing cultural and distinctly individualized interpretations on the part of the mother."[82] Like Knox, Hogenson is keen to stress that these innate responses do not in themselves include any conceptual content, and it is this which distinguishes the emergence model from the evolutionary psychology model. Human meaning and intentionality emerge out of a long evolutionary background of human sociality and cannot do so except in and through sociality.

These examples are both cited in the context of Hogenson's criticism of evolutionary psychology's reliance on Chomsky's theory of an innate grammar. Hogenson draws on several critiques but especially Terrence Deacon's argument that, for a feature to be reliably selected, the environment needs to remain stable over a long enough period for species-level genetic change to occur; the constant development and change of living languages does not provide such stability.[83]

To my mind, however, the most illuminating of all Hogenson's examples of emergence is the work done by Rodney Brooks in designing robots. Previously, computational models of cognition had been unable to solve the problem of how to design robots that could move around. Computers could beat a grand master at chess but were unable to move across a room without bumping into obstacles. Brooks proposed that rather than designing an elaborate cognitive module with a host of algorithms to account for any situation the robot was likely to encounter, (like the modules proposed by evolutionary psychology), all that was needed was to link perception directly to the motor action of the robots, thus eliminating the cognitive module altogether.[84]

In his debate with Anthony Stevens at the IAAP Cambridge Conference in 2001, Hogenson showed a short video in which a group of small robots, each basically consisting of a light sensor on wheels, gradually self-organize so that they all join together in pushing a box into a corner.[85] It looks for all the world as if they are guided by some kind of intentional program for collective action concerned with "box-pushing" but in fact all they have are simple instructions for action on encountering obstacles, such as "push-left" or "push-right." When I saw this, I suddenly understood what "emergence" was and realized the potential of dynamic systems theory to revolutionize the way we think about archetypes. "This," I thought, "is the future."

Hogenson's conclusion is that the archetypes *do not exist* in the sense of being located anywhere whether in the brain, the genome, or a neo-Platonic transcendent realm. "Rather the archetypes are the emergent properties of the dynamic developmental system of brain, environment, and narrative."[86] The implication of this view, it seems to me, is that it will no longer be possible to distinguish between archetypes and archetypal images since the only ontological reality is the emergent images, whether these are the patterns of action or symbolic representations constructed via the imagination. We may recognize certain regularities that reliably emerge but there is nothing "behind" or "underneath" those regularities other than our own abstractions.

At this point, Hogenson seems to draw back from the radical implications of his conclusion, reassuring his readers that of course the archetypes exist or we would not be able to understand our basic human narratives. By this, he means that archetypes do exist as emergent phenomena with demonstrable regularities even if they are not discrete entities "in the unconscious" with any behindological force. In his subsequent work, he has sought to show that these regularities obey mathematical laws, thereby retaining the idea of symbolic forms as shaped by universal structures, now redefined as emergent rather than pre-given.[87] Similarly, Knox retains the notion of archetypes for her image schemas, taking from the archetype idea only the notion of the "original form." Thus, for both authors, the concept of the archetype remains meaningful despite being reformulated in emergent terms.

The Redundance of Archetypes

In my view, the retention of the term *archetype* in such radically different explanatory models obscures the fundamental distinction between emergence theory and the inherently essentialist assumptions of any theory of archetypes. By definition, archetypes are pre-existent forms, not only because that is what Jung says they are but in the fundamental meaning of the word as "the original pattern or model from which copies are made."[88] Therefore, they cannot be equivalent to emergent forms which are definitively *not* pre-existent. We might perhaps speak of omni-types in the sense that certain emergent features are universally found but they can no longer be archetypes since there is now no original form of which they are the typical examples.[89] Without this, the term *archetype* becomes merely descriptive and misleadingly so since it implies that there is some primary form "behind" the phenomena in a way that emergence theory disputes. Jung proposed the existence of archetypes because he observed certain regularities and thought it was necessary to postulate an explanatory category for them that he named archetypes. But it now turns out that these patterns can be explained in an entirely different way that does *not* require an external or *a priori* ontological category to explain their emergence. Hence "the archetype" becomes the equivalent of phlogiston. The discovery that fire occurs through the combustion of oxygen does not "redefine" phlogiston, it enables us to see that we no longer *need* phlogiston as part of our explanation.

Let me give an example of a universal pattern of relating which is sometimes given as an example of "archetypal" behavior—the attachment system between mother and infant. Here the description *archetypal* adds nothing to the phenomena in question because the behavior is not driven by pre-existent forms. Attachment theory demonstrates by empirical evidence that young infants show consistent patterns of distress when separated from their mothers and, latterly, that these patterns are consistent over time and can be passed on to offspring. This is a robust theory backed by a large body of empirical experimental evidence. There are even elaborations to the theory which show the impact of attachment on brain development.[90] Attachment theory does not claim that attachment behavior is the expression of an archetype—it shows that it is the expression of a sequence of behaviors (including emotional responses) which are initiated and terminated in particular ways. As Knox points out, attachment theory does not refer to a "potential for content" but to behavior which is realized in actual experience.[91] Knox is not saying that there is nothing innate about infant attachment but rather that the innate elements can only be simple non-representational mechanisms, not complex elaborations of perception and behavior that give infants an "idea" of what they can expect to find in a mother. There is simply no job for the archetype to do here. It is redundant.

So it is misleading and inconsistent to say that archetypes arise out of brain, narrative, and environment since these are not the archetypes but the typical images and patterns of action that the concept of archetypes was supposed to explain. The original explanation proposed the existence of some other entity or force or principle, whether biological, psychological, or metaphysical that exists prior to the typical images or action patterns and is responsible for their emergence. But in the new explanation, the images and patterns are emergent from much simpler elements such as proto-grasping or the perceptual processing of the movement of objects in space. So to be logically consistent we would have to say that it is those simple elements which constitute the archetypes, not the images and actions that emerge from them. But, of course, these simple innate elements look nothing like archetypes as Jung described them. Even the emergent forms such as image schemas or proto-conversations look nothing like archetypes and these are already emergent from simpler features. So in order to arrive at anything remotely like the archetypes with which Jung's work is concerned, we have to look elsewhere – not to the purported original forms which symbols express but *to the symbols themselves.*

What all this amounts to is that we have nothing to lose by dispensing with archetypes and everything to gain. The loss frees us from having to keep faith with a hypothesis that has outlived its usefulness and redirects our attention to the actual phenomena that archetypes were introduced to explain. In my view, these phenomena primarily refer to the process and products of symbolic imagination— that is, symbols and their meanings.

In addition I would like to make an important extension to Hogenson's conditions for the emergence of archetypes out of brain, narrative, and environment. Curiously, he has left out the body which is the vital element of our being in the world. The brain plays a crucial part in the functioning of the body but it is ultimately no more than a single organ within the body and cannot function without it. The body includes the brain but the brain is not the body. Nor is it just the archetypes which are emergent from brain, body and environment—it is the mind itself. It takes more than a brain to make a mind as much as it takes more than a brain to make a body. That is the subject of the next chapter since, before we can have a position from which to consider the emergence of symbolic imagination within the mind, we need to have a deeper understanding of the mind itself. Like language and archetypal images, the mind is not located anywhere, yet it does most certainly exist.

CHAPTER TWO

EXPANDING THE MIND

In this chapter I intend to discuss a number of different theories that have in common the effort to break down the Cartesian barrier separating the thinking mind (*res cogitans*) from the sensory world "out there" (*res extensa*). Although virtually no one subscribes to this kind of Cartesian dualism anymore it has had a deep and pervasive effect on the way we think about and conceive of ourselves and the world we live in—that is, our being in the world—and it is extremely difficult to think ourselves out of our Cartesian presuppositions. Elsewhere I have discussed how I think Jung struggled with this in his attempt to formulate a satisfactory explanation for synchronicity, and it is also implicit in the critique of archetypes as innate structures in the brain that I outlined in the previous chapter.[1] The emergence model is part of a wider response to this residual Cartesian problem and its ultimate aim is to enable us to think about ourselves in the world in a more holistic way that breaks down the division between subject and object and reconstitutes our model of the mind as embodied, embedded, situated, and contextual. It challenges the dominating view of the mind as located in the brain and, *a fortiori*, the even more extreme yet commonplace belief that the mind *is* the brain; instead, it relocates mind in the natural world of which we are ourselves a part.

Dualism, Idealism, Materialism

Descartes' formulation of mind and matter as wholly separate and different entities is the first modern articulation of a problem that is still unresolved today—how is an immaterial mind related to a material body? One way of considering this question would be to ask "what kind of thing is the mind?" This was not, however, the main problem with which Descartes was concerned. His primary aim was to establish that only the soul can think. What follows from this is that material objects, including the human body, are better understood by considering them in terms of their own mechanisms rather than imputing to them extraneous qualities of a purposive mind appropriate only to the soul. This did not mean that Descartes questioned the *reality* of the body or that he doubted that body and soul were united in one being. When challenged on the question of how the mind can move the body or the body can transmit its sensations to the mind he replied that there is also a union of soul and body by means of which "the soul can act and suffer with the body."[2] Although he never argued the point in much detail, he clearly did not doubt that mind and body constituted a unity even if he could not provide a satisfactory explanation that followed from the way he had separated them. And he also gave a reason *why* he had "said almost nothing" about the connection—that it would have been harmful to his main intention which was to challenge the Scholastic-Aristotelian view of bodies acting according to soul-like qualities such as the "heaviness" of a physical body.[3] It seems then that the Cartesian dualist legacy with which we all struggle today is a by-product of the main thrust of his thought which was concerned with the philosophy of scientific method as much if not more than the philosophy of mind.

Descartes' aim was to provide a secure philosophical foundation for the newly emerging experimental science based on mechanistic principles. He achieved this by the use of skepticism as a method that enabled him to rebuild a system of belief from the established first principle that the one thing that cannot be doubted is one's own existence. It is, though, highly significant that, for Descartes, "I exist" was equated with "I think"—that is, he grounded existence in rationalist thought and relegated emotion and sensation to the separate realm of the body. The body thus becomes part of the material world that is not mental and therefore cannot guarantee one's own existence. This is what Antonio Damasio called "Descartes' Error," arguing that emotion is an integral aspect of thought and therefore that the mind must be fully embodied.[4] Emotion and embodiment are just as much a guarantee of our existence as thought and, furthermore, have the considerable advantage of grounding us in the material world.

So it is a great irony that someone who was so concerned with the exploration of the material world should have constructed a philosophy of mind that severs us from feeling grounded in our material existence. Descartes is not really responsible for this, of course; he simply articulated a key moment in the transition from the medieval world of Aristotelian scholasticism to the modern world of scientific materialism. He helped to make possible the scientific revolution by showing the previously unthinkable possibilities that could be opened up by seeing the world as a non-mental system of mechanisms, ultimately a *machine*. And it is this, rather than dualism *per se*, that has increasingly left those who wish to maintain a place for the soul fighting a rearguard action against the apparently unlimited triumphs of materialist science. This can be traced through the conflict between Idealist and materialist views of the world since the early eighteenth century, the challenge to Christian religious truth posed by Darwin's theory of evolution in the nineteenth century, and, not least, the uneasy relationship between twentieth-century psychology and a scientific method based on the mechanistic principles of materialism initially laid down by Descartes.

Thus, to greatly oversimplify some very complex philosophical debates over several centuries, the advance of materialist science has led to attempts to get rid of the problem of the mind by incorporating it in matter, for which, latterly, neuroscience and artificial intelligence have provided the means as well as the need. Neuroscience cannot hope to provide a full explanation of mental functioning if it cannot explain how the mind exists in the first place, while the notion of artificial intelligence ultimately relies on being able to prove that computers can think in a way that is indistinguishable from the human mind. Both disciplines come up against the obstacle of consciousness, hence the title of Daniel Dennett's 1991 book *Consciousness Explained* which drew on both disciplines in an intellectual *tour de force* that has been said to explain everything *except* consciousness.[5]

Against the advancing tide of materialism, Idealist philosophers have striven to maintain the supremacy of the mind or Spirit by arguing that, since the material world can only be known through the mind, the mind (or psyche) has a prior claim to be the fundamental reality (metaphysical Idealism) or, at least, that the mind is an irreducible element of how we can know the world at all (epistemological Idealism). An alternative strategy is to seek a sort of truce by arguing that mind and matter are both aspects of some other fundamental reality which we are unable to know directly (dual aspect theory). The theories that I discuss in this chapter are all attempts to escape these alternatives by reformulating the nature of mind so that the problem of dualism does not arise. These approaches argue that the mind/body problem is really a conceptual problem that derives from Cartesian dualism—that we have become trapped in Cartesian ways of thinking about the mind and need to learn to think about ourselves and our place in the world in a different way. They could also be described as a way of re-conceptualizing materialism so that it does not exclude the mind—hence the emphasis on embodiment, being in the world and material engagement—but also on expanding our conception of the mind so that it is no longer cut off from the material world.

Berkeley and La Mettrie:
Esse est Percipi vs. Man a Machine

The conflict over the status of the mind is illustrated particularly well by two opposing thinkers from the eighteenth century, both of whose work was in part a response to Descartes: the Anglo-Irish cleric Bishop Berkeley (1685–1753) who formulated the first modern argument for Idealism in his *Principles of Human Knowledge* (1710) and Julien Offray de La Mettrie (1709–1751), a French physician who was the first to propose the completely materialist and atheist view that man is a machine in the 1740s.

Writing in the first decades of the eighteenth century, in the wake of Locke and Newton as well as Descartes, Berkeley recognized that the growth of materialist science posed a threat to religious belief in a Supreme Being through its assertion of matter as a fundamental reality. Against this, Berkeley questioned the existence of matter as a necessary conceptual entity. He did not question the reality of things in the world (houses, mountains, rivers, apples, trees, stones, etc.) but argued that such things could not exist independently of the mind. In his famous phrase, *esse est percipi* (to be is to be perceived), things only have existence in and through the minds that perceive them. Berkeley's answer to the problem of what happens to the tree in the forest when there is no one there to perceive it was that, ultimately, all things are held in the Mind of God. Thus, the ultimate guarantee of existence and reality is God Himself. In this way, Berkeley could vanquish the doctrine of Matter and prove the necessity of God in one stroke.

Few subsequent philosophers have dared to propose such an extreme version of Idealism as Berkeley. Yet, despite the apparent absurdity of the notion that things only exist through our perceiving them, his philosophical arguments are serious ones and still respected by philosophers today. For example, Wittgenstein regarded him as a much deeper philosopher than Schopenhauer, whose post-Kantian philosophy of the "World as Idea" a century later bears some similarities to Berkeley.[6] Schopenhauer regarded him as the father of Idealism because of his insistence on the absolute necessity of subjectivity. For his part, Schopenhauer was one of the first German Idealist philosophers to reinterpret Kant's strictures "banning" speculation about a transcendent reality by arguing that the world was created/driven by a transcendent Will whose operation could be recognized and known—a view that has much in common with Jung's view of the psychoid archetype. And, of course, the central importance of subjective experience is a *sine qua non* of psychoanalytic practice even if it may be theoretically reducible to drives or archetypes.

Berkeley's concerns about the implications of materialism were borne out within his lifetime by the equally daring proposition asserted by Julien Offray de La Mettrie, who was the first to take Descartes' view of matter to its logical conclusion. La Mettrie asserted that man himself is a machine who can be studied and understood in wholly mechanistic terms without the dualist intervention of a separate non-material soul. By observing his own reactions to a severe fever, he concluded that not only were his mental faculties affected by his physical condition but that these mental processes were actually caused by organic changes in the brain and nervous system. In his first book *L'Histoire Naturelle de L'Âme* (The Natural History of the Soul) published in 1745 he put forward the claim that there is no separate soul or metaphysical essence and that men, like animals, can be studied in entirely mechanical terms. Where Descartes had argued that animals were mindless machines from which men were distinguished by the possession of a soul, La Mettrie countered that animals can also think and communicate their passions without requiring a soul, so why should humans be regarded any differently?

His ideas were greeted with universal outrage and he was forced into exile in Germany where he published his definitive work

L'Homme Machine (1747) which produced an even greater scandal. This stated that men, like animals are mechanical automatons. As he put it in a subsequent book, "[nature] made without thinking a machine which thinks."[7] Since all human behavior, including reasoning, is based upon sensation, it can be explicated strictly by reference to physiology without supposing any divine intervention.[8] Even more controversially, he anticipated Darwin by a century in pointing out the similarities between apes and humans and even suggested that apes could be trained to learn languages[9]—a claim that is still being tested today, albeit with rather limited results, as discussed in the next chapter.

Since the mind is subject to the forces of the body, La Mettrie argued that the study of how men function was best conducted by physicians, rather than by philosophers or theologians, a point that has striking echoes with the views of Sigmund Freud. Intriguingly, La Mettrie is also reminiscent of both Freud and Jung in the importance he gave to imagination:

> I always use the word 'imagine,' because I think that everything is the work of imagination, and that all the faculties of the soul can be correctly reduced to pure imagination in which they all consist. Thus judgment, reason, and memory are not absolute parts of the soul, but merely modifications of this kind of medullary screen upon which images of the objects painted in the eye are projected as by a magic lantern.[10]

Freud and Jung

The conflict of views illustrated by Berkeley and La Mettrie were still very much alive in the late nineteenth-century context from which psychoanalysis emerged. Freud and Jung took very different positions concerning the relation between mind and matter. Although initially influenced by Goethe's (Romantic) *Naturphilosophie*, Freud enthusiastically adopted scientific materialism as a medical student. For the rest of his life, he never wavered from the materialist convictions that made him a devoted supporter of the "anti-vitalist pact" proclaiming, just as La Mettrie had done, that living beings could be fully explained in chemical and biological terms without the need for any separate "vital" force responsible for life.[11] Freud began his career as a neurologist and his first attempts at formulating a scientific psychology were couched in entirely neurological terms.[12] He rejected this as unsatisfactory and, in making the shift to a purely psychological theory of the mind, he made an ingenious accommodation with his materialist views. Since the state of neurological science at the time was not adequate for the formulation of a materialist theory, it would be necessary to proceed in psychological terms but with the expectation that, in due course, all that he was postulating in psychological terms would eventually be demonstrable in physical terms. In my view, it was for this reason that he insisted on fidelity to his theory of libido, not, as Jung disparagingly claimed, because he was obsessed with the "numen" of sexuality. The libido theory was, for Freud, the link to a material foundation for his psychological theory; libido was the bridge between instinct as a physical phenomenon and its representation in the mind as unconscious wishes. As he wrote in *Three Essays on Sexuality*, "The concept of instinct is thus one of those lying on the frontier between the mental and the physical."[13]

For Jung, the situation was much more complicated as he oscillated throughout his life between his allegiance to science and his more personal (and experiential) convictions of the reality of the spirit. Furthermore, his view of science was very different from Freud's staunch materialism, owing much more to the scientific thinkers of German Romanticism and *Naturphilosophie*, such as Goethe and Humboldt.[14] Their approaches to science included a close interrelationship between the subjective and objective, a holistic view of natural systems, and a view of empiricism in which phenomena are allowed to "speak for themselves."[15] Thus, for Jung it was no contradiction with scientific empiricism for him to assert that psychic reality is the primary datum of experience. He states that "the psychic alone has immediate reality and that psychic reality is "the only reality we can experience immediately."[16] He was also scathingly critical of materialism as an unjustifiably one-sided view:

> Just as formerly the assumption was unquestionable that everything that exists originates in the creative will of a God who is a spirit, so the nineteenth century discovered the equally unquestionable truth that everything arises from material causes. Today the psyche does not build itself a body, but on the contrary matter, by chemical action, produces the psyche. This reversal of outlook would be ludicrous if it were not one of the unquestioned verities of the spirit of the age.[17] ... We delude ourselves with the thought that we know much more about matter than about a "metaphysical" mind or spirit, and so we

overestimate material causation and believe that it alone affords us a true explanation of life.[18]

He comes closest to an Idealist position when he argues that psychic factors are the *sine qua non* for the existence of the world and therefore "we are steeped in a world that was created by our own psyche."[19] Nevertheless, he draws back from a complete eschewal of matter à la Berkeley, espousing a more agnostic Kantian reticence about the ultimately unknowable nature of the "thing in itself." "But matter is just as inscrutable as mind. As to the ultimate things we can know nothing."[20]

Despite the strong Idealist tinge to his thought, Jung usually professed a version of neutral monism (that there is a fundamental reality but we don't know what it is) or, latterly, dual aspect theory, as in the following comment from *Mysterium Coniunctionis*: "The common background of microphysics and depth-psychology is as much physical as psychic and therefore neither, but rather a third thing, a neutral nature which can at most be grasped in hints since in essence it is transcendental."[21] And in the Tavistock Lectures he says,

> It is due to our most lamentable mind that we cannot think of body and mind as one and the same thing: probably they are one thing, but we are unable to think it. ... Body and mind are the two aspects of the living being, and that is all I know. Therefore I prefer to say that the two things happen together in a miraculous way ... we cannot think them together.[22]

Jung's difficulty in being able to think beyond the separation of mind and body is largely due to the way he remained trapped in Cartesian assumptions of an encapsulated mind that was at odds with his intuitive sense of a body-mind unity (as might even be said of Descartes himself as I indicated earlier). This encapsulated view of the mind is apparent when Jung remarks, "Consciousness has no direct relation to any material objects. We perceive nothing but images, transmitted to us indirectly by a complicated nervous apparatus."[23] He also says,

> It is my mind, with its store of images, that gives the world color and sound; and that supremely real and rational certainty which I call 'experience' is, in its most simple form, an exceedingly complicated structure of mental images. Thus there is in a certain sense, nothing that is directly experienced except the mind itself.[24]

From this it follows that the real nature of material things can only be determined through chemistry and physics. In true Cartesian style, he writes, "These disciplines are really tools which help the human intellect to cast a glance behind the deceptive view of images into a non-psychic world."[25]

Jung's boldest attempt to resolve the apparent conflict between matter and spirit was his concept of the "psychoid," developed through his collaboration with Pauli and his work on synchronicity. The term *psychoid* was originally coined by Hans Driesch for whom it had an explicitly vitalist meaning. As Addison has argued, "The fact that [Jung] chose to adopt the same terminology suggests that he still wished to retain a vitalistic basis for his ideas, in spite of the fact that he eschewed the entirely vitalistic notion of Driesch."[26]

At one level, the psychoid refers to the area of overlap between the mental and the physical and is therefore similar to the way Freud used instinct as a borderline concept of this kind. But for Jung the psychoid is much more than this since it indicates a potentially non-psychic aspect of the archetype on the one hand and, via synchronicity, the apparently psychic aspect of the material world on the other. This is the basis for his conclusion that matter and spirit are two aspects of the same thing:

> Since psyche and matter are contained in one and the same world, and moreover are in continuous contact with one another, and ultimately rest on irrepresentable, transcendental factors, it is not only possible but fairly probable, even, that psyche and matter are two different aspects of the same thing. The synchronicity phenomena point, it seems to me, in this direction, for they show that the non-psychic can behave like the psychic, and vice versa, without there being any causal connection between them.[27]

To my mind, this only succeeds in introducing further complications and confusion. For one thing, it involves Jung in a Kantian contradiction in which he claims that it is possible to have knowledge of the psychoid as a "transcendent factor" which by definition is beyond knowledge.[28] Secondly, it involves the introduction of a principle of meaning or "meaning in itself" that is apparently divorced from any intentional agent for whom anything might be meaningful— unless it hints at the existence of a transcendent God.[29] This would be reminiscent of Berkeley's argument that the things of the world are held in being through the mind of God, another indication of Jung's inclination towards Idealism.

The Problem of Consciousness

The fundamental problem with Jung's concept of the psychoid is that it starts from a dualistic Cartesian view and then attempts to bridge it rather than challenging that viewpoint at its source. The same issue crops up in recent debates about how to solve the so-called "hard problem" of how the material brain "creates" immaterial consciousness.[30] As philosopher Evan Thompson shows, any attempt to create a "third thing" (such as the psychoid) to resolve the problem is doomed to failure:

> Dualistic conceptions of consciousness and life ... exclude each other by construction. Hence there is no way to close the gap between them. To reduce conscious experience to external structure and function would be to make consciousness disappear (materialism); to reduce external structure and function to internal consciousness would be to make external things disappear (idealism); *and to inject some third ingredient between the two is a desperate effort to bridge an unbridgeable chasm.* The hard problem is thus not so much hard as impossible: the problem of making comprehensible the relation of mind and body cannot be solved as long as consciousness and life are conceptualized in such a way that they intrinsically exclude one another. For this reason it is crucial to realize that this chasm is a philosophical construction going back to Descartes. We need to look more closely at this Cartesian legacy for it remains a powerful force in many contemporary treatments of the problem of consciousness.[31] [italics added]

One of the most fundamental assumptions of the Cartesian legacy is that the mind exists "in the head" and, latterly, this has become increasingly identified with the brain. This frequently results in absurd claims that attribute agency to the brain as if it is the "real" actor in the human drama. So, for example, it is said that "the brain makes sense of things and, when it is unable to do so in relation to such questions as 'why are we here' it resorts to superstitious beliefs."[32] The implicit image here is the brain as a sort of malfunctioning computer that is attempting to act beyond the limits of its programming. This replicates the mind-body split as a brain-body split, although there is also a wisp of a ghost in the machine that is supposedly asking the computer-brain questions it can't answer, questions that "don't compute."

It may be objected that this is simply a figurative way of speaking but such figures of speech are persuasive and easily elide the fact that brains do not think, people do.[33] In this sense, brain activity is confined to the transmission of chemical and electrical impulses, albeit in the context of a breathtakingly complex and differentiated architectural organization. Even though we could not think, imagine, or act without it, that does not make the brain the agent of our thoughts and actions which are only possible through our embodied engagement with the world. The confusion is apparent in frequent references to the so-called "brain/mind" implying that there is no difference between them. At best, this strategy may be adopted as a kind of agnostic stance, as if to say that, since we do not yet know the difference between brain and mind and since it is apparent that the mind is dependent on the brain, we can speak of them *as if* they were one. But more commonly, it is simply a fudge, a way of pretending that the problem of the relation between mind and brain does not exist, as if the electrical and chemical activity in the brain *is* the mind, thus avoiding the "hard problem" of how the one becomes the other.

Computational Theory of Mind

A further aspect of the Cartesian legacy is the equation of the soul with rationality. Descartes identified the soul with thought ("only the soul can think"), and the body with feeling as a form of sensation which was thus placed on the other side of the mind/matter divide as purely mechanical. It was La Mettrie's observation that his supposedly purely thinking soul was actually affected by his bodily feeling that led him to dispense with the idea of the soul altogether.

Computer science has, in one sense, gone in the opposite direction, dispensing with bodily feeling and focusing entirely on the thinking soul but ending up with the same conclusion that there is nothing more than the material machine. There is nothing, in principle, about machines that can carry out the same functions as humans do that denies the non-material aspects of consciousness (the "soul"). The philosophical question arises when claims are made that such machines are *the same* as humans. This claim asserts that since the soul thinks and computers can carry out the operations that humans undertake when they think, then computers can also think. Since only the soul can think (according to the Cartesian legacy), this means that computers that can think must have souls or, in modern parlance, that such machines would also be conscious.

The question of machine intelligence was first addressed from a scientific point of view by Alan Turing in 1950.[34] Turing's paper, which virtually founded the field of Artificial Intelligence (AI), was concerned with demonstrating how computers could be programmed to rival human intelligence. Its most famous element was the Turing Test in which a human being and a computer would each be interrogated by a series of textual messages. Turing argued that if the interrogator could not distinguish between the computer and the human on the basis of this test then the computer could be deemed intelligent, since this would be no different from the way we judge other humans to be intelligent by external observation.

Turing's work has been seminal for AI for good reason, but the Turing Test reveals several questionable assumptions about human intelligence and consciousness. Firstly, mind is conceived, as Descartes did, in entirely rational terms, excluding the body, emotion, and sensation. Secondly, it is seen as an internal property of mechanical bodies that is only discernable by deduction—an important assumption that lies behind a great deal of developmental research on when children develop a "theory of mind" and, more generally, how we know that other people are conscious. In philosophy of mind, this is known as "the zombie problem"—i.e., how do we know that other people are not "zombies" who merely give the *appearance* of possessing minds like our own since our only direct knowledge of mind is through our own consciousness and we cannot experience other people's experiences? Hence the further assumption that mind and consciousness exist "in the head" and that is where we should look for it. Inevitably, this has led to the popularization of the now almost ubiquitous metaphor of the brain as a computer, reflecting the dominant assumption in AI that the mind itself is a computer. These assumptions have made for an unholy alliance with the more radical versions of materialism known as physicalism and eliminativism which argue that an explanation of properties and functions of the brain *is* an explanation of consciousness and that nothing further would be required. This is, of course, an example of the reduction of conscious experience to external structure and function mentioned by Evan Thompson: the strategy whereby mind can be (theoretically) made to disappear.

The assumption of the Turing Test, adopted by the AI community, that a digital computer could have a conscious mind merely by simulating a human ability has been repeatedly challenged by the "Chinese room" thought experiment devised by John Searle. Searle invites us to imagine him in a room in which he receives Chinese characters (say, through a slot in the door). He has a set of rules that enables him to process them in the same way a computer program would do and then to issue a further set of Chinese characters as a reply so that someone receiving the characters would be convinced that a conversation was taking place with an intelligent interlocutor. In this case, however, Searle does not understand a word of Chinese and therefore is entirely unaware of the *meaning* of the conversation. The argument is designed to show that being conscious, having a mind and thinking, requires a capacity for understanding, a sense that the conversation is about something (known as "intentionality" in philosophy of mind) and that since the computer does not understand the program it carries out, it cannot be regarded as having a mind. [35]

Searle is not arguing that no machine could think, since he is enough of a materialist to believe that human beings are themselves machines. His point is that in order to think, a machine would have to be constituted like the only machine we know that does think—a human being—so he remains hopeful that a biological explanation for consciousness will one day be forthcoming. His argument is that the computational model of the mind will not help us achieve such an explanation.

From a rather different perspective, Rodney Brooks has come to a similar conclusion through his work in robotics that I mentioned briefly at the end of Chapter 1 in relation to emergent properties of dynamic systems. Brooks' success in getting robots to imitate the movement of living animals was achieved by throwing out the cumbersome super-structure of cognitive modules undertaking the formal processing of symbol representations and creating a direct link between external sensors and movement. Not surprisingly, Brooks has come to question the dominance of the computational model as a suitable metaphor for understanding living systems.

> If we look back over recent centuries we will see the brain described as a hydrodynamic machine, clockwork, and as a steam engine. When I was a child in the 1950s I read that the human brain was a telephone switching network. Later it became a digital computer, and then a massively

parallel digital computer. A few years ago someone put up their hand after a talk I had given at the University of Utah and asked a question I had been waiting for a couple of years: 'Isn't the human brain just like the world wide web?' The brain always seems to be one of the most advanced technologies that we humans currently have. [...]

The metaphors we have used in the past for the brain have not stood the test of time. I doubt that our current metaphor of the brain as a network of computers doing computations is going to stand for all eternity either.[36]

Brooks does not doubt that there are mechanistic explanations for how we think but his comments draw attention to the power of metaphors to guide our thinking along certain lines and how difficult it can be to extricate ourselves from these modes of thought. His work in robotics suggests that in order to understand how the mind thinks, we need to think about what the mind does, that is, we need to reconnect thinking with action. This approach was developed by Horst Hendriks-Jansen into a model of the mind based on situated action. This serves as my starting point for a discussion of how to reconnect mind and world so that the dualistic mind-body problem and the conflict between materialist and Idealist views of the world need not arise. Mind is emergent from action in the world and in this sense, mind is in the world and part of the material world. Yet with the development of human consciousness, the world can also be represented in the mind via the imagination. These two aspects of the mind are nevertheless only possible through active engagement in the world.

Situated Action

The atomistic approach by which things are understood by being reduced to their elements can only take us so far before the usefulness of the original "clockwork" metaphor on which it is based is exceeded. Then we need to put mind, body, and world back together again in order to see what is really going on. Hendriks-Jansen gives a telling example of how our understanding of living creatures is affected by the context in which we study them—a real understanding of the meaning and purpose of behavior requires that the behavior is contextualized in the situation for which it is "intended" (what it is "about").

Neurophysiologists have been studying the visual system of the horseshoe crab for over fifty years due to the size and relative simplicity of the photoreceptor clusters called ommatidia. These are

100 times larger than the rods and cones of the human eye and there are only 1,000 of them. By the 1970s it was thought that the mechanism of the horseshoe crab's eye was fully understood but it turned out that no one had studied how the eye worked when it was still attached to the crab! Only then did vision scientist Robert Barlow discover that, *in situ*, the receptivity of the horseshoe crab's eye varied on a daily cycle using a number of complex and previously unsuspected mechanisms. So Barlow began to investigate what the horseshoe crab's eye was actually for. He began to study not only the eye *in situ* with the animal but the animal *in situ* with its natural environment. Every summer he moved his lab from Syracuse University to the Marine Biological Laboratory on Cape Cod to observe the visual behavior of horseshoe crabs during the mating season.[37] Over several years' study Barlow was able to show that the horseshoe crab's visual system is optimized for mate selection; it is optimized to recognize objects of a certain size and speed of movement that correspond to another (female) horseshoe crab.[38]

Amongst the conclusions Hendriks-Jansen draws from this story are two which demonstrate the limitations and misconceptions involved in models of animal functioning based on the computational manipulation of internal representations (the idea that mind is located in the head/brain).

1. The only way to makes sense of what the eye was really doing was by understanding what the horseshoe crab was doing when it made use of the eye.
2. There is no internal representation that could correspond to the actual event of a another crab moving across its field of view at the rate a horseshoe crab would be likely to travel. Thus, the entity to which it responds *comes into being only through the crab's own behavior in particular circumstances.*[39] [italics added]

There is, then, no "image in the brain," no mating vision "module"—it is neither necessary nor possible. Rather the situated activity of the horseshoe crab creates the entity-event for which the eye is adapted. So in order to understand what is going on, we need to look at the entire situation that includes the crab's visual system, its mating intentions, its movement in the sea, and the female crabs to which it responds. This is the situation which has "meaning" for the crab and which makes its own visual behavior meaningful. These are "not entities that can be reduced to events inside the creature's head."[40]

Hendriks-Jansen's model of situated action is intended to replace the traditional models of cognitive science and AI that attempt to describe cognition in terms of formal task definitions based on symbol manipulation of the kind that Searle was critiquing in his "Chinese room" argument. For an alternative approach he turns to ethology and developmental psychology to show how infant thought and behavior are emergent from species-typical, sub-cortically mediated activity patterns.[41] Hendriks-Jansen argues that these simple mechanisms do not have meaning or intentionality in themselves but provide the scaffolding for meaning and intentionality as emergent phenomena. So, for example, infants have an innate tendency to focus on faces (or face-like objects) and a tendency for their gaze to become locked on the face of the mother, thus engaging the mother's interest and encouraging her attempts to engage him in conversation. This early mechanism is thus not "about" the mother but simply about the innate tendency towards face-gazing. Hendriks-Jansen clarifies the point by comparison with the mother duck's behavior towards her ducklings:

> The mother duck's behavior with respect to her duckling can be shown to be a conglomerate of independent activity patterns, each of which has its own distinct, action-specific sign stimulus. The only reason these activity patterns converge on her duckling is that all those sign stimuli are situated on the duckling. Our intentional descriptions of animals can thus ascribe an aboutness to their actions that does not correspond to the operations of the underlying mechanisms. The mechanisms of the mother duck's behavior make no reference to the duckling, just as the mechanisms of wall following in Mataric's robot do not refer to walls and the focusing mechanisms that cause a young infant's gaze to center on his mother's face are not about the mother.[42]

This makes it look as if we are back to the Cartesian idea of animals having no souls because they are simply a collection of mechanisms, only now this is being extended to infants as well, along the same lines as La Mettrie. But this would itself be a Cartesian misapprehension that reveals how difficult it is to grasp the idea of situated emergent meaning. It is not that the duckling has no meaning for the mother duck. It is simply that such meaning is not to be found in the conglomerations of mechanisms but is emergent from them. "Such intentional description of the mother duck's behavior (that it is "about" the duckling) is applicable only because of its interactive nature and the fact that the various constituent activities are situated in a particular environment."[43]

Meaning is not inherent to the duck (in its brain, for example) but is distributed throughout the system constituted by mother duck and duckling operating within their species-specific environment (the milieu or *Umwelt*). If we apply this to infants this suggests that meaning is emergent and distributed *between* mother and infant. So it would then become very difficult to say where the "intention to grasp" is located when mothers interpret their infants' proto-grasping as expressing a wish to grasp the objects towards which they are reaching. In fact, it would probably be best to say that it is not "located" anywhere. Even though the mother does have such an intentional idea and the infant may not, the intention consists of the meaning of the whole situation not simply the mother's conception of what is happening. For both parties, mind is emergent from situated action. The difference is that the mother is able to use a special aspect of mind—her imagination—to relate to her infant well before the infant has developed an imagination of their own. But the absence of intentionality on the part of the infant does not mean that the infant does not have a mind; rather, it means that the infant mind is in a process of development *pari passu* with grasping objects and turn-taking "conversations" with its mother. As Hendriks-Jansen says, "With the aid of the dynamic scaffolding supplied by the mother, the infant thus performs intentional acts long before he is capable of intentional thought."[44]

Part of the difficulty here is distinguishing between the kind of intentionality possessed by conscious beings able to form mental ideas that are "about" something (intentionality in the philosophical sense) and intentional activity that has no conscious purpose. Does the mother duck *intend* to care for the duckling? Is that the *purpose* of her activity even if that activity is built out of simple mechanisms that *in themselves* are not "about" the duckling? Here I think we need a broader conception of the relation between mind and life that allows us to connect psychological life more closely with body, affect, and meaning.

The Enactive Approach

The enactive approach applies phenomenology to the study of biology to develop an approach which reveals the "deep continuity between life and mind."[45] In common with all the approaches I will discuss in this chapter, the fundamental theme is that mental processes do not take place "in the head" but are emergent activities of the organism's engagement with the world.

The enactive approach builds on Maturana and Varela's concept of autopoiesis as the defining characteristic of living cells. Autopoiesis refers to the necessary features of a system that is able to define a boundary with the environment and to maintain that boundary by continually recreating the difference between itself and everything else. A cell produces its own components which in turn produce the cell in an ongoing circular process.[46] This definition is then extended to living systems as a whole that are the source of their own activity and define their own modes of being and, to that extent, meet the definition of "self." They are therefore *autonomous systems* in contrast to machines that require an outside agent to specify their mode of operation. The latter are heteronomous systems that function by means of inputs that produce outputs. So, computational models of the mind that attempt to explain its functioning in heteronomous terms are inappropriate for the understanding of living systems. For living systems, the environment is not a pre-specified external realm represented internally in the brain by means of sensory inputs but "a relational domain enacted or brought forth by that being's autonomous agency and mode of coupling with the environment."[47]

Mental activity is therefore best understood as a form of action. As Thompson says "cognition is the exercise of skillful know-how in situated and embodied action."[48] In terms that are very reminiscent of Barlow's work on the visual system of the horseshoe crab, Thompson writes, "In all animals neuronal networks establish and maintain a sensorimotor cycle through which what the animal senses depends directly on how it moves, and how it moves depends directly on what it senses."[49]

The central role of *sense-making* in the enactive approach also leads to a view of autonomous living systems possessing an intrinsic purposiveness. The creature has a relation to the environment that is defined by its own self-creating and self-maintaining activity and this brings the world into being for it as a meaningful environment, a milieu or *Umwelt*. Kurt Goldstein who developed von Uexküll's original idea of the *Umwelt* via Gestalt psychology writes, "The environment (*Umwelt*) emerges from the world through the actualization of the being of the organism—[granted that] an organism can exist only if it succeeds in finding in the world an adequate environment."[50]

Evan Thompson illustrates the operation of meaningful intentionality (sense-making and intrinsic purposiveness) at the simplest level of autopoietic living systems—the activity of a humble bacterial cell, *Escherichia coli* (*E. coli*):

> When swimming in the presence of a sucrose gradient, these cells will tumble about until they hit upon an orientation that increases their exposure to sucrose. At this point they will swim forward up-gradient ... towards the zone of greatest sucrose concentration. While sucrose is a real and present condition of the physicochemical environment, the status of sucrose as a nutrient is not. Being a nutrient is not intrinsic to the physiochemical structure of the sucrose molecule; it is a relational feature, linked to the bacterium's metabolism. ... It is something actualized at another level. Specifically, it is enacted or brought forth by the way the organism, given its autonomy ... couples with the environment. Sucrose belongs to the physical environment but sucrose-as-nutrient belongs to the living order. Sucrose has meaning and value as food but only in the milieu that the system constitutes for itself.[51]

This example clearly describes the function of sense-making which "changes the physiochemical world into an environment of significance and value, creating an *Umwelt* for the system. Sense-making ... is none other than intentionality in its minimal and original biological form."[52] This distinguishes the activity of mother ducks and infant face-gazing and proto-grasping from the activity of a wall-following robot. While all these systems are generating their environment through the feedback loops of sensorimotor activity, the environment of the wall-following robot has no significance or value for the robot in terms of its self-maintenance. It is not an autopoietic system and neither the environment nor its own activity has any meaning or purpose for it. It's "purpose" is nothing other than its own activity. It can demonstrate what emergent meaning looks like but only to an external observer. In this respect it remains a heteronomous system despite its motor autonomy. By contrast, the activity of the mother duck towards her duckling and the proto-gestures and responses of the infant have an overall intentionality that transcends the mechanisms themselves. This is related to the intrinsic purposiveness of autonomous living systems that is "a constitutive property the whole system possesses because of the way the system is organized."[53] This makes it legitimate to talk about the mother duck caring for her duckling and to regard the infant as being intentional from the start in seeking to develop relationships and skills that facilitate its own development. This provides continuity to the infant's behavior that is missing from Hendriks-Jansen's account of how a non-intentional infant carrying out simple mechanisms like face-gazing can somehow turn into a human subject who loves his mother. For the enactive approach, emotion is inseparable from cognition and arises out of more basic functions of sense-making due to the common element of value-motivated action.

> What has salience and value also has valence: it attracts or repels, elicits approach or avoidance. Such action tendencies in relation to value are the basis of emotion. Hence, as Walter Freeman argues, emotion is essential to all intentional behaviors. To describe cognition as embodied action implies that cognition comprises motivated action tendencies and thus is also essentially emotive.[54]

Thus the enactive approach provides a view of meaning and intentionality that shows the continuity between life and mind; all living systems possess elements of interiority and self-directedness that are characteristic of mind, while mind is "a form or structure of engagement with the world and thus resembles life."[55]

Synchronicity and Enacted Meaning

The implication here is that meaning-making is an intrinsic element of being alive, from the humblest bacterial cell to the vast complexity of a human being. Furthermore, meaning arises directly from our engagement with the "life-world" in which we are situated and is a fundamental aspect of our adapted fittedness to our environment. This view is helpful in understanding those most puzzling forms of psychological phenomena that Jung called "synchronicity" since it replaces the Cartesian dichotomy between mind and world with a more holistic view in which mind is a function of the biological system's engagement with the world. There is no longer the need to bridge the unbridgeable chasm with the purported "third thing" of the psychoid. Meaning arises out of embodied intentionality towards the world in terms of the organism's species-typical ways of coupling with the environment. So in the same way that Thompson describes the difference between sucrose as a real and present condition of the environment and sucrose as a nutrient, we might say that coincidence is a real and present feature of the environment but synchronicity is not. Synchronicity is a relational feature actualized at another level, enacted or brought forth by the way the organism couples with its environment. Specifically, it is the enactive skill of identifying congruent correspondences between similar events, especially with reference to states of heightened emotion through which we form meaningful gestalts. Hence emotion is the meaning of experience.[56] This is not a question of attribution—for example, we would not say that a rabbit "attributes" a meaning of danger to the swooping hawk. The rabbit *knows* what the hawk means as a given of the animal's sense-making and intentionality expressed as an emotional response within its specific environment. For humans, the recognition of similarity and analogy is such an inherent feature of our way of being in the world that we experience certain events as meaningful in terms of our own intentional stance towards them. It is only from the Cartesian perspective in which the material world is severed from the experiential world of the psyche that the meaningfulness of such correspondences can be denied. But this perspective fails to encompass crucial ways in which humans couple with their environment.

In this sense, the emergence of new meaning is a microcosm of the emergence of mind itself through our complex form of engagement with the world, involving brain, body, and an environment that, for humans, is as symbolic as it is material. Thus, synchronicity can be understood in ways that arc through psychic and physical aspects of the world without being reducible to one or the other and without requiring the intervention of a third element—the so-called "psychoid."

While the human life-world (and human consciousness) is distinguished by the extent to which we enter into a historically created world of symbolic meanings, other animals enact their own form of consciousness through engagement within their own milieu or *Umwelt*, the species-specific environment of what has significance for a particular animal. The *Umwelt* and the animal's own development are in a continual dynamic interaction, each one fashioning the shape and form of the other through the way the animal acts within its own environment. As Thompson describes it "[autonomous systems] enact an environment inseparable from their own structure and actions. ... They constitute (disclose) a world that bears the stamp of their own structure."[57] This world is the *Umwelt*, "the lived phenomenal world as it presents itself to that animal thanks to its sensorimotor repertoire,"[58] as revealed in Barlow's close observation of the world of horseshoe crabs.

Looking at how creatures operate within the sphere of their own *Umwelt* can transform the way we see them. It is not a question of having no presuppositions, for that would be impossible and we would not be able to understand anything at all. It is more a question of putting ourselves in their place as far as is possible without importing our own species-specific ways of being in the world into how we see other animals. Nevertheless, as living bodies ourselves we have "inside knowledge" of living processes and this provides a perspective that is quite different from the Cartesian method of disembodied objective analysis.[59] This is not to say that one approach is "better" than the other, but they reveal different aspects and so it depends on what we want to find out. The distinguishing feature of our human way of being in the world is that we *imagine* the world in a particular way in order to find out about it. The dominating power of the Cartesian imagination is such that we have forgotten that the Cartesian method is a particular way of imagining the world.[60] To apply this method, we have to follow Descartes by imagining ourselves as disembodied, rational minds that do not have an inner relation to the world through our bodily life within it.. Descartes recognized that this was necessary for the advancement of an understanding of the world based on experimental science. This was his great achievement but it has also increasingly become a limitation, not only at the boundaries of science but in the way it has affected our overall relation to a de-spiritualized world imagined as being without meaning and purpose.

A Study in Enactive Phenomenology:
Joe Hutto and the Turkeys

If we wish to understand the *Umwelt* of other creatures (including other human beings) we need to thoroughly immerse ourselves in the situated activity from which their particular *Umwelt* is emergent. This kind of participatory involvement is rare in animal studies and is often dismissed as "subjective," which rather misses the point, of course. One outstanding example is Joe Hutto's extended study of the life-world of the wild turkey in the Northern Florida Flatwoods.[61] Hutto is himself a native of this area where wild turkeys have resided for more than twenty million years. As a child he was taught to hunt wild turkeys and this may well have provided the basis for his method of study. Hunters have to learn to think like the animal they are hunting by imaginatively entering into its world in order to understand how it is likely to behave when hunted.[62] So Joe Hutto was already something of a "casual authority" on the wild turkey when he had the opportunity to spend almost a year with a young family of turkey poults who had been imprinted at birth to regard him as their object of attachment. Although he had many previous experiences of imprinting a wide range of mammal and bird species before, this study was unique in terms of the degree and extent of his involvement, living at close quarters with "his brood" through most of every day for a year until they reached adulthood. In his field notes he says,

> I have never attempted to keep an imprinted animal's experience so completely insulated from my own. I do not want them to share my life but instead defer to theirs as much as possible. Attempting to do what they do, go where they would go and even speak their language, I have been very careful to keep them isolated from my world.[63]

Although the title of the DVD re-enactment of his study, *My Life as a Turkey*, is a bit of an exaggeration, it is not that far off the mark. Joe Hutto spent almost all day every day with the turkeys from birth until maturity by which time they were able to take their places as the wild creatures they are in their own habitat. His deep knowledge of the forest habitat and his deep respect for animal life as fellow sentient beings who dwell together with him in that world makes for a fascinating and moving account through which the life-world of the wild turkey in its natural habitat is revealed. Hutto's approach to his charges is one of finding understanding through immersing himself in the world of the Other as much as possible. He did not attempt any kind of scientific "objectivity," but his passionate love affair with his young charges reveals so much of their nature in a way that no attempt at "objectivity" could hope to do.

The difference between how the turkey develops and functions in the world for which it is adapted and how it might appear in captivity is sobering and humbling; it is the difference between ordinary human living and life in a concentration camp, stripped bare of all that makes us human. It is a vivid indication of the way any animal can only become "itself" and be fully understood via the *Umwelt* of its particular being. Seen through the eyes of their own way of relating to a world to which they are highly adapted, the turkeys are revealed as highly intelligent creatures. That is, Hutto sees that intelligence needs to be assessed in terms of the world as it is for the animal that uses it, not as it is for the human beings "observing" them. This participative approach has huge implications for the way in which the scientific study of animals, including humans, can produce a distorted picture by subjecting them to its own assumptions and requirements. The attempt to remove extraneous variables through scientific objectivity is itself a variable which is not taken into account; scientific objectivity can be a distorting factor in its own right and cannot therefore be truly "objective."

Among the many remarkable things Hutto discovered was the young wild turkey's intense interest and curiosity about many aspects of its surroundings combined with an ability to "take in" what was seen and remember aspects of the environment for the future. The turkey's ability to pick out all kinds of snakes, for example, was far beyond what Hutto could do, despite a life-time spent in the same habitat and an encyclopedic expertise with its flora and fauna. The turkeys were remarkably alert; at no more than a week old they "exhibited … an awareness that at once includes the smallest crawling particle on a leaf and the red tailed hawk soaring a half mile up the field."[64] While most of these capacities are innate and will have been honed for evolutionary survival over millions of years, they cannot develop without the opportunity to use them. It is only through their daily foraging walks in the forest that they were able to accumulate the knowledge and skills to become the wild turkeys they were born to be. Isn't this reminiscent of Jung's apparently paradoxical remarks regarding individuation as the process of becoming the person you already are? Hutto regards the detailed knowledge, distinctions, and behaviors exhibited by the turkeys as evidence of genetically-stored information. It is more likely, however, that the knowledge and intelligence displayed by the turkeys was, as Thompson puts it, emergent from their active involvement with a suitable environment that discloses a world bearing the stamp of their own structure.

In this way, the turkeys disclose for Joe Hutto a forest different from the one he thought he knew so well—it is the milieu as constituted by the turkeys' intentionality towards it. There is thus no "objective world"; there are only multiple ways of being in the world. Furthermore, the turkeys themselves are constituted by the world of the Flatwoods at the same time as constituting the world of the Flatwoods through what has meaning for them within it. Creature and context together make up a dynamic system that needs to be seen as a whole if we are to understand it.

Many aspects of this world could only be revealed by the emotional connection that was established between man and bird. From the start, Hutto describes the process of imprinting, not in terms of a biological mechanism, but through each hatchling identifying him as the object of its complete devotion by which he is deeply moved.[65] He becomes deeply attached to them, and they to him. For a long time, they seek physical closeness and comfort from him and regularly display what he can only describe as "affection."[66] By describing their reactions in emotional terms like our own, Hutto opens up their world to us with new eyes—when they use their "lost call" they are upset and frightened, when they spot something new they are excited or apprehensive. They are sometimes relaxed and sometimes out of sorts and irritable. They are like us, but at the same time they are entirely unlike us. Despite his own involvement, Hutto is careful to avoid attaching human attributes to animal behavior, but, on the other hand, he aims to overcome any intellectual presumptions and above all "our condescending human arrogance." "Whether attempting to achieve understanding of an exotic culture or an unfamiliar species," he writes, "a position of superiority is always a recipe for failure."[67] Despite the many revelations of his time with the turkeys, there is much that remains unfathomable and beyond his comprehension. "There is more going on with them every instant than I can possibly follow or comprehend. I am beginning to suspect that no matter how much time I spend with these birds, they will always remain a mystery to me."[68] No matter how closely he accompanies them on their daily journeys in the Flatwoods, he is frequently surprised by their reactions—reactions which display an endless variety, subtlety, and complexity.

There is much here that is reminiscent of the appropriate attitude for doing psychotherapy. Of course, Joe Hutto was not attempting to do any kind of therapy with the turkeys—on the contrary, he was allowing them to influence *him* while attempting to keep his own influence to a minimum. What is similar is the belief that in order to truly understand another, one has to put aside one's own beliefs, attitudes, and preconceptions as far as possible and try to see and feel the world through the mind of the other.

In one respect, though, Hutto's admiration for the turkeys' intelligence leads him to disregard an important distinguishing feature of his own—his capacity for imagination. He inhabits their world so much that he does not consider one of the most crucial distinctions between these very different species: while the man can learn to live as a turkey, the turkey cannot learn to live as a man. That is, through imaginative engagement, humans can *adapt* their way of being in the world, and this alters their way of seeing the world—and *vice versa*. Here again, we see the way consciousness (how we see) is enacted through our way of being in the world. Unlike other animals, however, humans are capable of seeing and experiencing the world in remarkably different ways, enabling us to shape and adapt to very different environmental contexts. It is true that Joe Hutto was not terribly good at being a turkey, but the very fact that he could even think of doing so, let alone the extent to which he succeeded, reveals a kind of consciousness beyond the ken of any other animal. This flexibility is no doubt key to our evolutionary survival. And this suggests that evolutionary biologists who attempt to account for human traits in terms of the context in which humans first evolved are likely to be on the wrong track. We have not evolved for one particular environmental milieu—we have evolved to adapt and shape the milieu in which we find ourselves through our imaginative engagement with it.

Having given examples from the simpler life-forms of crabs, ducks, and turkeys, I now want to turn to specific theories of human intelligence that take the process of cognition "out of our heads."

The Extended Mind

The thesis of the extended mind is that the mind is not bounded by "skin and skull" but is extended into the world. A precursor of this view can be found in Samuel Butler's notion of "exosomatic evolution," the idea that in humans the endosomatic evolution of bodily organs has been supplanted by the exosomatic evolution of tools and machines. This was taken up by Karl Popper who comments,

> But man instead of growing better eyes and ears, grows spectacles, microscopes, telescopes, telephones, and hearing aids. And instead of growing better memories and brains, we grow paper, pens pencils, typewriters, dictaphones, the printing press, and libraries.[69]

Andy Clark takes this idea further to suggest that these extensions are not merely *adjuncts* to the mind but part of the mind itself. Clark quotes a conversation between physicist Richard Feynman and historian Charles Weiner in which Feynman makes the same point. Weiner was excited to have found a batch of Feynman's original notes and sketches that he said "represented a record of Feynman's day-to-day work." Feynman corrected him—the notes were not a *record* of the work, he said, but the work itself. "I actually did the work on the paper. ... It's not a *record*, not really. ... You have to work on paper and this is the paper. Okay?"[70] Cognition is not merely dependent on external tools and props but takes place across the boundary of "skin and skull" so that "the mind" literally includes these extended environmental elements. Feynman was not thinking "in his head" and recording the results on paper—he was thinking on the paper and therefore the pen and paper were an intrinsic part of his thinking process. As Clark and Chalmers put it in their original 1998 paper, the features of the environment play an active role in *driving* cognitive processes, not just facilitating them.[71]

Nevertheless, it could still be argued that the pen and paper were merely aids to a cognitive process that was determined by states of Feynman's brain and that therefore any truly mental process must be an internal one. To counter this, Clark and Chalmers give an example that has become emblematic of the Extended Mind thesis known as Otto's notebook.[72] Otto suffers from Alzheimer's disease and so he relies on a notebook to fulfill functions previously supplied by his memory. He records new information in the notebook and, when he needs it again, he consults the notebook to find it. So, when he wants to go to an exhibition at the Museum of Modern Art, he consults the notebook which tells him that the museum is located at 53rd Street and off he goes to the museum. Now compare Otto's case with that of Inga who hears that there is an interesting exhibition at the Museum of Modern Art and so, recalling that it is on 53rd Street, she sets off for the museum in exactly the same way. The essence of the argument is that Otto and Inga both hold a belief about the location of the museum that is functionally identical. Each of them consults his or her memory to activate the belief, but whereas Inga's memory is located in her brain, Otto's is located in his notebook. Since beliefs are considered to be definitively mental states, Otto's mental state is therefore contained not "in his head" but in his notebook. In an argument known as the parity principle, Clark and Chalmers state that

> If, as we confront some task, a part of the world functions as a process, which, were it done in the head, we would have no hesitation in recognizing as part of the cognitive process, then that part of the world *is* (so we claim) part of the cognitive process.[73]

They further suggest that extended cognition may be a specific feature of human evolution; "the brain has evolved in ways which factor in the reliable presence of a manipulable external environment." They suggest that language may be a key example of this kind of extended cognition as an external feature which couples with the brain to produce a form of cognition that is constituted by both elements. Ironically, we would be more like Cartesian "inner" minds relying on purely internal cognitive resources if we were without language, in which case Descartes would have been unable to formulate the *cogito ergo sum* on which his internalist doctrine depends.

Finally, they consider the implications for the self which, they point out, thus becomes co-terminous with the environment. If we are always coupled with an environment, then that environment becomes, in one sense, part of ourselves. As we saw with the turkeys, they could only "individuate" in a suitable environment. As humans, we make our own environments to some extent, though not under circumstances of our own choosing (in Marx's famous phrase.)[74] Thus, just like the turkeys, if our environments are disrupted, our selves are disrupted. Alva Noë gives an example of this in relation to his father's difficulty in adapting to a new environment in America.[75] He was, as we might say, a fish out of water. Like the fish for whom the water is undoubtedly its *Umwelt* so that fish and water together make a coupled system, the immigrant who loses his *Umwelt* may have considerable difficulty refashioning a self in the new environment. More profoundly, we might consider the plight of indigenous peoples such as Native Americans or Aborigine Australians who suffer severe loss of self when they are severed from their traditional environments and ways of living.

This last point indicates an aspect of the "extended mind" approach that is rarely part of its considerations—that the human mind is not simply a cognitive apparatus for high-level problem solving but an embodied emotional responsiveness deeply intertwined with its environmental milieu. More usually, Clark's conception of the extended mind (and the considerable debates that have grown up around it) remains rooted in the disembodied cognitive science tradition whereby cognition is regarded as a system of computational functions which could, in principle, be carried out by any apparatus that met the conditions specified by a sufficiently detailed description of those functions. So it is perhaps not surprising that most of Clark's examples concern tools and technologies. Functions such as perceptual recognition of shapes on a computer screen, intellectual problem-solving, and memory are highlighted at the expense of embodied skills and the emotional aspects of the way we come to know our world. These reveal the essentially relational aspect of cognition, as described in the enactive approach, where the coupling of the organism with the world is always intentionally motivated and therefore emotionally meaningful. In this regard, Thompson and Stapleton refer to research which shows the interdependence of brain regions concerned with cognition and emotion as well as Damasio's work on the role of emotion in monitoring and responding to changes in bodily homeostasis. They question the assumption that cognition can be either internal or external, suggesting instead that "cognition is not an event happening inside the system; it is the relational process of sense-making that takes place between the system and its environment" and is therefore not "located" either in space or matter.[76]

Human cognition also involves far more than problem-solving. While there is growing evidence of the remarkable problem-solving abilities of other species such as crows and parrots, their intelligence is almost entirely evidenced in tasks which provide food as a reward. They are motivated by survival needs.

The distinguishing feature of human activity is that we are interested in so many things that are not directly related to our survival, even if they might arguably have some kind of ultimate evolutionary advantage. It seems probable that the areas of human endeavor that we now differentiate as religion, art, and science were once all of a piece. Knowing the world (science) was united with a spiritual reverence for the world (religion) and expressed through group activities involving figurative representation (visual arts), narrative, singing, dancing, and the use of musical instruments.

Musical instruments provide a good illustration of the extension of the mind through tools and technologies whose use and purpose go well beyond problem-solving and might not even be thought of as "cognition" at all, although they are certainly activities involving intellectual and bodily skills and at least part of their purpose is the expression and communication of emotional states. This widens the definition of cognition to include "any interaction or engagement that produces meaning for the agent."[77] Music may have begun with the human voice or it may have begun through the discovery of interesting and pleasing sounds from material objects that were then developed into what we now recognize as musical instruments. At present, the oldest known musical instruments are 35,000-year-old bone flutes discovered in the same area as the Lion Man. Astonishingly, some of these flutes are constructed to play a modern pentatonic scale.[78] Any such form of musical notation is necessarily an inherently extended mind phenomenon. It cannot exist except through the fashioning of objects capable of making such sounds. Rather than music being composed "in the head" and then played on an instrument, the affordances of an instrument (its particular features and possibilities), reveal the music that can be played on it; the music is emergent from processes of material engagement. In this sense, music is created by musical instruments as much as it is created by musicians. The composer who *imagines* music before it is played is a late addition to the musical process. Even then, the music that can be composed is contingent on the reconfiguration of music in the world that has previously been heard. So the nature of music is dependent upon the tools and technologies through which it is expressed. Musical instruments are active agents in the creation of music, a good example of "the cognitive life of things."[79]

New technologies can transform the nature of music. For example, the introduction of electrical amplification in the latter part of the twentieth century turned the guitar into the dominant solo instrument of the era. Electrification didn't just make the guitar louder; it enabled the development of technical affordances such as distortion and sustained feedback that greatly increased the palette of sounds available, creating a synergy between these new possibilities and what musicians could imagine. Nowadays every major guitarist has their own "rig"—an amplification system for the particular sound they are aiming to achieve—and this is as much a part of what makes musicians unique as their physical techniques in playing their instrument.

For improvisational musicians, it is still the case that the cognitive process of imagining music and the bodily activity of producing it are directly linked. The instrument is an intrinsic element in the compositional process, shaping the music according to its own affordances. At its best, there is no point at which musician, instrument, and music can be separated—the process is an enacted, embodied unity in which the instrument functions as a part of the musician's mind revealed directly through the instrument. Thus music is a relational and emotional form of cognition *par excellence* and the musician is a good candidate for what Clark describes as "nature's very own cyborgs: cognitive hybrids who repeatedly occupy regions of design space radically different from those of our biological forbears."[80] For this reason alone, Clark questions the evolutionary psychology model that interprets modern human behavior in terms of our adapted fittedness for the environment in which humans originally evolved. He argues that "our technologically enhanced minds are barely, if at all, tethered to the ancestral realm" or "constrained by the limits of the on-board apparatus that once fitted us to the good old Savannah."[81] The way that we couple with artifacts and symbols has not only transformed our environments, it has transformed us.

Furthermore, there is clear evidence that the development of particular skills in particular environments can actually change the brain—a far more plastic and adaptable organ than suggested by the pre-specified massive modularity model of evolutionary psychology. Music again provides a good example. Musical training before the age of seven produces thickening of areas of the brain associated with language skills, executive functions, hearing, and self-awareness. Musicians exhibit greater sensitivity to the nuances of emotion in speech through differential neural processing of auditory response in the brainstem.[82] And musicians have increased gray matter (size and number of nerve cells) in the auditory, motor, and visual spatial areas of the cerebral cortex.[83] As Oliver Sacks writes, "Anatomists ... could recognize the brain of a professional musician without a moment's hesitation."[84] Another well-known example is the increase in the size of the hippocampus amongst London taxi-drivers, due to the demands made on their brains by "the knowledge," the detailed memory of London streets, which they are required to learn before they can be granted a license. These examples show once again how we are adapted for adaptation and that a key feature of our evolutionary success is the plasticity of the human brain in conjunction with the transformations brought about through our artifactual, symbolic cultural environment.

Distributed Cognition

Music provides a further illustration of an important addition to the idea of the extended mind—that our cognition is not only extended via the tools we use but is distributed through group activity and the practices and processes that become embedded over time in social institutions. As Thompson reminds us, "Behavior does not exist *in* the nervous system or *in* the body any more than a conversation exists in the individual speakers (or their brains) or a jazz improvisation exists in the individual instruments or soloists."[85]

So, improvisational music illustrates the way that meaning-making is distributed across the group. This is also the function of social and cultural institutions such as educational, scientific, and professional institutions, the legal system, and religious organizations, all of which act as repositories of previously established cognitive information. Learning to think within the rules and procedures of these established institutions greatly enhances the cognitive resources available to individual actors who do not have to rely on creating their own knowledge *de novo*. Shaun Gallagher argues that the distribution of knowledge (as sociologists would call it) is a further extension of the extended mind. For example, "legal judgments are not confined to individual brains, or even to the many brains that constitute a particular court. They emerge in the workings of a large and complex institution." Gallagher concludes that "human cognition relies not simply on localized brain processes in any particular individual, or on short-term uses of notebooks, tools, and technologies, but often on social processes that extend over long periods of time."[86]

This idea of cognition as distributed amongst a group of actors engaged on a shared task was developed by Edwin Hutchins in the early 1990s. His approach was to focus on "how people go about knowing what they know and the contribution of the environments in which the knowing is accomplished."[87] He applied this approach to a study of navigation on a ship, looking at the multiple cognitive resources used by navigators in conducting tasks such as defining lines of position. Other applications include airplane pilots, engineering practice, air traffic controllers, field archaeologists, and science lecturers, but the implications of these studies go far beyond these particular practices. Hutchins showed that the reasoning processes of navigators involved an interaction between embodied gestures, material objects (tools), and shared communications with colleagues working on a shared task.

Crucially, he argues that "interactions between the body and cultural artifacts constitute an important form of thinking. These interactions are not taken as 'indications' of invisible mental process, rather they are taken as the thinking processes themselves."[88]

For example, navigators reason about the relationship between various projected possibilities for future lines of position using hand gestures and bodily movement in conjunction with the plotting protractor placed on a map. These practices show a continual interaction between imagination and embodied action as a means of developing knowledge. Navigators and pilots are jointly engaged in a process of imagining the future—how to bring a ship to harbor or land a plane on a runway. In another example, a researcher in a molecular biology laboratory uses her hand to demonstrate two possible forms of motion for the molecule under investigation. Here the hand motion provides the means "to imagine dynamic properties of entities that cannot be seen or sensed directly." So here we see that imagination literally "bodies forth the shape of things unknown" as Shakespeare famously put it in *A Midsummer Night's Dream*. Bodily movements and the use of artifacts provide a means to bring "airy nothings" into material form, thus making it possible to think about intangible objects that could not otherwise be realized. Andy Clark suggests that religious artifacts function in this way, making it possible to conceive of non-material realms that we would otherwise find very hard to imagine, let alone believe in.[89] In all these examples, we see the way that bodily, material, and social practices, in conjunction with brain processes, act as an overall self-organizing field of cognition which, taken together, constitute the mind.

Hutchins argues that these forms of embodied cognition act as the prior scaffolding for the use of imagination *per se*.

> Once we have learned to interact with these things, we may learn to imagine both the things and our interaction with them. Then we can organize our thinking using internal resources in ways that previously required interaction with external cultural things. In this perspective, interaction with the material and social world comes first, and imagination of those interactions comes later. ... Imagining bodily interaction with things can become a form of conceptual thinking.[90]

This means that without the things that provide the images for symbols, there could not *be* any symbols. Symbols are imagined things, things which provide the possibilities for the transformational images that could not exist in the material world (e.g., a lion-headed man) and are able to "bring forth" abstract entities (e.g., god-images) that could not otherwise be imagined or conceived. As Hutchins says, it is not that thinking and imagining never happen in the absence of a material world but that they are necessarily *derived* from processes involving action with the world both ontogenetically and phylogenetically.[91]

By any account, this places the things of the world and our cognitive interaction with them *a priori* to symbolic imagination. If these interactions constitute the thinking process itself, it makes no sense to postulate some other realm of the "possibilities of ideas" (archetypes) from which symbolic thinking is derived. Rather, the practice of embodied thinking is prior to the emergence of symbols, and it is only through the use of symbols that anything like "archetypes" can come into existence, perhaps as the emergent regularities in symbolic patterns or the way in which thinking is implicitly structured by the particular symbolic systems into which each child is inducted, especially via language.

This argument is similar to Vygotsky's theory of the social origins of mind, an important influence on the development of the distributed cognition approach. Vygotsky argued that social processes give rise to individual processes and that both are mediated by artifacts. The child first interacts with others and with artifacts and only then develops the capacity to repeat the interpersonal process as an intrapsychic process.[92] This seems to be the case not only for humans but for other cognitively advanced animals as well, such as New Caledonian crows. Recent research has shown these remarkable birds to be second only to humans in their problem-solving abilities. Astoundingly, these crows not only use tools (sticks) to access food and tools to access other tools (metatool use) but even make some quite sophisticated tools from sticks and leaves. Furthermore, the tools they use vary between different groups, showing evidence of cultural learning. Young crows learn to use tools in this way by observing their parents and then trying to imitate what the parent crows have just done.[93]

Vygotsky's ideas were an important influence on the psychologist Rom Harré who argued that the self also develops through the appropriation of social interaction as a personal attribute—the self is first a public self that develops in interaction with others and only later becomes a private self.[94] Drawing on Harré's work, Louis Zinkin controversially challenged Jungian shibboleths regarding the origins of the self, arguing that, to begin with, the infant always displays its feelings publically and only later has the capacity to make this private by appropriating the pattern of interaction as his own. Hence the self is formed on the pattern of the child's early social context, much of which is prior to conscious abstraction and representation.[95]

Hutchins' work on distributed cognition has also shown how interactive cultural processes may facilitate an increase in cognitive abilities across several generations:

> Phenomena that are not predictable from the organization of any individual taken in isolation may arise in the interactions among individuals. Once having developed in this larger system, they may become elements of cultural practices and thereby become available for appropriation by individuals.[96]

In conjunction with Brian Hazlehurst, Hutchins conducted a number of computer simulations which show that cognitive evolution can occur without the necessity for genetic change involving "special modules" or "evolutionary miracles," for example, the argument that the cultural explosion of 50,000 to 100,000 years ago indicates an evolutionary change in the brain. One such study showed how learning about a natural phenomenon can be deposited in a culture for future generations by the production of artifacts so that, over time, a population would be capable of discovering things that no individual could learn in a lifetime.[97] The example they chose was the relationship between the phases of the moon and the levels of the tides. This information would have been particularly useful to the Native Americans who once used to come down to the beach adjacent to the University of California site where the simulation was conducted to collect shellfish at low-tides. Hutchins and Hazlehurst created a computer simulation in which each individual could represent their learning through the production of an artifact that could be passed on to the next generation. The results showed that if the simulation included a bias in favor of later generations choosing artifacts produced by those who had performed well on the task in previous generations, then predictive ability would spread through the entire community. In later generations, virtually all individuals would be able to predict the regularity with no greater innate learning abilities than the earlier generations. The simulation therefore showed how cognition becomes distributed via culture so that, over time, the cognitive abilities of individuals become greatly amplified by a combination of a small amount of direct learning and a greater amount of culturally mediated learning. In short, we are all standing on the shoulders of all the previous generations who provided the scaffolding for our own culturally mediated learning. Unlike the case of Baldwinian evolution where we become *biologically* adapted to cultural innovation (such as lactose tolerance increasing in dairy-herding societies), here there is no biological evolution but a clear evolution of cultural learning and sophistication.

Group-Specific Variability

Sociologist Norbert Elias makes a similar point in his distinction between biological evolution and social evolution.

> Humans are able to hand on knowledge from generation to generation not only by means of example here and now but above all by means of symbols which ... need not be bound to any particular time. ... Languages enable humans to transmit knowledge from one generation to another and thus make it possible for human knowledge to grow.[98]

And, of course, what the "artifacts" of Hutchins and Hazlehurst's simulation represent in the real world are *symbols* in the widest sense, especially, but not exclusively, language. Symbols thus open up the possibility of social and psychological change without any further change to the genome, giving humans a unique adaptive capacity that enables change and development to occur at a group-specific level rather than requiring overall species-specific changes at the genetic level. "In the case of evolution," Elias writes, "the chief instrument of transmission and change is an organic structure called the 'gene.' In the case of development, the chief instrument of transmission and change is symbols in the wide sense of the word."[99]

Elias points out that one cannot observe amongst animals the scope for such enormous changes in social living as the shift from nomadic hunter-gatherers to settled agricultural farmers or from tribes to empires.[100] And, unlike genetic change, social change is reversible— empires can fall, technologies can be lost, societies can fragment, etc. As Elias puts it, "Human beings are biologically capable of changing their manner of social life. By virtue of their evolutionary endowment they can develop socially."[101]

As human social life became established, it provided the evolutionary pressure for the development of symbolic communication and the larger brains required to use it. This then became a central aspect of the human species-specific environment of evolutionary adaptedness. Symbolic communication provides the platform for the development of precious cultural innovations which humans carried with them from place to place, not in their genes but in their social groups. This is a much deeper form of transmission than the idea of particular ideas or symbols being transmitted via cultural diffusion. Humans inevitably carry, not so much the possibility of particular ideas, as Jung thought, but the possibility of *having* ideas by virtue of being cultural animals immersed in socially-transmitted symbolic knowledge. Since actual ideas are emergent as symbols within group-specific cultures they are inevitably highly variable. And since it is precisely that group-specific variability that is species-specific, we are inevitably hard-pressed to find any fundamental unchanging elements. Although many social practices will be maintained and/or recreated out of the synergy between biological adaptedness and environmental circumstances, these are both variable and fragile. Human adaptability has enabled us to inhabit widely differing environments across the planet but the need for sufficiently large and varied social groups to maintain cultural innovation can also result in degradation of adaptive skills. An example of this occurred when the population of Tasmania became cut off from mainland Australia and it may also have led to the extinction of Neanderthals.

Culture does not arise from ideas in the mind but out of social and material practices which become embedded in symbols as carriers of meaning that can be transmitted to subsequent generations and transformed by future circumstances. So although ideas cannot be inherited, symbols can be—not biologically, of course, but through the medium of culture, the true medium for the emergence of the psyche.

Furthermore, this process of knowledge transmission begins in the prolonged period of infancy which is also species-specific to human beings. And there is an evolutionary synergy here between the development of a larger brain and the prolongation of infancy. For our hominin ancestors, the evolutionary increase in brain-size created what is known as the "obstetric dilemma"; upright walking requires a narrower birth-canal whereas increased brain-size requires a larger one. Hence human births are much more difficult than those of our hominin relatives. Yet this has also resulted in human infants being born at an earlier stage of development, so that some of their brain growth occurs post-utero. This makes brain-development subject to post-uterine influences, notably via mother/infant interaction which then becomes the crucible for much greater possibilities of cultural learning, such as language. Hence the unique "burst-pause" pattern of infant feeding mentioned in the previous chapter which is linked to the characteristic turn-taking pattern of human conversation. In turn, these new possibilities would have increased selection for bigger brains and longer periods of infancy that could make use of this new evolutionary potential.

I hope that by now it will be apparent that this emphasis on culture is not to be taken as a commitment to an old fashioned version of "nurture" over "nature" since the argument of this chapter has been that human nature can only emerge through nurture; in that sense, culture *is* nature. Humans are born with an expectation of culture in the same way that fish are born with an expectation of water—it is the medium in which we live and breathe and have our being and no human being could survive without it.[102] So the question of human nature then becomes one of discovering what is required for human beings to create and make use of culture, especially the capacity to use symbols since these are the prime means by which culture is transmitted to subsequent generations. In this respect, we are unlike other cognitive problem-solvers like the New Caledonian crows since there is so much more in our cognitive (and emotional) development than the imitation of tool-making skills. What these factors may be and how they may have evolved over the past two million years is the subject of the next two chapters.

CHAPTER THREE

FROM APE TO HUMAN I
LANGUAGE AND SOCIALITY

The origin of symbolic culture has both a social and a material aspect—it is concerned with the fashioning of material objects as artifacts and the development of social and cooperative living amongst human groups, necessitating new ways of understanding and communicating with each other, especially via language. These joint forms of embodied engagement made it possible and necessary for animal minds to become human minds with the kind of symbolic resources we might now recognize as *psyche*.

By the time of the Upper Paleolithic, human beings had arrived at the point where they lived in a material world that was partly of their own making, in which their mental lives were distributed across a social and material *Umwelt* that had become integral to their survival. One essential feature of this humanly created world was language. Understanding the origin of language presents formidable difficulties, partly because it leaves no trace in the archaeological record and partly because of its immense complexity. Nevertheless, it seems to me hardly possible that an exploration of the origins of symbolic imagination could ignore language and so I begin this chapter with a review of Terrence Deacon's theory of the Baldwinian co-evolution of language and brain, followed by a discussion of the work of Michael Tomasello who argues that language is built on a prior foundation of social cooperation creating the common ground and joint attention required for language to develop.

Signs and Symbols

The use of symbolic communication is the key distinguishing factor between humans and all other animals. We are, as Terrence Deacon has it, the symbolic species—*Homo symbolicus*.[1] Symbols come in many forms and represent every facet of our existence—from the use of words to represent material objects like "dog," "stone," or "banana" to the complex indeterminate symbols of religion and mythology that most interested Jung. The latter were, for Jung, "symbols proper," and, to indicate this, he distinguished between *signs* whose meaning was more or less specifically denoted by their signifier and referred to something known and *symbols* which represented something unknown and required symbolization in order to become thinkable at all. This can be confusing because Jung's definition of a sign is equivalent to what is usually seen as definitive of a symbol. Thus Deacon writes,

> When we say something is a 'symbol' we mean there is some social convention, tacit agreement, or explicit code which establishes the relationship that links one thing to another. A wedding ring symbolizes a marital agreement; the typographical letter 'e' symbolizes a particular sound used in words; and taken together, the words of this sentence symbolize a particular idea or set of ideas.[2]

The point about Jung's more specialized use of the term *symbol* is precisely that the relationship that links one thing to another is not defined—instead of a one-to-one correspondence between the signifier and the signified, symbols in Jung's sense have multiple referents and indeterminate meanings. Susanne Langer called these "non-discursive" or "presentational" symbols.[3] These present their meaning as a whole rather than being the sum of their parts, as is the case with discursive symbols. Discursive symbols such as words or mathematical signs are arbitrary conventions that act as abstract counters for what they represent and so can be inserted into a text (or discourse) with reference only to the conventional rules of the text itself. Each element has a discrete meaning or denotation, held together by rules of grammar and syntax within which these meanings can be combined into sentences or equations. The text can then be read as an assembly of the individual components it includes. Non-discursive symbols do not have specific meanings in this way. For example, in music, individual notes (unlike words) have no meaning of their own but acquire meaning only through the context of the whole presentation to which they contribute. Other examples of non-discursive symbolism include the visual arts, poetry, myth and dreams all of which provide multiple, indeterminate forms of symbolic meaning. As Rycroft explains, "Unlike factual statements like 'The

Battle of Waterloo took place on June 18th, 1815' or 'Arsenic is a poison' which have only one meaning, dreams poems and novels either have no meaning or several meanings."[4]

Whereas discursive symbols aim for precision, clarity, and singularity of meaning, in the case of dreams, myths, and works of art, the more multiple and indeterminate the symbolic references, the greater and more lasting is the significance of the overall presentation. No single interpretation can ever encompass their meanings, and, no matter how many interpretations are made, the meanings are never exhausted. The interpretation borrows its significance from the replenishing symbol itself, like drawing water from a well.

Non-discursive symbols of this kind make use of a specially developed capacity for analogy, associative connections, and pattern recognition, all of which make humans uniquely capable of using metaphor as a way of enhancing our understanding of the world. It may even be that we are sometimes *less* skilled at working out relations of cause and effect than other problem-solvers in the animal kingdom such as crows, squirrels, and the great apes because we see so many possible associations. From a purely rational problem-solving view of the world this results in "misunderstanding" and "misperceiving" the world—we see things that are "not there" or are "unreal" resulting in "false beliefs" such as superstition and belief in spiritual agencies.[5] But these pattern-making associative analogies open up new vistas that other animals do not possess, including not only the more sophisticated patterns of cause and effect embodied in modern science but also the symbolic meanings of ritual, myth, art, and religion.

Symbols, Imagination, and Consciousness

Symbols in this sense might be regarded as tools of the imagination—signifiers that enable us to conjure up and represent the unformulated intimations that come to us from an unknown realm that psychoanalytic psychology has come to represent (symbolize?) as "the unconscious" but has also been thought of as "the spirit world" or indeed the Imagination itself as it was conceived by the Romantic poets. Such complex and sophisticated symbols cannot emerge without an already well established symbolic language in which to formulate them. We create symbols out of already existing symbols in a complex layering of increasingly abstract meaning. Symbols enable us to present and represent that which is not directly perceivable by our senses but they cannot be created *ab novo* in the non-sensible vacuum of an "internal" mind.

Fundamentally, symbols exist for the purpose of communicating with other humans with whom we co-exist in a symbolic community. Now that we live in such a symbolically saturated world, in which symbols can also be used for solitary contemplation, we may fail to recognize this. Humans now have an imaginative "space" within which symbols can function in what appears to be an entirely internal way—via the process of dreaming, for example. Yet it is only through the use of symbols as a means of communication that imagination becomes possible as a solitary function that mirrors the communicative function of symbols in a communicative dialogue with ourselves. The private dialogue is derived from a prior public dialogue albeit it may subsequently deviate from it in significant ways.[6] Imagination is an extension of this, making possible the creation of innovative forms that go beyond the sensible world, of which the Aurignacian Lion Man is so emblematic.

Imagination is also directly linked with the specifically human form of self-reflexive consciousness. Here is a description of the function of consciousness given by Antonio Damasio in which consciousness shades into a description of the function of imagination. Damasio describes anxiously watching a frail old man boarding a ferry in the rain, observing his difficulty and uncertainty and how two men on deck ease him into the safety of the cabin. He comments,

> Now let your mind wander and consider that, without consciousness, the old man's discomfort, perhaps humiliation, would simply not have been known to him. Without consciousness, the two men on deck would not have responded with empathy. Without consciousness, I would not have been concerned and would never have thought that one day I might be him, walking with the same pained hesitation and feeling the same discomfort. Consciousness amplifies the impact of these feelings in the minds of the characters in this scene.[7]

The old man may not require imagination to feel discomfort (although his humiliation probably does involve imagining how others see him) but Damasio's account of the empathy of his helpers already implies imagination and his description of his own thoughts and feelings is clearly one in which he not only imagines the states of mind of those he observes but goes on to imagine his own future possibilities, creating an imagined identification with the old man that strengthens his empathic engagement with him.

This capacity to imagine possibilities that are not yet present may exist in rudimentary form in other creatures who engage in problem-solving activities. I am dubious whether the crow *imagines* a solution to the puzzle of how to use one tool to acquire another in the sense of rehearsing actions in thought, but when a chimpanzee goes off into another room to find a suitable tool for a food-extraction problem, it is reasonable to propose that she carries a mental representation of the problem with her.[8] Even so, it is questionable whether such a representation exists in any symbolic form as something that she can communicate with, or that she experiences her mind as some kind of internal space where such reflective consultation about the task at hand can occur, or needs to occur. Rather it seems more likely that what is "represented" is her bodily engagement with the task at hand (quite literally) and the "feel" of the object needed to complete it. This would be an example of a sophisticated form of enactive engagement in which mind is a function of brain, body, and the environmental situation. The neural correlates for this are close to those of image schemas, so it could be argued that the chimpanzee has a concept of the tool required as long as we remember that such concepts do not constitute any form of signification.

By contrast, the virtual world of human imagination depends on symbolization because, without it, it would be literally inconceivable. Symbols are the tools we think with or, to be more precise, symbols are the tools we *imagine* with. Symbols enable us to do far more than practical reason can achieve. And this is why it is not reason that makes us human, for other animals can reason. It is imagination that makes us human.[9] So, if we need symbols in order to imagine, the question is, how did we acquire the capacity to use them? The answer is almost certainly that all forms of symbolic thought are derived from language or at least that language is the condition for their emergence. This may seem counter-intuitive to those who are used to exploring the world of non-discursive symbolism through dream and fantasy where symbols seem to be associated with the representation of "primitive" unconscious phantasy, emotion, and sexuality. By this light, language might seem more associated with the rationality of the conscious mind and therefore not as "deep" as unconscious imagery (mere "signs" rather than symbols). Yet when we consider the evolutionary origin of symbolic thought it becomes clear that language must have come first. As Deacon argues, "species that have not acquired the ability to communicate symbolically cannot have acquired the ability to think this way either."[10]

This suggests that signs (in Jung's sense) precede symbols in evolutionary terms; more complex indeterminate symbols are built up out of many layers of signification that provide the referents to which more complex symbols refer. This is not necessarily the case in childhood development—ontogeny does not recapitulate phylogeny— since the child is born into a world where complex symbolic imagery is already available to represent the bodily, emotional, and relational concerns that come to be represented through imagination.

Indexical and Symbolic Communication

Language as a form of symbolic communication is distinct from those forms of communication used by other species which rely mainly on indicative forms of reference. For example, the alarm call of a vervet monkey indicates the arrival of a predator but does not enable the monkey to call about lions when there are no lions present. These are indicative communications that lack the all-important feature of symbolic reference. Humans also use these kinds of calls to express our emotional states, often much more effectively than is possible through the use of symbolic language. As Deacon explains, "Indeed even in our own species, a rich and complex language is still no substitute for a shocked expression, a muffled laugh, or a flood of silent tears, when it comes to communicating some of the more important messages of human social relationships."[11]

Whereas indicative or indexical communications rely on a one-to-one correspondence between the index and what it indicates, symbolic references operate on a higher level where a series of indexical references form a network of meaning with links between them. This enables the meaning to be defined and maintained by reference to other symbols in the network, even if what it represents is absent or lost. For example, a monkey can be taught to press a buzzer to get a nut, but if the buzzer ceases to work, the association is extinguished. The buzzer then no longer indicates "food" and so has no meaning in the context of the monkey's intentional world (his enactive engagement with a milieu). By contrast, the statement "press the buzzer to get the chocolate" means something to humans whether or not there are any buzzers or chocolates present. We are able to *imagine* buzzers, pressing, and chocolates simply by the words themselves. That is why words are symbols and symbols promote imagination.

Teaching Language to Chimpanzees

Deacon's argument for how language might have emerged in our evolutionary history is based on the most successful attempt to teach chimpanzees to communicate using a symbolic language system, conducted by Sue Savage-Rumbaugh and her team. Many previous attempts now seem naïve and exploitative in retrospect, riding roughshod over the species-specific difference between humans and their nearest relatives in the belief that learning was entirely driven by environmental factors. The distressing story of what happened to "Nim Chimsky" a young chimp introduced into a human family in the belief that he could be reared like a young human is an egregious example; as he grew bigger he attempted to have sex with his "mother" and attacked one of the research students assigned to his care. So he was returned to an isolated, caged existence and then sold for medical research. Only through the tireless efforts of one of his later caregivers was he able to find a more humane (sic!) existence together with two companions.[12] For a while it had appeared that he had learned a large number of words but on closer study, the scientist leading the research, Herbert Terrace, concluded that Nim's "language" did not go beyond pragmatic associations and imperatives that were involuntary demands for primary rewards.[13] He had no grasp of syntactic structure or the meaning of words apart from their associative context. He had not progressed from indicative to symbolic communication.

Chimpanzees do not have control of their vocalizations, and their limited vocal apparatus makes human language impossible for them. Previous experimenters used American Sign Language to overcome this limitation, but, in addition to this, Savage-Rumbaugh and her team introduced a system of "lexigrams," icons on a keyboard that the chimps would push to communicate with the researchers. After thousands of trials over a period of a year and a half, two of the chimpanzees, Sherman and Austin, succeeded in grasping symbolic reference. This meant that as well as being able to understand the association between a particular lexigram and its object (e.g., banana), they had also learned the way the lexigrams were related to each other, which amounted to a simple form of syntax—i.e., the sequences in which they could or could not be used.

Deacon argues that this token-token relationship is definitive of symbolic language in contrast to iconic and indexical reference which remains at the level of relating a token to a particular object. The shift to a token-token reference is what holds symbolic reference in place when its associative (indicative) context is extinguished (or merely absent). "Competing sets of overlapping associative relationships on the indexical level translate into mutually supportive higher-order semantic categories on the symbolic level."[14]

Deacon is particularly interested in the achievements of another chimp, a young bonobo called Kanzi. What was so protracted and laborious for Sherman and Austin to learn was picked up apparently effortlessly by Kanzi who was not even being directly taught but was simply together with his mother while *she* was learning. Kanzi has gone on to learn 350 lexigrams, and, according to Savage-Rumbaugh, he understands over 3,000 spoken words, including commands such as "put the soap on the apple" or "carry the TV outside."[15] Deacon believes that the explanation for this lies not in what the young Kanzi could do but what he couldn't do. It was precisely the immaturity of his learning abilities that provided just the right learning environment for the "un-learning" needed to grasp symbolic reference. This could not be due to any Chomskian "language acquisition device" for the simple reason that bonobo chimps could not possess any such innate module.[16]

Co-Evolution of Language and Brain

Deacon sees this as an indication of how language has evolved in a way that is adapted to the brain capacities of early learners: "children's minds need not innately embody language structures if languages embody the predispositions of children's minds."[17] Alongside the adaptation of language to the brain is the correlative process by which the brain evolves in response to the use of language, including a greatly enlarged prefrontal cortex and the adaptations that made vocalization suitable for linguistic expression. It is here that the effect of Baldwinian evolution comes into play whereby biological changes are selected as a response to behavioral adaptations rather than being the original cause of those adaptations. As humans begin to evolve language, subsequent generations are born into a community of proto-language users. Since language has evolved to confer an evolutionary advantage, those who are best adapted to take advantage of this innovation will prosper, creating a selection pressure for brain evolution in relation to a cultural innovation rather than anything in the natural environment. This is how the human species evolved into cultural animals living in socially created environments.

Pair Bonding and Shared Care ("Allomothering")

This may tell us *how* language evolved but it leaves open the all-important question of *why* it evolved; what was the selective advantage of using symbolic communication? Deacon proposes an intriguing answer that pushes the origin of language back to the point of transition from the more ape-like australopithecines to the very first *Homo* species, probably *Homo habilis*. He suggests that the shift to a meat-rich diet, correlated with the increase in brain-size during this period, meant that nursing females would have been unable to provide food for themselves, leading towards a change in sexual and social organization towards pair-bonding. But for females to be able to rely on males to provide for them and males to rely on their female mates to not propagate the genes of their rivals would have required a social contract that could only be demonstrated by some kind of symbolic communication. And since it takes a great deal of repetition for a non-symbolic ape to acquire the capacity for symbolic reference, Deacon suggests that this may have been provided through ritual: the establishment of repeated conventional gestures and activities that provided the symbolic communication needed to convey and confirm the "promise" of pair-bonding.

This is certainly an appealing hypothesis that places the sexual couple at the heart of what it is to be human, lending support to psychoanalytic theories about the importance of the primal scene as well as a Jungian conception of the syzygy in all those myths of the "first couple." It also provides support for the idea of ritual as basic to our humanity and the way that sociality and symbolization might have evolved in tandem with one another. Nevertheless, it seems to me that this is a theory with all of the right notes but not necessarily in the right order.[18]

Firstly, is it necessarily the case that nursing females would be dependent on male mates to provide them with the necessary nutrition? Sarah Hrdy argues that, on the contrary, humans evolved to be cooperative breeders who share infant care, including food-sharing with a wider social group, especially, but not exclusively, relatives.[19] Unlike other primate species in which mothers closely guard their infants for six months and will not let anyone else near them, modern humans seem to have evolved to share access to newborns; shared care or "allomothering" is common and widespread especially in studies of modern hunter-gatherers.[20] Hrdy argues that provisioning by male mates would not have been sufficient to provide the nutrition required by nursing couples. Again, a comparison with modern hunter-gathers shows that sixty percent of calories are provided by women and much of this is not meat but plants. This suggests a very different picture whereby it was the increased levels of social cooperation that facilitated distribution of resources. Rather than a traditional picture of the man who brings home the bacon, the inclusion of meat in the diet would require multiple hunters who pooled and redistributed food alongside groups of women gathering and sharing the more reliable sources of plant food. This pattern introduces a sexual division of labor at the same time as it strengthens mutual ties of cooperation within and between male and female groups. Hrdy concludes,

> A broad look at the most recent evidence has convinced me that cooperative breeding was the strategy that permitted our own ancestors to produce costly, slow-maturing infants at shorter intervals, to take advantage of new kinds of resources in habitats other than the mixed savannah-woodland of tropical Africa, and to spread more widely and swiftly than any primate had before.[21]

The potential achievements of this kind of social cooperation based on shared activities of food-sourcing and sharing do not in and of themselves depend on symbolic communication but may well provide a better basis for symbolic communication to develop more naturally and gradually. This suggests a more fundamental problem in Deacon's hypothesis. For symbols to have commonly accepted public meaning across a whole social group, there would need to be a great deal of common ground. If language itself is to be credited with creating some kind of social contract, how is that common ground to be achieved? How could there be shared agreement across the group as to what any particular symbolic gesture represented? And what would bring the whole group together in some kind of public ritual "marriage ceremony?"

This is where the theories of extended mind and, especially, distributed cognition outlined in the previous chapter are so relevant to the problem of how both society and symbol emerged. Symbols cannot create a system of distributed cognition *ab novo*; they must rely on its prior existence to create the kind of fertile ground out of which symbolic reference can grow. Symbolic communication is not the engine for the development of sociality; it is sociality that provides the engine for symbolic communication.

Interactional Intelligence

This is the view that has been developed by Michael Tomasello, Stephen Levinson, and their colleagues at the Max Planck Institutes of Evolutionary Anthropology and Psycholinguistics, respectively. Levinson draws attention to the peculiarly indeterminate quality of spoken language with its multiple ambiguities and continual adjustment and correction as people gather what their interlocutor is trying to say. Yet, remarkably, we seem to be able to understand the vaguest of communications. For example, Levinson refers to the "thing-a-me-jigg" phenomenon:

A: Where the hell's the whatdjacallit?

B: Behind the desk.[22]

We may also be able to derive significant meaning where there is no speech at all— e.g., a longer than expected pause before answering a question.[23]. This is because language is much more than a symbolic code; it relies on a context that allows for a mutual reading of intentions, as in Grice's theory of intentional meaning. Grice proposed that the speaker intends that the recipient will understand that something is being said that has relevance to their mutual context (their "common ground"). For example, if I am walking along the street with someone who suddenly says, "How about this one?," I will be able to understand that "this one" refers to the restaurant on the corner only because of the shared context of having recently arrived in an unknown city and needing to find somewhere to eat. Without these mutual assumptions of intentionality it would be impossible to work out what other people mean simply by what they say or do.

Linguistic communication assumes a background of mutual coordination, mutual salience, and cooperative intersubjectivity that makes language interpretation possible. Its prototypical mode is conversational in which speakers take turns at speaking and alternate handing over to another party for response at the end of each turn. This alternation allows for the continual checking that intentions have been successfully communicated and, perhaps even more important, allows for the necessary nudges and cues from the other party that ensure the conversation is on track or needs to be corrected to allow mutual understanding to proceed. Again, we only tend to notice this when it is absent; speakers who do not pause between turns frequently become difficult to follow or simply lose our attention.[24]

This is clearly very different from the kind of situation in which attempts are made to teach chimpanzees to use symbolic language. This suggests that the achievement of symbolic reference may not be quite so difficult a problem as Deacon assumed since, for humans, it arose within a context of social collaboration (e.g., food-sharing) that already distinguished early human groups from their hominid ancestors. Levinson argues that the crucial issue in the origin and success of our species is not to be found in our big brains or the origin of language but in the structure of everyday human interaction that he calls the human interaction engine: "Language didn't make interactional intelligence possible, it is interactional intelligence that made language possible as a mode of communication."[25]

One way of discovering what these species-specific aptitudes might be is to look at the differences between ourselves and our great ape relatives. Rather than trying to teach chimpanzees to behave like us, it may be more instructive to compare what comes naturally to them with what comes naturally to us and, especially, what it is that we do that they do not do.

What Chimps Don't Do

Cognition and Social Intelligence
Great apes have remarkable cognitive capacities that compare very well with those of human children in areas such as perception of space, quantity, and causality. Their cognition evolved mainly in the context of foraging for food and enabled them to become some of the most skillful problem-solvers in the world.[26] Like other species adapted for problem-solving such as crows and cockatoos,

they have unusually large brains for their body size. Great apes are especially skilful at using and finding tools to forage for food. Numerous experiments of this kind demonstrate that chimpanzees understand causality and are able to make inferences. In addition, we have already seen the remarkable results achieved with getting chimpanzees to communicate with humans, whether or not that is regarded as language *per se*. However they do it and whatever it is they do, they are certainly very smart.

Chimpanzees are also capable of understanding the goals and intentions of others but in a purely competitive way. This makes them able to deceive each other. If a chimp knows where a banana is hidden, he will wait until the dominant male is out of the way before retrieving it.[27] This means that he not only can predict what another chimp will do but what the other chimp can see and cannot see—that is, he is able to recognize that the other has a different perspective from his own—an important element in developing a "theory of mind." Further evidence that they are able to make inferences about the goals of others is provided by a series of experiments that yield similar results to those conducted with young children. For example, in an experiment originally designed to test human children, the chimps were shown a human operating an apparatus to produce an interesting result (e.g., a light or a sound) and were then given a turn themselves. Although the easiest way of operating the apparatus was with their hands, the human instructor used another body part, such as their feet. The chimpanzees, however, were able to distinguish between occasions when the human was unable to use their hands (e.g., they were holding a bucket) and those when they chose not to do so. In the former situation, the chimps used their hands anyway because they could understand that the human was unable to use their hands whereas they could. In the latter situation, they were more likely to copy the unusual behavior. This suggests that, like human infants, the chimpanzees understood not only what the experimenter was trying to do but why he was doing it in a particular way—the reason for his action in pursuing the goal.[28]

As the deception experiment indicates, chimpanzees can also follow the gaze direction of another and can understand that others see, hear, and know things from a perspective different from their own; however, while they can understand what another knows, they cannot understand what another *believes*, as demonstrated by the well-known "false-belief" test. In the standard human version of this test, children see a character ("Sally") leaving some chocolate in her basket before leaving the room. Another character removes the chocolate and places it in a box. The children are then asked to predict where Sally will look for the chocolate when she comes back. Typically, children under four years old will expect Sally to look in the box. They cannot distinguish between what they know and what Sally knows, so they cannot understand that Sally has a false belief. This is actually a rather difficult and complex task that may involve other factors than false beliefs.[29] More recently, simpler versions of the test have indicated that even one and two year old children can understand something in the direction of false beliefs.[30] Various chimpanzee versions of this test have all yielded negative results; the chimpanzees can distinguish whether another knows or does not know where the food is hidden (knowledge-ignorance), but they cannot distinguish between being uninformed (not knowing) and being *misinformed* in situations where the food has been moved without their knowledge.[31]

One interesting possible implication of this test is that chimpanzees (and very young children) are limited in what they can *imagine* about another, in particular in relation to non-existent entities. In the knowledge-ignorance version, the subjects only need to know where the food *is*, whereas in the false-belief version they need to hold in mind both where the food is and where it is *not*. They have to imagine an imaginary state of mind alongside the actual situation and compare the two, and it is this they seem unable to do.

Symbolic Play and Fantasy

The most obvious sign of imagination in human children is the development of fantasy play, as early as the second year, and the use of objects to enact social scenarios, such as feeding a doll. This kind of play seems to be almost entirely unique to humans though there are some rudimentary elements of it already present in chimpanzees (and therefore it is likely to have been present in the common ancestor). In their review of fantasy play in apes, Gómez and Martín-Andrade define symbolic play as "actions carried out with the intention that they *stand for* other actions, objects, or situations that are not present at that moment."[32] This is clearly a necessary basis for the development of symbolism in the full (non-discursive) sense but it does not yet have the more complex form in which there is a *metaphorical* use of symbolism whereby the object has a metaphorical relation to what it represents, rather than simply "standing for" it in a one-to-one signification. For example, a young child who is told the story of the tiger who came to tea (and eats up everything in the house) may not consciously recognize the symbolism of her own greedy impulses, but her delight in a story in which no harm comes to anyone and the tiger remains an object of affection will have the same kind of unconscious resonance as a dream, albeit the latter may be more frightening.[33] Symbolic images of this kind require an implicit metaphorical linkage in which the symbolic manifests a particular *aspect* of what it "stands for": the tiger is hungry like the child is hungry, hence the tiger stands for hunger rather than the child herself. So we need to remember that even fully fledged "symbolic play," in Gómez and Martín-Andrade's sense, is a far cry from the kind of symbolic meaning that a child as young as three or four can begin to understand and use in their own dreams and made-up stories. Stories require narrative and narrative requires language; symbolic images in dream and fantasy acquire their significance through being embedded in the narrative structure of language.

Examples of the kind of pre-linguistic symbolic play referred to by Gómez and Martín-Andrade include a young child using a stick as a spoon to feed a doll or, possibly in the case of apes, when an ape uses a log to "stand for" a baby. Even for this to count as symbolic play, however, there would have to be an intentional symbolic relation—that is, the object is being used to stand *for* something rather than merely stand *in* for something else, or, as Gómez and Martín-Andrade put it, there is a distinction between "using instead" rather than "using as if." A human parallel would be the use of a blow-up doll as an aid to masturbation that is used instead of a real person but without the sense of "as if." This way of using objects can be applied to actual persons too as in the phrase "sex object," and it is a familiar experience for analysts when patients attempt to use them as "stand-ins" for some scenario in their own world. The counter-transference experience then is one of coercive communication, as Knox calls it, where there is no sense of the symbolic or "as if" and no space for the analyst's own mind.[34] This refers to what Tomasello calls the "individual intentionality" that characterizes great ape ways of relating to others, rather than the "shared intentionality" that characterizes cooperative human communication. For humans, being used in this way is an uncomfortable and unpleasant experience that can create a feeling of offence or intrusion that might be described as a denial of one's own humanity and is in striking contrast to situations in which two participants enact a shared drama together in a spirit of "as if" play.

Although there are a few examples of apes in the wild using objects in a substitutive way—usually the use of objects to substitute for babies—there are very few examples of anything that could be considered as examples of pretend or symbolic play.[35] Gómez and Martín-Andrade suggest that instances involving the application of maternal behaviors to inanimate objects or inappropriate animals may not involve any symbolic or imaginative content at all but are merely applications to inanimate objects of patterns that were evolutionarily designed to catalyze maternal behavior. In that respect, they would be similar to the kind of play fighting that is found in the behavioral repertoire of virtually all mammals and has an adaptive function that is separate from symbolic pretend play.

There are, however, more examples amongst apes that have been "enculturated," especially those that have learned to use symbolic communication such as Sherman, Austin, and Kanzi, although even here they are not particularly common. In the most extensive and detailed study with both bonobos and chimpanzees involving three linguistically trained and two non-linguistically trained young apes of both species, Lyn, Greenfield, and Savage-Rumbaugh analyzed ninety-nine hours of videotape and recorded twenty-seven examples of some kind of pretend play, although many examples were quite rudimentary.[36] Significantly, all but three examples came from the linguistically trained apes. Some of the most "advanced" examples are reminiscent of what Kleinian analyst Hanna Segal called concrete symbolic equations, where there is no distinction between the symbolic object and what it represents.[37] For example, Panbanisha, a two-year-old bonobo is shown a picture of a gorilla and told that there is a "monster video" she might watch. Panbanisha hits the picture which drops to the ground where she hits and stomps on it, then bites the picture, tearing it. Here it seems that Panbanisha regards the picture as equivalent to the object it represents, although there does also seem to be some kind of representation of the symbolic idea "monster." In another example, Panbanisha, now three and one-half, says "snake" at the keyboard and when asked where the snake is points to a cupboard. When her caregiver goes to the cupboard, Panbanisha clings to her neck and becomes obviously scared. Here, as is familiar with human children, what may be an attempt to master fear through the use of a symbol (perhaps the lexigram "snake") is overwhelmed by the real emotion and any possibility of "as if" is lost.

A third example from Panbanisha, now age nine, shows her capacity to enact situations involving an imaginary food object when she "eats" blueberries from a photograph, first bringing her mouth to the picture and making chewing movements and then acting out picking the blueberries off the picture with her fingers and eating them. In a well-known example from a previous study, a chimpanzee called Viki was seen playing with an imaginary version of a pull-toy on several occasions, even making attempts to "free" it when it became stuck.

What do these examples tell us about what great apes can and can't do in the area of pretence, imagination, and symbolic play? Or to put it another way, what can we learn from their limitations about what further evolutionary development was needed for the full development of symbolic imagination in humans?

The first point is that the acquisition of some kind of symbolic language seems to be required for the development of symbolic play. This makes it possible for a more extensive form of interspecies interaction to take place. The development of pretend play begins to occur in the shared space that humans and apes come to inhabit together. Gómez and Martín-Andrade conclude,

> The combination of symbolic tuition and human patterns of interaction may be especially relevant for the case of imaginative play. The teaching of symbolic action ... and the encouragement and promotion of symbolic games may explain well the apparently superior imaginative play of trained apes. ... But for the rearing and training conditions to have an effect the apes themselves must contribute something.[38]

I suggest that this shared cooperation between ape and human is an example of extended and distributed cognition. The normal limitations of the apes' imaginative capabilities are extended by operating in an environment with much more imaginatively developed humans. Yes, the apes have to have some rudimentary cognitive-imaging capacity to be able to engage in this way, but this is only part of the story; the mental events that these examples of imagination demonstrate are not going on in the apes' brains but in their social behavior with humans, a milieu that goes beyond their species needs and adaptations. This creates a kind of "hybrid mind" that is part-chimpanzee and part-human but a hybrid in which the direction of influence seems to be only one way—the humans attempt to induct the apes to be more human-like without much sign of them making efforts to become more ape-like. This makes it rather a one-way form of collaboration, if indeed it is genuinely collaboration at all.

To my mind, this gives all the examples that involve the interaction between humans and chimps a rather uncomfortable and "unnatural" quality. When the humans behave with the chimps as they would with human children, they themselves are acting "as if"—as if they are pretending that these creatures in their care *are* human children. Perhaps the apes are happy enough since all animals like to play and many species get along well with humans as long as they are treated with love and kindness. (Charlotte Freeman, personal communication, October 2013) Yet these attempts to scaffold developmental progress often seem forced and disregarding of the species-specific differences between apes and humans in a way that contrasts with Joe Hutto's study of the wild turkeys. In both cases, the humans had to use their own human imaginative capacities, but whereas Hutto strove to understand what it was like to be a turkey, the apes' companions strove to imagine how apes might behave more like humans. In some respects the apes obliged, but it may be that key differences became obscured in the process.

Helping, Sharing, and Collaboration

One of the most crucial of these differences is brought out by another set of experiments with chimpanzees that can be summed up as demonstrating that *chimpanzees do not cooperate with one another.* For example, young chimps show no interest in social games such as bouncing a ball together. When the ball is bounced to the chimpanzee, they simply do not "get the idea" that they are supposed to pass it back again. They will synchronize their behavior with a human in a problem-solving task but if the human stops participating they will make no attempt to re-engage them. In contrast, human children will readily collaborate in both problem-solving and social games but show *more* interest in social games since they will turn the instrumental task into a social game, and if the adult stops participating they will try to re-engage them.[39]

Nor do chimpanzees understand when a human is trying to help them. If a chimpanzee knows that food is hidden in one of two buckets but does not know which one and a human helper points to the correct bucket, the chimpanzee will take no notice of this gesture and search for the food randomly. They do not possess the kind of "interaction engine" that would enable them to infer the significance of the pointing gesture and its relevance to their search for food. Tomasello explains that,

> Apes simply do not understand that the human is communicating altruistically in order to help them toward their goals. That is, they themselves communicate intentionally only to request things imperatively, and so they only understand others' gestures when they are imperative requests as well—otherwise they are simply mystified as to what the gesticulating is all about.[40]

The only examples of chimpanzees themselves using a pointing gesture are in captivity (as when Panbanisha pointed to the snake) and these are always for imperative purposes rather than for informing, helping, or sharing as humans do. In contrast, human children learn to point around the age of one year and frequently use pointing in declarative as well as imperative ways. They will point out features of the environment that delight them purely for the purpose of sharing their delight with others and they will only be satisfied by a response that communicates to them that the recipient has understood their intention; if the recipient simply looks at the object or at the child, the child is not satisfied. Only if they look at *both* the object and the child does the child know that they have understood that the intention is to share pleasure.[41] Declarative pointing is also used in conjunction with language learning; a child may point out an object of delight and the parent will add the word "Yes, it's a *bus*!" And on a later occasion the child will point and say to the parent, "Bus!"

Some domesticated animals such as horses, goats, and dogs can learn to understand human pointing and will follow the direction of the point.[42] Most intriguingly, though, is the case of elephants who understand pointing without any prior tuition at all. Given the same "food in the bucket" test as apes, they will unerringly pick the bucket with the food from the first trial.[43] This may suggest a level of social cooperation amongst elephants that is not seen even in our closest relatives, although it is yet to be established whether elephants use pointing with their trunks to communicate amongst themselves. It is well known that elephants take a great interest in their own dead; when they come upon the remains of another elephant they will gather round and spend some time examining the remains in an apparently reverential manner. There are also reports of them travelling long distances to locate lost members of their group. All this would indicate a level of mutual care and concern amongst elephants that has, until now, seemed unique to humans. Since the genetic divergence between elephants and humans is 100,000 million years, this would be a case of convergent evolution. That is, helping, sharing, and empathic concern would have evolved separately in each species due to the exigencies of a particular kind of group-living.

Although evidence of mutual support is contested in chimpanzees, there is clearer evidence of caring and sharing amongst bonobos. The two species are very closely related but have very different social organizations; bonobos are much less aggressive, do not have dominant males, and frequently use sex as a kind of social "glue." Young bonobos offer consolation and comfort to others that have been hurt, and they are also more inclined to share food than chimpanzees.[44] The evidence certainly indicates that "a sensitivity to the emotions of others and the ability to provide appropriate consolatory behaviors emerges early in [their] development."[45] The fact that bonobos are more likely to share food with strangers than friends, however, suggests that sharing is being used in a very different way and is not necessarily a form of active collaboration.

Tomasello's research shows that even where it is possible to get chimpanzees to work together they show no interest in sharing with or helping their partner. His team has designed a test of collaboration where two apes have to pull on a rope in a way that enables each of them to get a reward. The rope is strung across a moveable plank with pieces of banana on it but in order to get the reward the apes have to pull together. This is because the rope is strung through hooks so that if one individual pulls on their own, it will just pull the rope out. The chimpanzees will pull together when they are each given the end of the rope, and they will get the reward. But if something goes wrong with the process such that only one of them can reach the food, the fortunate chimpanzee will do nothing to help the other reach the food—they will only cooperate for selfish ends.

When a similar experiment is done with two- or three-year-old children with marbles rather than food as a reward they will collaborate in a similar way in pulling the rope. The big difference is that if the reward is unequal—say one child gets three marbles and the other gets only one—the children will usually want the rewards to be equally split and the fortunate child will voluntarily give the other child one of his marbles so that the rewards are equal. So even though children may hold on to their own belongings and squabble with their peers over the use of a toy, when they are specifically collaborating with each other, they will help and share—something that only humans do.[46]

The same applies to groups of chimpanzees hunting monkeys in the wild. Although it looks as if the group are cooperating and dividing roles between them, in fact, each is pursuing their own individual goal and attempting to get into the best position they can in order to make the kill since he who makes the kill gets the best spoils. Any food-sharing that goes on afterwards is on the purely instrumental basis that it is in the winner's interest to share some food rather than have to fight to retain what they already have.[47]

Putting this together with ape abilities to deceive each other and hide their own motivations has lent support to the idea of the "Machiavellian intelligence hypothesis."[48] This idea proposes that primates living in groups needed to develop social intelligence in order to achieve reproductive success in a socially competitive environment. Nicholas Humphrey first proposed this hypothesis in 1976 as an explanation for why primates have such large brains.[49] The more general idea of social intelligence has become focused on strategies of deception, lying, cunning, and manipulation based on the same assumptions as Dawkins' notion of "the selfish gene"—the idea that evolutionary selection is a competitive struggle in which those who are able to outwit others will prosper and pass on their genes, thus selecting for increased capacities for deception and manipulation.

Tomasello's research proposes a radically different hypothesis that is equally supported by natural selection. He argues that the major innovation in early hominin groups was a shift from competitiveness to cooperation that created entirely new ways of living together requiring new forms of communication that paved the way for the development of language, culture, and symbolization. Tomasello does not attempt to date these developments, but the fact that brain-size almost doubled from *Homo habilis*, the earliest stone tool-makers of 2.5 million years ago, to the fully developed *Homo erectus* a million years later makes it clear that there had been a key shift in primate evolution in that time. The question is what was that shift and what were the selection pressures that drove it? Tomasello suggests there may have been competition from other terrestrial monkeys such as baboons that pushed early hominins towards meat scavenging as a source of food, requiring a coalition of individuals to ward off other animals and thence towards more active collaborative hunting of game and foraging for plants. The advantages of being able to pool their efforts through shared intentionality by informing, helping, and sharing with others would have conferred an advantage on those individuals who were good at sharing and receiving information and had a reputation as being good cooperators. Those that regularly deceived others or failed to share would be shunned. Of course, this doesn't exclude forms of Machiavellian intelligence, but, as Tomasello points out, lying to others is only possible on a) the assumption that their information is expected to be trustworthy and b) having the shared communicative skills to make lying possible.[50]

I have already considered the evidence gathered by Sarah Hrdy of shared childcare and shared foraging amongst human groups. In addition, Tomasello systematically compared the social structures of great ape and human forager societies and concludes,

> In every domain where apes behave mostly individualistically, humans behave mostly cooperatively. ... Humans but not apes engage in cooperative communication in which they provide one another with information that they judge to be useful for the recipient. Humans but not apes actively teach one another things helpfully, again for the benefit of the recipient. Humans but not apes make group decisions about group-relevant matters. And humans but not apes create and maintain all kinds of formal social structures such as social norms and institutions and even conventional languages using agreed-upon means of expression. In all, cooperation is simply a defining feature of human societies in a way that it's not for the societies of the other great apes.[51]

From the perspective of humans then, the ape way of living would be unbearably lonely. This may account for the peculiar sense of disjunction in observing the efforts of humans to engage chimpanzees in pretend play. The apes are just doing their own thing really—there is no sense of a dialogue in which a shared activity can grow and develop with a life of its own. For example, compare the strenuous efforts to engage chimps and bonobos in fantasy "as if" play with this typical example of pretend play with a two year old imagining bath time with a Teddy Bear:

> Having made a twiddling gesture at one end of a shoebox, we seat a Teddy Bear in the box. We ask "Where's the

soap?," pick up a wooden brick and rub Teddy's back
with it. The two year old joins in by lifting Teddy out of
the box announcing that "He's all wet" and wraps him in
a piece of paper.[52]

Here there is a sustained sense of make-believe that is shared
between both participants. The cooperative sharing makes it possible
to create an imaginary narrative world that exists alongside the "real"
world in which the unfolding chain of events is recognized by the
child who joins in with her own creative contribution ("he's all wet").
This world of "in-between" or transitional space is, as Winnicott
stipulated, not simply "made up" by the child any more than it is
"found." Although the child is "cued" in a similar way to the cueing of
Savage-Rumbaugh's chimpanzees and bonobos, here the child makes
her own imaginative contribution to a shared, collaborative activity
that takes place in the mutual space of shared intentionality. Thus,
the imaginative world arises in the social context of playing *with*
another; without these mutual communicative intentions it would not
be possible to develop an "inner" symbolic life or indeed any kind of
symbolic life at all.[53]

This taken-for-granted expectation of helping and sharing means
that, for example, should we ask a stranger for directions or to pass
the salt, we expect some sort of collaborative reply. Similarly, humans
communicate merely to share with each other and gain pleasure from
doing so. No ape would ever communicate with another about the
weather, for example, or, for those in captivity, whether the humans
are in a good mood today. They lack not merely the communicative
means but more profoundly the motivational intention to do so. By
contrast, humans routinely need others to take pleasure and interest
in their activities.

This fundamental tendency towards operating in a shared world
gives a much more acute dimension to the anguish of abandonment
in humans, beyond the anxiety and distress of mother and infant
separation that is common to the attachment system of all mammals.
It is notable that other animals do not communicate as a means of
helping each other. For example, if a whimpering chimpanzee child
is searching for its mother, no nearby female will point her out to the
child even though she knows her location and is perfectly capable
of making pointing gestures.[54] Similarly, Cortina and Liotti report
an incident originally observed by Cheney and Seyfarth in which a

troupe of adult baboons in the Okavango Delta swam across to another island, leaving the juveniles stranded.

> Not surprisingly, the juveniles found this separation very distressing, and they gave agitated bark and scream calls that signal separation distress and huddled together at night. *To the consternation of the research team*, the adult baboons heard the calls and looked toward the juveniles, but except for one baboon, none answered the calls nor made an effort to swim back to get the juveniles (the danger is real because lions often take advantage of these situations).[55] [italics added]

Thus humans respond even to the distress of other species, whereas amongst the baboons, even the juveniles' own parents appear serenely undisturbed. For humans, such implacable unconcern is the stuff of nightmares and evil, a common terror amongst psychotherapy patients with early experiences of traumatic abandonment. All of us enter into the world of shared intentionality to some degree just by possessing a (more or less) shared language and the means to (more or less) function in the world. But at a deeper level, children who have not had sufficient early experience of reciprocal sharing can feel a lifelong sense of being shameful and shunned as if they have fallen out of the human community, a pariah beyond the pale. The emotional anguish of this state has an intersubjective dimension as well as an attachment one; it is vividly captured by images of a lone human in a world of aliens or, in a neat reversal, by Steven Spielberg's story of E.T., the lone alien in a world of humans.

Human Sociality—Common Ground and Shared Intentionality

The development of cooperation and collaboration amongst early humans fostered the emergence of common ground and joint attention which, in turn, made it possible to infer communicative intentions. This would have been the origin of the "human interaction engine," the development of the kind of interactional intelligence that enables participants to recognize that pointing, or other forms of gesturing, *mean* something—that they have an intention to communicate that the recipient can understand by reference to the shared context in which they are made. While I was reading Tomasello's book *The Origins of Human Communication* I had an experience of this kind while on holiday in a country where I do not speak the language. I arrived at the toilet block in a public park where there was a long queue. A man began speaking to me but I had no idea what he was saying. As he spoke, however, he began to make a sort of curved pointing gesture from which I immediately understood that there was another toilet round the other side of the block where I found there was no queue. Probably, he too had recognized from my initial lack of response that I could not understand the language and so began supplementing his speech with gesture. This is a typical example of the kind of sharing of information amongst humans for no other motive than to help each other. Since we share not only the immediate context but the underlying communicative inferences that strange gestures have a purpose that is relevant to our current concerns (the "Gricean intention"), we are frequently able to understand each other even without language.

Since the capacity for voluntary, flexible vocalization did not develop in humans until the last 500,000 years at the outside, it is almost certain that language began with the use of these kinds of pointing and pantomiming gestures—i.e., gestures that imitate the object or action that is being referred to. If, for example, I am out foraging with a partner who begins making a peeling action and putting his hand to his mouth, I am likely to assume that he has spotted a good banana tree and will follow the direction of his gaze and point to locate it. As we have seen, it is possible to get chimpanzees to make these kinds of pantomiming gestures in pretend play but there is no sense that they are doing so to communicate helpfully with their partners or even to communicate at all. I would therefore question whether such gestures could be regarded as "symbolic play" since symbols have a quintessentially communicative function—they *mean* something, which means they mean something to someone—they enact a communicative intention.

Nevertheless, the presence of such gestures amongst chimpanzees is extremely significant since it supports Tomasello's contention that the development of new communicative functions in early hominin groups would have been possible without the need for the physiological evolution of cognitive skills and would not have been dependent on a random mutation in the brain conferring a selective advantage. The evolutionary process would have been a *social* occurrence due to the selective pressures of competing for resources with other primates occupying a similar ecological niche. This leads to a Baldwinian form of evolution where, as with Deacon's model, there is a co-evolution of language and the brain that is a response to social pressures within the group requiring greater levels of cooperation. Whereas Deacon sees symbolic language as a *pre-condition* for social cooperation (the securing of pair-bonding promises), both Levinson and Tomasello see language as *emergent* from cooperation, making the problem of symbolization less of a formidable leap. Deacon puts the cart before the horse.

In Tomasello's model, language begins in the context of a shift towards cooperation that refashions the individual intentionality of great apes towards shared intentionality or, as John Searle calls it, "*we* intentionality."[56] [italics added] The selective pressure is initially towards helping and sharing, especially in the context of sharing food resources, but this brings into being an entirely new form of mental existence in which "mind" exists in the context of the cooperative activity of more than one individual and, eventually, the whole group—in short, an extended mind with distributed cognition.

Searle argues that "we intentionality" is essential to the existence of any kind of social fact, even something as simple as taking a walk together where there is an implicit assumption of togetherness that is quite different from two people who just happen to be going in the same direction. If we are going for a walk *together*, it would be considered odd and rude if I suddenly went off in another direction without any "by your leave." Doing something together constitutes the existence of social rules that can be obeyed or broken—the notion of something being "rude" is itself something that exists only in the context of tacitly agreed social norms. This is what Searle means by a social fact—something that has meaning only in the context of human social activity, as opposed to the intrinsic facticity of what he calls "brute facts" of the physical world that exist independently of human activity. We may regard Mount Everest as a challenge to be climbed, a pretty sight, a geological structure of rock and molecules, or a living entity with its own spirit, but it is at least ontologically *there* in the first place, howsoever we relate to it. The physical reality of Everest would remain a "fact" even if there were no humans to recognize it, (albeit it takes a particular kind of imagination to conceive of the world as separate from our intentional sense-making presence within it). By contrast, social facts only exist as long as there are humans to recognize their existence. Nevertheless, they are just as real.

Crucially, Searle argues that shared intentionality cannot be reduced to individual intentionality, although he does so without questioning the assumption that "all my mental life is inside my brain and all your mental life is inside your brain."[57] Searle is a philosopher of speech acts and his solution to the problem of shared intentionality is a linguistic one; he argues that certain elements of this "in the brain" mental life can take the form of "we intend," "we are doing so-and-so," and the like. Even so, his challenge to the traditional philosophical objection to "we intentionality" is a most instructive one. He suggests,

> It has seemed that anybody who recognizes collective intentionality as a primitive form of mental life must be committed to the idea that there exists some Hegelian world spirit, a collective consciousness, or something equally implausible. ... It has seemed, in short, that we have to choose between reductionism, on the one hand, or a super mind floating over individual minds on the other.[58]

This critique speaks directly to the problematic aspect of Jungian psychology. If a collective consciousness is implausible, how much more so is a collective *unconscious*? The idea of shared intentionality therefore offers a more plausible explanation of the kind of psychic phenomena which fascinated Jung and to which he sought an explanation. It is not necessary to presuppose any kind of "super mind" if psychological life can be rooted in social life. The phenomena of the collective unconscious can be explained in social and material terms without requiring an ill-defined notion of a "collective psyche." These phenomena arise out of human actors working together to solve material problems in ways that require them to develop enough imagination to be able to symbolize things that are "not there" in a material sense but can be recognized as real through being represented in symbolic form.

Psychic Facts Are Social Facts

Furthermore, this approach has the additional advantage of closing the gap between psychology and sociology as two distinct or even opposed approaches to human behavior. The simple notion of social rules, based on shared assumptions and expectations are both *psychological* facts that exist within an individual mind, as Searle wants to insist, and *social* facts that have a social existence that is distributed through the group and not reducible to individual intentionality. Of course, I would want to go further than this and question whether such psychological facts can be located within an individual mind at all. The development of social life simultaneously creates the development of psychological life. The human mind is a social mind and so psychic facts are *ipso facto* social facts. *A fortiori*, since symbolic language is a form of social communication, the capacity for symbolization is socially acquired ("appropriated" in Vygotsky's term), and psychic symbols have an intrinsically social aspect. This is why the imagery of dream and fantasy is dependent on the scaffolding of symbolic language.

This may also explain the puzzling phenomena of people who are unable to symbolize and yet capable of having apparently symbolic dreams. Giles Clark provides a good example of this in a paper on borderline states of mind.[59] A man who lived a chaotic, compulsive, and destructive life, incapable of stable relationships and fueled by explosive, aggressive outbursts, dreamed that he was fucking a cathedral. The next day he went and "pissed and yelled my guts out in a church." Clark understands the dream as an unconscious metaphorical image of how he experiences others and behaves towards them, including his analyst. He comments that the dream depicts something "almost not even proto-symbolic" that is a somatic attack on the body-mind of himself and others.[60] This patient epitomizes the state of mind of those whose agency and intentionality cannot be represented symbolically but can only be evacuated through physical action (pissing in the church, etc.).[61] Yet, if that is the case, how could he possibly formulate such a rich symbolic image? One possibility is that the dream relies on a basic semantic capacity in which one object can be substituted for another, a basic property of language. Because language is a web of associative relationships whose meaning is held in place by their relation to each other (the token-token relationship), it is possible to construct sentences (and therefore thoughts and images) which reference what Deacon calls "impossible things," from a lion-man to a cathedral that can be fucked.[62] Tomasello makes the same point, arguing that abstract constructions provide slots which allow atypical construals, thus facilitating metaphorical or analogical thinking:

> In all, this system of conventionalized abstract constructions
> … enables the kind of creative conceptual combination
> by which humans may think, or at least try to think, of
> everything from flying toasters to colorless green ideas
> sleeping furiously.[63]

Thus symbolic imagination combines material things (lions, cathedrals, toasters, etc.) and linguistic structures (flying, fucking, sleeping, etc.) allowing endless reconstruction of new imaginative possibilities. Imaginal things are freed from the limiting affordances of material things but made possible and held in place by the abstract structure of language. So it becomes possible to think an image even without having the "third perspective" that makes it possible to place it in a wider context of understanding. Clark is able to formulate an interpretation of the dream through the use of metaphorical analogy in which the cathedral "stands for" a mother, an analyst, or, more generally, some body in whom the patient needs to have his explosive emotions contained. The patient, however, is unable to take a "third position" in which he can see the image from the perspective of another and so the interpretation makes no sense to him at all. In a sense, he lacks common ground with his own intentions, a reflection of a lack of common ground in his early relating. Unless there is sufficient coordination of joint intentions towards a third object (e.g., a toy) between adult and infant, the infant cannot develop a third perspective, the basis for self-reflexive consciousness.[64] So although he has been inducted into language sufficiently to be able to dream of impossible things, he has not been inducted into the shared play that forms the basis of a symbolic life. He has not made the transition from sign to symbol (in the non-discursive sense). He can only formulate a sensory narrative (fucking the cathedral) but cannot make sense of his analyst's efforts to transpose it into a symbolic one.

The notion of collective intentionality also offers a rather different perspective on the development of the self-monitoring function of the super-ego that places the exigencies of the incest prohibition in a much wider context of social cooperation. In order to improve their chances in the group,

> early humans simulated the evaluative judgments that others made of them with regard to their cooperative proclivities—precursors to norms of morality—and also with regard to the intelligibility of their communicative acts—precursors to norms of rationality.[65]

The need to monitor one's own behavior in a social context would therefore originate from cooperative primates engaged in tasks requiring joint attention and common ground. In order to work together as partners, we have to think about how we are viewed by others. This suggests that the development of a self-monitoring capacity is inherent to being cooperative communicators. Those that learn this early, through intra-familial interaction and sanctions, will be at an advantage. That is, just as symbolic meaning is held in place through shared linguistic usage in a community, so norms of behavior ("super-ego" functions) are held in place through processes of socialization within the group—another example of an extended and distributed mind that does not exist "in the head" but operates between people in a social context.

Features of social life that generate the need for greater self-monitoring necessarily generate greater self-awareness as *I* come to consider myself in the context of cooperating with *you*. Thus, ultimately, even the great mystery and miracle of human self-reflexive consciousness is socially generated; it is not a given of the human brain. Although the enlargement of the prefrontal cortex is clearly associated with the development of reflexive consciousness (and imagination), and reflexive self-consciousness would not be possible without it, a human being not immersed in a social culture would have precious little opportunity to develop such a consciousness. *I* can only exist because *you* exist, or, in Searle's terms, *I* exist because *we* exist. *I* exist in the context of social living with other humans who cooperate with each other and use symbolic communications to do so.

Alongside the development of sociality and language, humans were becoming skilled tool-makers and beginning to transform their material environment through the use of tools and other means such as the control of fire. These are all matters which can be studied via the archaeological record and, despite the paucity of evidence, enable us to create a possible time-line for human development in tandem with the development of language and sociality, even though the latter leaves no material traces. In the next chapter, I consider how a symbolic culture might have arisen from the earliest tool-makers of the Oldowan delta 2.5 million years ago to the cultural flowering of Upper Paleolithic art some 40,000 years ago.

CHAPTER FOUR

FROM APE TO HUMAN II
MATERIAL ENGAGEMENT

I f we accept Tomasello's hypothesis that the shift from ape to human coincides with the development of cooperation and socially organized collaboration, when might this have occurred in the archaeological record? One possible supposition is that it coincides with the earliest use of stone tools, many of which were found at the Olduvai Gorge in East Africa from which they take their name—Oldowan tools.

The Oldowan Stone Tool-makers

These tools date from as far back as 2.5 million years ago and are commonly associated with a species called *Homo habilis* although this is not certain. They consist of a core which has been struck at a precise angle using another rock as a hammer, shearing off a number of flakes and leaving a sharp-edged chopper. These could be used to dismember a carcass or smash bones to extract marrow.

Food Sharing and the "Home Base" Hypothesis

In 1978, archaeologist Glynn Isaac suggested that the Oldowan tool-makers may also have been the first species to have developed the distinctively human practice of food-sharing.[1] His argument for this centers on the claim that the Oldowan tool-makers did not, like other apes, "eat and go," consuming their food as and where they found it, but, like modern human hunter-gatherers, they maintained a "home base" to which food would be transported and shared within the group. If so, this would suggest a quite different form of social organization than is evident in the social arrangements of the great apes. Both stones and bones seem to have been carried from one site to another in an apparently purposive way. The presence of bones from several different species at a single site suggests that this was, at least, a preferred feeding location. There is also evidence that the stone cores from which the tools were made were carried from sites up to ten kilometers away since the tools were found at sites devoid of stones from which they could have been made.[2] This suggests a considerable advance in planning and forethought over that of other tool-using species, although recent evidence shows that chimpanzees are also capable of planning ahead by collecting useful objects before they are needed and taking them to a potential feeding site such as a termite nest.[3]

Isaac's hypothesis was that the evidence that food had been carried to a home base indicated a division of labor such as is evidenced amongst hunter-gatherer groups today in which females contribute the majority of gathered foods while males contribute most of the hunted food. Males and females range in separate groups and join up again at the home base. Nevertheless, Isaac was cautious about whether the Oldowan tool-users obtained their meat by hunting, in which they made the kill themselves, or opportunistic scavenging of carcasses hunted by other animals, such as lions. Nor did he consider these early hominins to be anything more than "protohuman." He concluded from the relatively primitive form of their tools that "the first tool-makers lacked the highly developed mental and cultural abilities of more recent humans." He did consider, however, that there might be a link between the ability to exchange food and the ability to exchange information, and concluded that "[f]ood sharing and the kinds of behavior associated with it probably played an important part in the development of reciprocal social obligations that characterize all human societies we know about."[4]

Subsequently, Isaac's claims were disputed by Lewis Binford, a major figure in Paleolithic archaeology in the 1980s and arguably "the most influential American archaeologist of the twentieth century."[5] Binford analyzed the bone fragments from which Isaac had drawn his hypotheses and concluded that *Homo habilis* were not merely scavengers but "marginal scavengers" who would not have had significant amounts of meat to transport from one location to another. In that case, the evidence for a "home base" form of social organization collapses.[6] Inevitably, these issues have been the subject of detailed debate over many years in the archaeological world and it remains frustratingly difficult to prove one assertion over another due to the limited amount of evidence available and the long time scale over which it might have accumulated. Isaac probably over-estimated the level of social and cognitive development of the Oldowan tool-users and his comparisons between modern hunter-gatherers and early proto-humans are difficult to justify today. One alternative theory is that the stones were transported to create caches that could be rapidly accessed to exploit a carcass before other predators arrived.[7] Even if such caches were created unintentionally, the fact that they would have become available for use by subsequent generations shows the way that culture may quite literally accumulate—the idea of a base or cache comes not from an idea in the brain of one or even several individuals but from the way the material circumstances lend themselves to such an idea—the stone cache itself might contribute to the development of the idea of a central base.

Kanzi, Stones, and Phones:
Mental Modules or Extended Mind

What is certain, though, is that, despite their comparative simplicity, the Oldowan stone tools mark a definite change in hominid skill. For all his ingenuity, this is a task that defeated Kanzi, the bonobo star-performer of Savage-Rumbaugh's lexigram method who has lived with humans all his life. Even though he can order a menu via an iPhone or light a fire with matches and toast marshmallows over it, learning how to strike a flake from a cobble core proved to be beyond him.[8] Kanzi understood what he was supposed to do readily enough and he does not lack manual dexterity since he can do things like tying shoelaces or undoing shirt buttons, but he could never achieve the skill of finding the right striking angle or controlling the amount of force in striking the core for acute angles. Instead he developed his own method; hurling a stone core against a concrete floor.[9]

Steven Mithen regards this difference as evidence for the development of "intuitive physics" in the mind of *Homo habilis* and perhaps the development of a specialized technical intelligence, cognitive modules that chimpanzees lack.[10] His is an intriguing and well-argued hypothesis, but it relies on the idea of a specialized modular mind. He proposes a model of separate, domain-specific "chambers" of intelligence on the analogy of walled-off chapels in a cathedral.

From the time of *Homo habilis* until the emergence of *Homo sapiens*, humans developed three specialized modules—natural intelligence, social intelligence, and technical intelligence, but these all operated separately so humans were unable to use the skills of one domain in the service of another. For example, he suggests that the reason that tools were consistently made from stone rather than other materials such as bone until the last 100,000 years or so was because, for earlier humans, bones belonged to the domain of natural intelligence and humans were unable to make the link between a material they used for food and one they used for technology. Similarly, they would not have connected an animal with their social world to produce an image like the Lion Man. He maintains the assumption of a " big bang" in cultural development that gave *Homo sapiens* the edge over their competitors, even their almost-modern close relatives, the Neanderthals, and argues that this is due to a cognitive shift in the brain that dissolved the walls between the separate domains, making it possible to link one cognitive domain with another. This created the distinguishing feature of the modern mind: our capacity for forming analogies and making links between one domain and another. Mithen names this *cognitive fluidity*. This would account for the development of metaphor and symbol since these make use of analogy virtually by definition.

I think Mithen is right to point to cognitive fluidity as perhaps *the* distinguishing feature of what makes us human: symbolic imagination would certainly not be possible without metaphorical analogy, and, as Lakoff and Johnson have shown, metaphor is also a basic feature of language. There are, however, two major problems with his theory. Firstly, there is no evidence for any such dramatic cognitive shift in the brains of modern humans, and , secondly, his theory relies on the questionable notion of mental modules and an internalist model of the mind. As Lewis-Williams points out, it assumes too exclusive an emphasis on rational intelligence, an essentially Western view that looks at early human development as a process of becoming more and more like (Cartesian) scientists.[11]

How else then might we think about the developments that began 2.5 million years ago, even allowing for the great uncertainty about precisely when our hominin ancestors embarked on the long road to collaboration and symbolic communication? Perhaps Kanzi's difficulty—and his solution—might provide a clue. One important reason why Kanzi can't make stone tools is that he is not physically equipped to do so. Despite his manual dexterity, he lacks the precision grip that characterizes the human hand. Chimpanzee and bonobo hands have long fingers and short thumbs, adapted for tree climbing, whereas the human hand is adapted for precision grip, perhaps initially adapted for throwing and clubbing.[12] By the time of *Homo habilis*, these changes were already fairly well-advanced, showing that their intentional goals were different from those of chimpanzees. The two species are pursuing different goals in their embodied action, just as they came to do in their use of communicative devices.[13]

So the deeper reason why Kanzi cannot make stone tools is that it is outside his species-specific intentional goals. He is not operating in an environment where the pressure towards making stone tools is a matter of survival. He can only be manipulated into doing so by being set a task whose solution encourages him in that direction, a task he pursues for quite different reasons than those which impelled early hominin groups living in the wild. The solution he finds by using the concrete floor would certainly not have been part of the milieu of *Homo habilis* but has its own kind of affordance as something very hard against which things are likely to break. He uses the floor in the same way he uses matches and iPhones, in his own species-specific way in an environment very different from his natural environment of adaptation. In so far as an iPhone is a feature of the extended mind, Kanzi is not using it in any recognizably human way but as part of his own extended bonobo mind whose intentionality is rather different from that of humans.

The idea of the extended mind does not imply that things *are* the mind; the extended mind is to be found in the synergy *between* human bodies with human brains and the objects they utilize and create for their own purposes. When we marvel at Kanzi's skills, we project those aspects of the human mind that are located in the iPhone into the thing itself. But for Kanzi, the iPhone is just another lexigram board through which he can make his requests known. He is never going to send someone a text saying "Where's the picnic?" or "Have a great time!" because his mind just doesn't work like that. Only humans express opinions or ask questions. No other animal uses communication to say things about the world, as opposed to just signaling a direct emotional state or need.[14] What is special about Kanzi is the environment in which he has been raised and, it should be said, the sensitivity to his own needs that seems to have enabled him to live contentedly within it. So, although Kanzi remains 100% bonobo, his mind cannot be that of a typical bonobo because his environment is not that of a typical bonobo. If the mind is emergent from embodied engagement with the environment, then to understand the emergence of the human mind, we need to look at the environment in which it emerged.

Cognitive Archaeology

The attempt to understand the development of the mind through its relation with the material objects in the environment is an application of enactive, extended, and distributed notions of mind to archaeological theory known as Material Engagement Theory, developed by Colin Renfrew and Lambros Malafouris.[15] Their approach is a recent innovative development in what is itself the relatively new field of cognitive archaeology of which Mithen's book *The Prehistory of the Mind* was another ground-breaking example.

In the first half of the twentieth century, archaeologists were mainly concerned with describing ancient cultures in terms of the time and place in which their artifacts were found. This was what Lewis Binford rebelled against. He argued that although archaeologists "cannot dig up a social system or ideology" the material items of archaeological excavations functioned together with these more behavioral elements and therefore make it possible to yield a systematic and understandable picture of the total extinct cultural system.[16] Isaac's "home base" theory was a similar effort to go beyond what the paleontologists had been able to do by making anthropological as well as archaeological deductions about how the long-extinct species might have lived. But the study of cultural systems and behaviors is still not a study of the mind, a more ambitious undertaking altogether.

Cognitive archaeology seeks to reconstruct the prehistory of the mind, taking as its cue the pattern of brain expansion over the past two million years, beginning with *Homo habilis* and accelerating during the million year history of *Homo erectus* with another spurt around 500,000 years ago coinciding with the emergence of *Homo heidelbergensis*, the common ancestor of ourselves and our Neanderthal cousins. Similarly, both Deacon and Tomasello speculate that the most likely candidate for the beginnings of language (in whatever form) would be *Homo erectus*, pointing to the considerable change in brain size from early to late *erectus*.

Renfrew has defined cognitive archaeology as "the study of past ways of thought inferred from the surviving material remains."[17] On the face of it, this seems a daunting task; however, if, as I argued in the previous chapter, cognition is extended and distributed, then material artifacts are not merely the effects of the mental causes that produced them but are part and parcel of the cognitive process itself. In accord with Feynman's rejoinder to Charles Weiner, material objects are active contributors to the psychic processes with which they were interacting. Rather than there being a pre-existing cognitive state or intention which shapes what humans do with material objects, the objects themselves are constitutive of the mental states that engagement with them brings into being. This clearly opens up a rich and fascinating avenue of research for cognitive archaeology since it means that much more can be derived from material remains than had previously been thought. Humans have left behind not merely a record of their cognitive process but a crucial aspect of the cognitive process itself which can be partially reconstructed.

Material Engagement Theory studies the deep connection between the mind and things—a view of mind that, as discussed in Chapter 2, takes it out of our heads and into the world in which we live. Acknowledging an intellectual kinship with developmental systems theory, Malafouris argues that instead of a unidirectional formula whereby genes drive and determine behavior, there needs to be a bi-directionality of influences in which physical, social, and cultural aspects of environment and behavior play fundamental roles in triggering the expression of genes.[18] He develops a strong argument for things having their own cognitive agency that shape the mind as much as being shaped *by* the mind, a synergy that is "a constitutive intertwining of brains, bodies, and things that unfolds in real time and space."[19] My suggestion of the way that accidental stone caches may have influenced the development of concepts of a home base would be a case in point. Nor is it possible to classify the tools themselves according to any definite set of pre-existing intentions as Nicholas Toth discovered when he attempted to replicate them. He concluded that "their final shape depends not on a template in the maker's head but on the shape of the raw pebble ... or rock fragment with which the maker starts." [20]

In this way, things may be said to constitute the mind or, more precisely, engagement with things constitutes the mind. Psychic life emerges from the particular way in which humans first began to engage with objects as tools. Symbols too are a form of tool—they are tools to think with. This suggests that the use of tools and the development of language are likely to have developed alongside each other. This may be because of the way tool use drove the development of certain areas of the brain associated with language, but it may be more to do with the way that the manipulation of objects and the use of gestures with conventional meaning are both forms of tool use. They indicate the way that humans had begun to transform their environment, to *make* things. They had already begun to be more creative than any other species. For, as Malafouris says, "Even the most highly trained nonhuman nut crackers couldn't equal the abilities seen in the earliest hominin makers of stone tools."[21] On the other hand, Iriki and Sakura question how creative these early tool makers really were. They argue that the early stone tool users were merely passively adapting to the tool-using niche they had created in the same way that beavers are adapted to life inside the elaborate dams they build.[22] This, they suggest, is the reason why there was so little innovation in the use of stone tools over hundreds of thousands of years. Glynn Isaac remarked that over this period "toolkits tended to involve the same essential ingredients seemingly being shuffled in restless, minor, directionless change."[23] Even so, it is through our relationship with tools that we eventually come to be human. This, suggests Malafouris, makes us more *Homo faber* than *Homo sapiens*.[24]

Before there could be thinking "in the head," that is, thinking that takes a non-material form, there had to be material engagement with physical objects to provide the basic metaphors out of which symbols are constructed. Symbolic objects are tools to think with, just as linguistic symbols are. Even now, most of the symbolic furniture of dream, fantasy, and myth consist of material things (including living things) put to symbolic use. Symbols are imagined things.

On a purely material level, the use of manual tools enables the progressive emergence of forms that could not exist prior to their use. For example, the use of stone tools made it possible to cut the hide away from animals and this in turn opened up the possibility that hides could be used as clothing, making it possible for humans to dwell in climates that previously would have been too cold for them. Recent discoveries of stone tools and fossilized footprints at Happisburgh in Norfolk have shown that humans were living as far north as Britain around 850,000 years ago, almost 500,000 earlier than previously thought.[25] They could not have done so without the use of some kind of clothing. When *Homo sapiens* greatly improved on the use of animal skins by inventing needles and thread, they were producing a tool that would have had no meaning or significance without the stone tools that had made animal hides available for use many thousands of years earlier. Furthermore, it may well have been through the wearing of animal hides and animal heads, that the idea of a lion-headed man arose, not merely as a man wearing a lion's head but as a being of an entirely different order.

Thus the introduction of clothing does not only open up new possibilities in the material world—living in colder climates—but also in the psychic world where it may open up imaginative possibilities for taking on different identities, including those of the spirit or "other" world. Clothing may even shape our metaphors and emotional responses in relation to nakedness and shameful feelings of exposure. While such feelings may exist in other forms, the extended mind perspective enables us to see how our material engagement is *constitutive* of emotional and spiritual states of mind as well as cognitive ones. In order to apprehend a spirit world, to be able to "think" a spirit world, there have to be means of representing those spiritual beings in a material way and these are further enhanced by the use of visual representation.

So we begin by using things and the use of things gives us ideas about how to use them. Only once this has been sufficiently established does it become possible for things to be used in other ways as ideas. The possibilities for mental elaboration that tool use promotes are described by Hutchins.

> By interacting with particular kinds of cultural things, we can produce complex cognitive accomplishments while employing simple cognitive processes. Once we have learned to interact with these things, we may learn to imagine both the things and our interaction with them. Then we can organize our thinking using internal resources in ways that previously required interaction with external cultural things. In this perspective, interaction with the material and social world comes first, and imagination of those interactions comes later ... *Imagining bodily interaction with things can become a form of conceptual thinking.*[26] [italics added]

And just as the use of material tools enables an elaboration of material forms that create a cultural habitat (e.g., in which people make and wear clothing), so the use of symbolic tools brings into existence an imaginal habitat by means of a conceptual elaboration in which "one thing leads to another." In both domains, tool use produces increased cultural complexity over time by means of the ratchet effect, the process whereby innovations become established by imitation so that over time they become the cultural baseline from which future generations begin.[27]

As humans began using things, these would gradually have become not merely an occasional addition but a regular and necessary feature of their way of living until eventually they became constitutive of a specifically human way of being in the world. Perhaps Isaac locates that point rather too early, but his hypothesis that the transport of food and tools (whenever that occurred) implies a requirement for things in which they can be carried is an important one. It shows that material engagement with things promotes further development through the agency of things themselves.[28] It is not only the need of humans to carry things that is promoting change—it is the needs of the objects themselves to be carried.

Homo erectus—Hand-Axes and Compassion

Despite their use of stone tools and the possible development of more sociable ways of living, *Homo habilis* remained close to the australopithecine apes that preceded them. It is the species that evolved around 1.8 million years ago that are more often thought of as the first true humans—*Homo erectus*. One of their most notable innovations was the Acheulean hand-axe, typified by their symmetrical teardrop shape and bi-faced sharp edges. These multi-purpose tools were in use for 1.5 million years and were still being used 60,000 years ago, despite a proliferation of more specialized and complex tools that had been developed along the way. That must make the hand-axe the single most important technological advance of all time.

Many of these tools are so pleasing to the eye (and hand) that it seems as if they must have been made with conscious intention by people with a well-developed aesthetic sensibility. Yet it is more likely that their shape and form were determined by the practical engagement of the knapping process—the striking of flakes from cores. The activity of butchering carcasses itself drove the need for more varied and effective tools. Malafouris argues that knapping activity does not arise "within" the mind and is then enacted—it is the actual practice of knapping that shapes the knapper's intentions as he or she discovers what the stone itself requires. "The best angles for flake removal are neither identified nor imagined in the knapper's head before the act ... they are embodied and therefore they must be discovered in action."[29] The knappers learn the feeling or tacticity of the stone and this guides their emergent intentions and thus eventually shapes the mind.

> The stone projects toward the knapper as much as the knapper projects toward the stone and together they delineate the cognitive map of what we may call an *extended intentional state*. The knapper first thinks *through* and *with* the stone before being able to think *about* the stone and hence about himself as a conscious and reflectively aware agent.[30]

The suggestion here is that the self-reflective mind arises from the material action of shaping the world via the use of tools. Rather than seeing these intentions as internal in origin as if the image or form in the mind comes first and is then imposed on the stone, this is an embodied view of mind and matter that are conceptually inseparable, in which act and image are mutually constitutive.

It is certainly the case that higher levels of intentional organization associated with prefrontal cortex activity is present in the use of late Acheulean knapping methods in contrast to Oldowan methods where strategic action-planning activation is absent. But rather than seeing this as a purely internal, genetically driven change, it should be viewed in the overall context of a developing human cultural milieu.

> These higher levels of intentional organization ... can emerge only through deliberate practice and skill acquisition, which would have been greatly enhanced and facilitated by joint action and communication; this adds support to the view that human technological, social, and linguistic capacities evolved together in a mutually reinforcing way.[31]

Care and Compassion

One of the most interesting features of *Homo erectus* and another species, closely associated with them, *Homo ergaster,* is that some of the skeletal remains that have been discovered in recent years show evidence of individuals suffering from incapacities that would have required care from others for them to have survived. One of the most well-known examples is a female *Homo ergaster* dated to around 1.5 million years ago. The deformation of her bones shows that she was suffering from an advanced case of hypervitaminosis (caused by an excess of vitamin A). The symptoms of pain, dizziness, blurred vision, and loss of muscular coordination would have taken months to develop so she could not have survived alone without someone to care for her, feed her, and protect her from carnivores. Cameron and Groves conclude from this that "the group dynamics of early *Homo* must have been based on some form of mutual support."[32]

An even older example of compassionate care comes from an important site at Dmanisi in Georgia that has yielded numerous remains that have been dated as far back as 1.8 million years ago. To date, five skulls have been found, most likely belonging to the species *Homo erectus*, predating previous human finds outside Africa by 800,000 years. Their presence in Western Asia shows that these early humans began to disperse out of Africa relatively soon after their earliest appearance in West Africa. One of the most remarkable of the finds at Dmanisi is the skull of an elderly male that is virtually toothless—only one canine was left. Yet this must have happened years before his death because the jaw has shrunk as the result of tooth loss. How could such an individual survive? These people were mostly dependent on meat and this was almost a million years before the use of fire. It would have been a real struggle for this elderly man to survive, especially in hard winters, so he must have been helped by others, providing indirect evidence of altruism and cooperation—a significant shift from great ape societies and very much in accord with the theoretical model proposed by Tomasello. So, these discoveries are a strong indicator of a form of social organization involving shared intentionality and collaborative cooperation.

David Lordkipanidze, the leader of the Dmanisi excavation is "sure that someone was taking care of this individual. Maybe this person had knowledge which others needed."[33] He sees this as early evidence of compassion amongst humans, which goes further than simply mutual cooperation, because taking care of someone suggests that this was not simply an exchange based on rational considerations of mutual need but had an emotional component too, even if the emotional component served the selective function of preserving knowledgeable individuals.

This is perhaps not so surprising considering that chimpanzees are known to offer consolation to distressed individuals who are socially close by kin or affiliation, despite their strongly individualistic, competitive social relations.[34] As might be expected, this behaviour is even more marked in bonobos. When young bonobos are attacked, others may rush to hug and comfort them. Those that have been mother-reared recover more quickly and are more likely to offer comfort to others, showing evidence that secure attachment increases the capacity for emotional self-regulation and empathic concern for others.[35] So compassion of the kind that Lordkipanidze thinks may have kept the toothless early human from Dmanisi alive might indicate a coalescence of attachment-based emotional expressions with more specifically human intersubjective collaborative and cooperative living. Furthermore, if the elderly were valued for their knowledge, then this would also suggest a means of communicating that knowledge—i.e., some kind of language based on common ground and shared intentionality. For now, all this must remain speculative, awaiting further discoveries of our earliest human beginnings.

The tools at Dmanisi are more like Oldowan choppers than the later Acheulean hand-axes usually associated with *Homo erectus* which may indicate that they left Africa before hand-axes were developed. Only recently, archaeologists from Dmanisi caused a considerable stir that was widely reported in the media when they suggested that the variation between the five skulls was no greater than that found amongst modern humans or chimpanzees.[36] Yet had these skulls been found at different sites indicating different time-layers, they would almost certainly have been assigned to different species. They concluded that many of the species previously regarded as separate and different, including *Homo habilis* might therefore all belong to the same species, *Homo erectus.* This would confirm *Homo erectus* as the great pioneer and predecessor of our own species—the human species that began using stone tools, developed the capacity to walk long distances (moving out of Africa, across Asia, as far as China, as well as up into Europe), began using fire (evidence for which has recently been pushed back 200,000 years to a million years ago),[37] and may well have begun to develop gestural forms of linguistic communication. And all the time, their brains were becoming larger, not as a cause of these developments nor simply as the result of them but in a synergy of emergent co-evolution between brain, body, and the changing material, ecological, and social environments with which they were engaged.

The Emergence of Modern Humans

Around 600,000 years ago, a new species emerged, remains of which have been found in Africa, Asia, and Europe. *Homo heidelbergensis* is now thought to be the common ancestor of both Neanderthals and modern humans. While those in Europe evolved into *Homo neanderthalensis*, a strong, stockily built human species well adapted to living in cold climates who were already present in Britain by 400,000 years ago, *Homo sapiens* evolved in Africa somewhat later, no more than 200,000 years ago and did not begin their voyage "out of Africa" until 60,000 years ago.[38] Much of this is uncertain because of the fragmentary nature of the fossil remains in Africa, although the once controversial "out of Africa" proposal that all modern humans are of (relatively) recent African origin was confirmed by mitochondrial DNA evidence in the 1980s. While the "multi-regional" origins theory clings on in a few isolated quarters, like the last Neanderthals pushed to the edge of Europe and scratching a living in the Gibraltar caves some 30,000 years ago, it is now generally accepted that we are all descended from a hypothetical "mitochondrial Eve" who lived in Africa some 200,000 years ago.

By the time of *Homo heidelbergensis*, humans were becoming increasingly sophisticated. They had probably been regularly using fire for thousands of years which would have provided not only warmth and cooked food but opportunities for social gathering around a hearth—perhaps the original meaning of the "archetypal" idea of "hearth and home." If those that eat together, stay together, then sharing food around a hearth would provide a strong basis for the growth of social cooperation and communication. Fire also provided opportunities for important technological advances. Around 300,000 years ago, people began making composite tools with wooden handles, using plant gum and red ochre as adhesive. Heating was also used to improve the quality of stone tools by burying them under a hearth for many hours at high temperature and leaving them to cool, thereby facilitating the removal of finer flakes and "giving more control of the final shape and cutting edges." These activities "imply a high level of knowledge, planning, and thought" and are "a sign of their increasing ability to shape their local environment—a key factor in the development of our modern human capacity to adapt to almost any place on Earth."[39]

From this period too came the use of wooden spears. The tip of one of these was found in Clacton, England in 1911, but in 1997 three complete two-meter wooden spears were discovered in Schöningen, Germany. These must have been javelins of some kind although whether they were thrown or used close-up to pierce a hunted animal is not known. It is certainly possible that tools of this kind existed much earlier since wooden tools are obviously much less likely to survive the ravages of decay over long periods of time. And it is probable that by this time humans had progressed from scavenging to hunting since the shoulder blade of a horse with what is thought to be a puncture wound from a spear has been discovered at the Boxgrove site in Southern England.[40] This remarkable site, dated to 500,000 years ago contains over 400 beautifully made flint hand-axes, found exactly where they had been left and showing that their makers were dividing up space in an organized way. Those makers were identified as *Homo heidelbergensis* when a tibia (leg-bone) and two teeth were found there in the mid-1990s.

The more that is discovered about these ancient ancestors, the more sophisticated and similar to ourselves they seem to be. The historical decline of the presuppositions and prejudices of imperialistic European supremacy have given us a greater appreciation not only of our living indigenous counterparts in the Americas, Africa, and Australasia but of our ancestral predecessors too. Increasingly, representations of what these earlier humans might have looked like have emphasized their "modern" features where earlier representations emphasized what was "primitive" about them, seeking to depict them as being as ape-like as possible. Surely "we" could not be the same as "them." Nowadays, we seek to find more of what we have in common than what divides us—even with apes, as we have seen with changing attitudes towards chimpanzees. This is evidenced by the use of familial terms such as *relatives*, *ancestors*, and *cousins*—terms of which I have made much use myself.

At the same time, the more we find the commonalities, the more we seek to identify the points of difference, for in all these enquiries we are seeking to answer the fundamental question, "What is it that makes us human?" What is it that distinguishes us from all these others that are so like us? What was the special spark that turned us into the unique, cultural beings we are today with the symbolic languages that have given us science, religion, and the arts, and have taken us to the moon both literally and symbolically? This is no longer to claim that we are superior to other living beings; anthropological and ecological thinking increasingly shows us that this is a myth particular to our own Western prejudices. Indigenous cultures still feel themselves to be fellow participants in the natural world with others who are animated in the same way as themselves, a sensibility we have lost to our increasing cost—and theirs. Yet we are certainly different from our fellow beings in the "more-than-human world," as David Abram calls it.[41]

Are Neanderthals Us?

Nowhere is this question more acute than in considering where (if at all) the dividing line might fall between ourselves and our nearest relative of all—the Neanderthals, a species who had already been living in Europe for nearly 400,000 years when *Homo sapiens* arrived some 40,000 years ago and who survived alongside us for a further 10,000 years. Why did we survive when they did not? What was it that we had—and have—that they did not? Or might it have all been due to happenstance and historical accident? Had things been different, could it have been the descendents of Neanderthals digging for evidence of their predecessors and wondering what happened to their human cousins who died out in Africa around 60,000 years ago, despite showing modern features even earlier than they developed in Europe a mere 20,000 years ago?

To begin to address this question, we need to identify those distinguishing modern features that begin to appear in the historical record in the last 100,000 years and ask whether they were unique to *Homo sapiens* or might have been shared with our co-descendants from *heidelbergensis*. There are four prime candidates: language; burial; the symbolic use of objects, especially for personal ornamentation; and, last but not least, the creation of figurative representations that reach their earliest spectacular apogee in the cave paintings of Southern Europe from 35,000 years ago. All of these features have in common one overriding factor: symbolic representation and communication.

Language

There is growing evidence that Neanderthals are likely to have possessed the same capacity for speech as modern humans. The two physiological features that make complex speech possible are the position of the larynx in the throat and the function of the hyoid bone which is attached to the tongue and enables the fine muscle control that speech requires. These features are unique to humans and had begun to evolve in *Homo heidelbergensis*. Only one Neanderthal hyoid bone has been found (at Kebara) but a recent study has shown that it functioned in much the same way as it does in modern humans today, a finding consistent with a capacity for speech in Neanderthals.[42] Neanderthal DNA has also shown the presence of the FOXP2 gene associated with the fine muscle control required for complex vocalization. This too is thought to have been present in the common ancestor (*heidelbergensis*).[43] This suggests a much earlier origin for vocalized language than had been previously thought and, if vocal language was preceded by gestural communications, supports the view that this must have become part of the repertoire of even earlier species such as *Homo erectus* at some stage of its million-year evolution.

Burial of the Dead

Here the evidence is rather more equivocal. Burial of the dead has particular significance when it is indicative of belief in an after-life or at least a sense that the dead person has a spirit that deserves care of some kind even after death. Such feelings and beliefs are indicative of an awareness of "the other world," a realm that may be thought about in a variety of ways. These may or may not involve specifiable religious beliefs but necessarily rely on a capacity for imagination. That is, there has to be a capacity to imagine or conceive of aspects of reality that "do not meet the eye."[44] In relation to burial, there are two issues—the first is whether burials are intentional and the second is whether the intention was related to concern for the dead person's spirit, however conceived. For example, some burials may have simply been a means of disposal or a health measure of some kind.

The sign of a spiritual intention is usually taken to be the deliberate inclusion of grave goods. There is a spectacular example of this dating from 28,000 years ago at Sungir in Russia where two adolescents and an adult male were buried in clothes each adorned with 3,000 ivory beads and mammoth ivory bracelets and accompanied by several hundred fox teeth pendants. Given the huge amount of time and effort involved in making these beads, there can be little doubt that this burial is evidence of dead persons being given very special treatment indeed, which, presumably, would have been a continuation of their special status in life, indicating another element of modern human activity, the symbolic use of objects.

The earliest examples of burials with grave goods are found at the sites of Skhul and Qafzeh in Israel. At Skhul, some 115,000 years ago, the jawbone of a massive wild boar was placed with the body of an adult male, while at the 100,000-year-old site at Qafzeh, the antlers of a fallow deer were placed in the hands of a child. Both of these individuals were anatomically modern.[45]

Evidence from Neanderthal burials is less clear. Reports of a Neanderthal buried with flowers 60,000 years ago in Iraq have subsequently been questioned on the grounds that it is equally likely that the flower-pollen found with the skeleton may have drifted into the cave unintentionally.[46] There is certainly some evidence of intentional burial by Neanderthals[47] and this suggests that they may have felt an emotional connection with their dead relatives and companions but there is little sign of the unequivocal use of grave goods such as those found at Skhul and Qafzeh, let alone that of Sungir.[48] The evidence is far from conclusive, however; it may simply be that Neanderthals practiced funerary rites other than burial such as exposure in the open.[49] These would have less archaeological visibility, indicating a common problem in tracing the past—absence of evidence is not evidence of absence.

Symbolic Use of Objects

Long before the Aurignacians began sculpting figurines from bone and wood, humans had been using red ochre for body-painting and shell beads as necklaces. These forms of personal ornamentation have become the focus of intense archaeological debate about the origin of symbolic behavior. Almost no one disputes that the use of personal ornamentation has a symbolic significance, but the question of when it was first used and by whom has become a kind of counter for when humans became "*Homo symbolicus*" and whether this trait was shared with Neanderthals or is definitive of *Homo sapiens*. Shell beads have become a symbol of the symbolic. It is notable that this debate rages independently of the growing evidence for Neanderthals having spoken language, a further indication of the special significance of the social use of objects for symbolic purposes.

Generally, personal ornamentation is seen as a way of signaling personal and social identity and status to others, implying a degree of social stratification and, crucially, its representation in symbolic form. It may also indicate the development of symbolic forms of social exchange and reciprocity insofar as this can be projected back from their use by modern hunter-gatherers. Amongst the !Kung, for example, ostrich shell beads represent reciprocity between neighboring or distant bands of people, a lightweight, portable token of mutual obligations.[50] If used in this way, shell beads might also indicate the emergence of symbolically structured relationships over long-distance social networks, suggesting more complex forms of social organization.[51]

Until only fifteen years ago, it was believed that symbolic objects of this kind came into use no earlier than 40,000 years ago. Since the late-1990s, however, a series of discoveries in North and South Africa have provided conclusive evidence that shell beads and red ochre used as forms of personal ornamentation date back as far as 100,000 years ago—or even longer. The finds at Blombos cave in South Africa are dated around 75,000 years ago while at Taforalt, in Morocco, the same kind of shells showing signs of the same kind of use (nassarious marine tick shells, intentionally perforated, with traces of red ochre) have been dated to 82,000 years ago. These finds are related to different cultures of anatomically modern humans, living at different times with different tool industries in widely separated locations. Even older shells have been identified in Algeria and at the Skhul site in Israel where the earliest human burial with the boar's jawbone was also found, probably 100,000 years ago. These finds provide strong evidence for the existence of a widespread bead-working tradition in Africa and the Levant well before the arrival of anatomically modern humans in Europe.[52]

Blombos cave has also become famous for its many pieces of ochre that have been intentionally marked with criss-crossed lines suggesting the possibly deliberate creation of abstract geometric patterns. These enigmatic features, which would originally have been a vivid blood-red color,[53] seem to suggest some kind of symbolic significance, but, if so, its purpose and meaning remains unknown. Evidence of humans using ochre goes back as far as 260,000 years ago at Twin Rivers in Zambia and about sixty pieces have been found at Pinnacle Point in South Africa dating from the time of the earliest anatomically modern human fossils around 160,000 years ago. This may have been used for functional purposes such as treating animal skins or as part of compound adhesives for making composite tools,[54] although Lawrence Barnham, who discovered the Twin Rivers site, believes that the variety of colors used and the processing effort involved in ochre use argues in favor of ritual use rather than a merely functional explanation.[55]

In the Upper Paleolithic period, red ochre was used very extensively, and, like shell beads, it is still in use today, as a pigment for body-painting.[56] Since body-painting is often associated with the symbolism of religious rituals, there is a good likelihood that red ochre is a sign not only of body-painting but of symbolic ritual practices in the distant past.[57] Since there are so many other possible uses for red ochre, however, I prefer to take perforated shell beads as the most unequivocal evidence for symbolic forms of personal ornamentation, especially where the perforations show signs of wear associated with being strung on cords as pendants or necklaces. Here there can be no doubt about the purpose, if not the meaning, of their use.

So what about the Neanderthals? If it could be established that they too used symbolic forms of personal ornamentation, it would be hard to maintain any significant difference between them and us. Not only would they be "rehabilitated" to a fully human status but it would more or less put an end to attempts to establish the emergence of modern humanity in terms of any definitive anatomical or neurological differences. As might be expected, then, the evidence remains uncertain and fiercely controversial. Neanderthal use of red ochre is now well documented for the period between 60,000 and 40,000 years ago and a recent study has found evidence at sites in the Netherlands of similar antiquity to the oldest occurrences amongst *Homo sapiens* (over 200,000 years ago).[58] As noted, though, this does not establish whether it was being used in any symbolic, non-utilitarian way.

Perhaps the most striking evidence of Neanderthal use of personal body ornaments comes from a site at Grotte du Renne in France, featuring several animal teeth and bones that have clearly been pierced to wear as pendants, as well as a number of bone awls. These were found at a site that is almost certainly of Neanderthal origin and includes skeletal remains (which is not the case at Blombos cave, for example). Unfortunately, though, the pendants were excavated fifty years ago and there is an ongoing controversy over their dating as they might have come from a higher (more recent) level of Aurignacian origin. João Zilhão, a strong proponent for the cognitive equivalence between *sapiens* and

Neanderthals, argues that this is an example of a residual prejudice left over from the nineteenth century when Neanderthals were regarded as "sub-human."[59] He cites, for example, the argument that is often made that if Neanderthals did exhibit apparently symbolic behavior, then they must have been imitating the recently arrived *sapiens*, like a child wearing their mother's pearls without understanding their significance. He also points to the double standards to which evidence of Neanderthal symbolism is subject—far more stringent tests than even more fragmentary or equivocal evidence attributed to modern humans. Furthermore, the Grotte du Renne pendants are not the only evidence of Neanderthal ornamentation. At two sites in Spain and one in Italy, perforated shells colored with pigment have been discovered dated to around 50,000 years ago (10,000 years before the arrival of "modern humans") and a bone stiletto with pigment on its tip that is most likely to have been used for the application of body-paint. There are also suggestions that Neanderthals decorated themselves with bird feathers, on the basis of cut-marks found on the wings of choughs and red kites in Gibraltar.[60] In short, there is growing evidence that, if body-painting and personal ornamentation are signs of symbolic behavior, then this applies just as much to Neanderthals as *Homo sapiens*.

Figurative Representation

There remains one area that is apparently unique to modern humans—the use of figurative representation that appears not long after the arrival of modern humans in Europe. Whether these representations were "art" in any sense that their makers would recognize or were an expression of some kind of spiritual-symbolic meaning, they display an astonishing level of technical skill, indicating that they were of great importance for their makers. The deep location of cave paintings show that they were special places almost certainly associated with ritual significance—for example, some of the caves seem to have been chosen for their unusually good acoustics, suggesting that singing and the use of musical instruments may well have been part of the rituals. The Aurignacians were certainly using musical instruments; the oldest ones known are bone flutes, discovered in the same area in Germany as the figure of the Lion Man, aged around 35,000 years old.

It used to be thought that this provided unequivocal evidence for the "human revolution." But here again, absence of evidence does not provide evidence of absence. Despite the fact that modern humans dispersed all over the world, this kind of sophisticated material culture does not appear anywhere else until thousands of years later. This does not necessarily mean that other humans were any less sophisticated, merely that they did not leave evidence of their sophistication behind in the archaeological record. Renfrew argues that since the dispersal out of Africa which took humans across the world occurred at least 20,000 years before the "creative explosion" and all these peoples have the same genetic make-up, the development of painting and culture in Europe cannot be taken as an indication of any kind of genetic modification that is responsible for modern human abilities. These developments must therefore belong to what he calls the tectonic phase of human evolution when cultural innovation and cultural transmission became the dominant mechanisms of human evolution rather than the speciation phase when change was associated primarily with genetic modifications.[61] For this reason, I would regard the culture of the Aurignacian cave painters in similar terms to the rise and fall of later civilizations across the world such as those of Mesopotamia and Egypt a mere 5,000 years ago. From the perspective of the post-Neolithic world, we are inclined to identify culture and civilization with the production of great monuments, but the evidence left behind by the Aurignacians of Western Europe and the Gravettians of Sungir suggests that the monumental civilizations of the near East were far from being the first great civilizations of humankind.

This was the error made by the colonial discoverers of indigenous peoples who assumed that because they were still using stone tools they were also more primitive biologically and culturally.[62] Only with the advent of twentieth-century anthropology was the complexity and sophistication of these indigenous peoples recognized by actually living with them and learning about their rituals, traditions, mythologies, narratives, and social organization. And it is even more recently that indigenous peoples have begun to have their own voice heard in post-colonial society. As Deacon points out,

> Most of the symbol use in a society, even excluding language, is not even embodied in any material but only in ceremonies, habits, and rules that govern everyday life. ... This is particularly true of foraging peoples, who move continuously from place to place. Like the words that prehistoric peoples spoke, the vast majority of their creative efforts would have produced results that vanished with them, or shortly afterwards ... The significance of this argument for interpreting archaeological data is that

artifacts are not reliable indicators of mental abilities, and
that lack of artifacts does not indicate a lack of the potential
to produce them.[63]

Take, for example the rituals studied by Victor Turner amongst the
Ndembu peoples of Zambia. These ritual practices certainly involved
the use of material objects, but these were natural objects put to
symbolic use, notably particular kinds of trees associated with white
or red sap.[64] The archaeologists of the future might find evidence
of their extensive use of pigment (white, red, and black), but they
would never be able to reconstruct the rituals with which these were
associated nor find any evidence that these people had as complex a
symbolic system of ritual as anything likely to have been associated
with the Aurignacian cave painters. Their symbolic ritual objects are
biodegradable and "leave not a rack behind."[65]

The example of human development in Australia is also
illuminating in this respect. The earliest human occupation of
Australia occurred some 40,000 to 50,000 years ago. This must
have been one of the most remarkable feats of early moderns since
it required building boats and sailing off into unknown territory for
some 100 kilometers. There can be little doubt that such people were
fully behaviorally modern. There is early evidence for the use of shell
beads in Australia, dating to over 30,000 years ago as well as one
of the earliest examples of ceremonial burial at Lake Mungo from
over 40,000 years ago in which a person was sprinkled with red ochre
and buried with hands clasped across the groin.[66] Yet these early signs
of symbolic and spiritual practices are not accompanied by the suite
of technological skills and diversification which occur both in the
South African cultures of Still Bay and Howiesons Poort (including
the Blombos caves) and even more clearly in Cro-Magnon Europe.
These developments do not seem to have occurred in Australia until
the last 10,000 years. As Brumm and Moore conclude "the Australian
record demonstrates that fully modern symbolling humans did not
necessarily produce a repetitive package of symbolic traces."[67]

What Makes Us Human? Culture and Genetics

To summarize, three strands of evidence accumulated over the
past fifteen years have increasingly challenged the idea of a "human
revolution" linked with the arrival of *Homo sapiens* in Europe
40,000 years ago.

1. Neither language nor the use of material forms of symbolism is specific to *Homo sapiens* but was also possessed by Neanderthals.
2. Cultures existing in North Africa at least 82,000 years ago and in South Africa 77,000 years ago were using personal ornamentation and, in the latter case, making use of sophisticated tools previously thought unique to the "creative revolution."
3. These cultures were fragile and patchy—they came and went, showing that there was no single advance that set humans irrevocably on the path to modernity.

In the light of all this, genetic explanations for what makes us human look increasingly unlikely. These explanations are strictly internalist (and *a priori*), focusing on supposed sudden and random mutation in the brain that gave humans a selective cognitive advantage over Neanderthals. Some, like Richard Klein, simply argue that a change in brain organization is the only possible explanation without specifying what it might have been, while others, like Wynn and Coolidge, propose specific cognitive functions that must be responsible for the "final leap," such as increase in working memory.[68] Mithen's proposal of an integration across previously separate modular domains allowing for the development of "cognitive fluidity" belongs here too, although it is interesting that his proposal does not rely so much on a "magic moment" of genetic mutation. Rather he proposes the use of language as the means by which "snippets" of information from one domain could cross to another, gradually producing the pressure by which the modular "cathedral" walls collapsed, allowing free movement between domains.[69] His theory, published in 1996 provides a good example of how quickly the archaeological field is moving since it relies on a) the now unlikely belief that Neanderthals did not have spoken language, and b) the absence of evidence of symbolic behavior outside Europe before 40,000 years ago, prior to the discoveries at Blombos caves published in 2002. This is not simply a matter of dating; these discoveries undermine the idea of a suite of skills and functions that arrived on the scene all together and once and for all.

A further difficulty in claims for a direct link between biology and culture is that the emergence of anatomically modern humans occurred around 200,000 years ago while the first known appearance of any of the characteristics associated with *behavioral* modernity did not appear until 100,000 years later. It would be a further 50,000 years before these became reliably established, and, even then, there are great variations between different times and parts of the world. For good reason then does Zilhão claim that "the emergence of symbolism cannot relate to processes of genetic or other biologically based, "flick-of-a-switch" change occurring in a geographically restricted ... population."[70]

Climate and Demography

This problem, dubbed the "sapient paradox" by Renfrew,[71] has led to a refocusing of attention on demographic factors as the means by which cultural innovations may be preserved or lost. By means of complex statistical simulations, a number of researchers have shown that population size and density are key factors in enabling cultural innovations to be preserved and developed. These models support and extend the Hutchins and Hazlehurst simulation I described in Chapter 2 which evidenced the role of distributed cognition in enabling cultures to provide support for learning that exceeds anything an individual could come up with in a single lifetime. This is linked to Tomasello's notion of the ratchet effect except that factoring in population size and density tells us more about what is needed for this to operate and be successfully maintained.

Henrich showed that even with errors in learning from one generation to the next, some learners will improve on the model they have been taught, thus allowing for individual innovation and creativity. If the population size is great enough, these innovations can travel through the population and enrich the overall culture. If it isn't, there will be a gradual degrading of skill—highly skilled individuals from whom to learn will become rarer and the "noise" in the transmission process will increase. An example of this is the degradation of technological skill amongst the population of Tasmania in comparison with that of mainland Australia after it had become cut off due to climate change.[72] Powell, Shennan, and Thomas built on Henrich's model to show that the accumulation of skill is dependent not only on the overall size of the population but also on migratory activity and the degree of interaction between subpopulations. Their results show that the periods of cultural innovation in Europe 40,000 years ago and in South Africa around 100,000 years ago do correlate with recent estimates of population size and density in these times and places. Their results also provide a possible explanation for the disappearance of innovation if population density, migration, and interaction between groups became severely reduced, probably as a result of environmental changes, especially climate change leading to inhospitable conditions.[73]

These models provide considerable support for the idea of an extended cultural psyche that cannot exist within the mind of one individual but is distributed throughout the social group. Nor is there anything *a priori* and given about it, as evidenced by the "now you see it, now you don't" pattern by which innovations appear and disappear throughout the period of the later Paleolithic from approximately 100,000 years ago to the Neolithic era of sedentary settlement and development of agriculture.[74] The pattern of innovation in all those areas which we might now regard as definitively human, ranging from technology to spirituality and including social, cultural, and symbolic forms of organization, is one of material engagement within a socio-cultural group where the group itself provides the requisite environment for creativity, innovation, and imagination to either prosper or fade. Nevertheless, men make history but not under conditions of their own choosing.[75] Given the fate of the Neanderthals, it seems that this is true even of the survival of the species itself. Depopulation within groups and increasing isolation between groups may have led to a terminal decline in the maintenance and refurbishment of the skill-base which eventually made them unable to survive changes in environmental conditions such as climate change.[76] These changes could have also included the arrival of a different population of humans competing for resources, although it now seems likely that there was a certain amount of exchange between the two groups. Recent sequencing of Neanderthal DNA has shown that modern human populations include up to 4% of Neanderthal DNA thus showing that the range of differentiation was not such as to render the two groups incapable of breeding with each other. In short, although there is clear divergence from the common ancestor, there is a good case to argue that Neanderthals and *Homo sapiens* belonged to the same species.

There must also have been some cultural exchange between the two groups. Contrary to the view that Neanderthals were simply "imitating" modern humans by copying some of their tools and their pattern of symbolic personal ornamentation without understanding their meaning, d'Errico and Stringer point out that evidence of Neanderthal's independent know-how displays an equivalent complexity to that of the incoming *sapiens* population.

> This indicates that even if it was demonstrated that the use of bone tools or personal ornaments by Neanderthals was the result of cultural contact with moderns, this would in fact reinforce rather than dismiss the modern character of their cognition, as it would show their ability, as observed in many historical instances among modern human populations, to incorporate external stimuli and reshape those influences in order to make them an integral part of their own culture.[77]

This is not to say that there were *no* differences between Neanderthals and *Homo sapiens*, but it does suggest that given a different set of environmental and demographic circumstances, Neanderthals may well have survived and prospered, eventually developing a form of modernity equivalent to but somewhat different from our own. It is impossible to say quite what those differences may have been, but, despite the similarities of the two sub-species' evolutionary trajectories, the genetic, morphological, and developmental differences may yet offer significant clues. Certainly the Neanderthal Genome Project has identified a number of genes that appear to be unique to the modern humans sampled and some of these appear to have as yet unresolved cognitive and physiological functions.[78] Perhaps these will turn out to be correlated with two important morphological differences in the fossil record identified by Stringer which point to the possibility for enhanced functioning in the realm of imagination.

The first of those concerns the different skull-shape of *Homo sapiens*. Unique amongst all other hominin species, *Homo sapiens* have a high, domed forehead with a distinctively globular-shaped skull, indicative of changes in the frontal, parietal, and occipital areas of the brain. In Neanderthals, the occipital lobes have a distinctive bulge, possibly associated with an enhanced visual cortex but in *Homo sapiens* the most significant change concerns not the frontal lobes, as might be expected given their importance in reflective thought and control, but the parietal lobes which are involved in, amongst other things, the function of episodic memories. Stringer considers that this might support the view of Wynn and Coolidge that the development of episodic memory may have been a key change in the development of the modern mind, especially in relation to the capacity to conjure up vivid inner-reality narratives and the "other world" scenarios of spiritual experience.[79]

The second feature identified by Stringer is the relatively longer childhood of *Homo sapiens* compared with Neanderthals. A recent study of the rate of dental growth in Neanderthal children has shown that they were maturing faster than their modern human counterparts. So, for example, a Neanderthal eight-year-old would be the equivalent of a modern eleven-year-old; overall, Neanderthal childhood would have been about three or four years shorter than ours.[80] The period of infant immaturity has been extending since the time of *Homo erectus*, in concert with the growth in the brain. In part this is due to the "obstetric dilemma" posed by larger brains, requiring infants to be born at a more immature stage. In turn, this allows for a longer period of childhood learning and development and enhances the opportunities for young humans to become adapted to a cultural environment.

This is one of the points of conflict with the evolutionary psychology (EP) model of evolution. EP proponents argue that the "pre-programmed" algorithms of brain modules are necessary because the "trial and error" learning of a "general purpose domain" for learning would be hopelessly inefficient, given how much young humans need to learn to function in a human environment (e.g., language). But, as we have seen, scenarios of cultural evolution enable humans to absorb the learning of previous generations "from time immemorial," as Jung might have put it, through culturally based learning mechanisms. For that kind of learning, what is needed is a maximally flexible body-with-brain that can adapt and absorb what is needed within a cooperative, pedagogic environment that allows plenty of time and space for creative experimentation. In addition to this offering opportunities for the natural history, social, technological, and linguistic skills identified by Mithen, it might also offer extended opportunities for the development of imaginative play, fostering the development of an expanded capacity to relate to symbolic representations, especially those concerned with the intangible, imaginal, and spiritual aspects of life.

Whether or not this capacity was specific to *Homo sapiens*, more developed, or equally shared with Neanderthals is not the major issue, since genetic and physiological factors are only part of the story. As with other aspects of behavioral modernity, the development of symbolic imagination must surely have been a long time coming and has been largely dependent on the social and material factors that fostered its emergence. As the Australian record demonstrates, it does not necessarily occur in concert with other changes in technological and social organization. And since absence of evidence is not evidence of absence, it is reasonable to assume that even a single piece of evidence in the archaeological record is sufficient to identify fully modern human behavior.

With this in mind, I now want to return to the significance of shell beads as indicative of a critical shift in the capacity for symbolic representation. Given that the earliest examples of their use dates to at least 82,000 years ago and probably longer, together with the likelihood that red ochre was used in non-utilitarian ways even earlier, we may tentatively conclude that fully modern symbolic humans have been living on the planet for at least 100,000 years and possibly longer. In the next chapter I use shell beads as a jumping-off point for a wider consideration of how symbols work and their role in the development of a specifically human form of consciousness. There are many aspects of how we became *us*, but from here on I will be focusing more directly on my main theme—the emergence of symbolic imagination.

CHAPTER FIVE

CONSTITUTIVE SYMBOLS AND THE IMAGINAL REALM

The use of personal ornamentation amongst early modern humans represents a step-change in symbolic communication. It is probable that language was already well-established by then, having begun in the gestural communications of *Homo erectus* and become increasingly vocal from *Homo heidelbergensis* onwards. But this would likely have been a language whose purpose and compass was to communicate about the visible, material world. As with the advances in technological skill, such forms of symbolic representation would have enhanced the growth of consciousness, laying the ground for conceptualizing *immaterial* aspects of the world, the intangible realities of emotional states, social organization, and the spirit world. This does not necessarily mean that these non-sensory conceptions were experienced or represented in any abstract way. David Abram argues that abstractions of this kind only emerged through the use of a written alphabet; for oral cultures, the world is experienced directly via sensory participation in which the sensible world remains alive with meaning and significance.[1] Thus, things which we now consider "immaterial" aspects of the world are experienced within a wholly sensuous world as we might expect, given the presuppositions of Material Engagement Theory and the extended mind.

Unlike linguistic signs that may (literally) point to what they represent, symbols of the immaterial, non-sensuous aspects of reality bring into being the realities they symbolize, even though they may not be thought about as being symbolic at all. The notion of the symbol has itself been abstracted from its original material referent— the token broken in half by two friends to enable one to identify a messenger from the other—and now usually refers to arbitrary signs which convey meanings according to an abstract code. That is, the concept of symbol itself may have been altered (and widened) by the introduction of alphabetic literacy. So in considering symbolic aspects of oral cultures we are referring to "spiritual" meanings that are non-separable from their "material" forms.

The symbolic component is indicative of the activity of imagination intertwined with and originally inseparable from the sensuous forms through which it reveals non-material meanings. In other words, imaginal symbols are emergent from the social and material conditions of early humans that made it possible and necessary to create them. That is, symbolic images, initially in the form of material objects (including living beings), are the outcome and expression of human intentional activity—hence the relation between *act* and *image* in this book's title.[2]

In order to demonstrate this I draw on John Searle's formulation of constitutive symbols—i.e., symbols which constitute the realities they represent—and Colin Renfrew's application of Searle's work to the field of cognitive archaeology. I then go on to argue that shell bead necklaces provide the earliest evidence of the use of symbolic objects to constitute intangible aspects of reality. This does not necessarily suggest that such objects are the *origin* of symbolization since the more we become aware of the deep engagement of oral cultures with their environment, the more we recognize a relationship that is wholly animated by a symbolic-spiritual relation between humans and the "more-than-human world."[3] So I am not arguing for the creation of something out of nothing here but for an emergent process driven by new forms of imaginatively enlivened material engagement that created new ontological realities, irreducible to the sum of their parts.

Constitutive Symbols

Renfrew gives an example of a constitutive symbol which dates from the Neolithic era—the emergence of the concept of *weight*. When archaeologists discover a series of stone cubes of regular, ascending sizes in some pre-historical culture, it is reasonable to assume that they were used as units for the measurement of weight and, therefore, that this particular culture had developed the concept of weight. But how, asks Renfrew, could the notion of measureable weight come about in the first place? His answer is that the symbol must relate to a physical property in the world—the experience of some objects being heavier than others, which is also the case with the stone weights that now *represent weight*.

> These stone cubes serving as weights are symbolic of themselves: weight as a symbol of weight. It may be appropriate here to use the term *constitutive* symbol, where the symbolic or cognitive elements and the material element co-exist. The one does not make sense without the other.[4]

So although the physical property of heaviness already exists "out there in the real world," it does not yet exist as the concept of *weight*, let alone mass. It is the material activity of weighing things in a social context where there needs to be some collective agreement of measure that instigates the use of objects that then count as weights. Thus the physical symbol of a weight creates the concept of *weight* as an emergent entity at a new level. The physical experience of heaviness now has a collective social meaning as *weight* and this is embodied in the use of the physical objects that constitute weights.

This is even more the case with the symbolization of immaterial properties such as emotional states, social relations, or intimations of the spirit world. As with heaviness, there is already something "in the real world" to which these symbols correspond but they can only be formulated once they can be symbolized. Only then can we "get a handle" on them by giving them material form. The crucial point is that the materialization of intangible states in the form of symbolic objects transforms them into tangible presences.

We can begin to get a sense of this in relation to symbols of social status which only exist as what John Searle calls "institutional facts."[5] These are factual realities that exist only through the collective intentionality of human social groups. For example, I was recently elected as the Chair of the Society of Analytical Psychology. This is a demonstrable institutional fact but its factuality exists only in and through rules which create the possibility for facts of this kind, rules which are set out in a *Constitution* of the organization in question. The "Constitution" thus "constitutes" the existence of the organization and can be appealed to as evidence of its existence, notwithstanding that none of these realities have any ontological status beyond the social agreements that constitute them and a body of written documents that substantiate those agreements.

Now we all realize that the term *Chair* (or *Chairman* as it used to be) must be derived from the physical chair in which persons of a particular status might once have sat. *That* chair is the king's chair, only the king is allowed to sit in it, and it is in the act of sitting in it that he becomes king. Not only does this confer special symbolic status on the physical object, be it chair, crown, scepter, feathered headdress, or lion's head, the physical object acts as the gathering point for the symbolic institutional reality of kingship which it thereby constitutes. And this is much more than simply a practical, political agreement in which the objects signifying status are conventional and interchangeable. Frequently, the physical symbols themselves take on a powerful affective aura that might be described as *mana* or even *numinous* that serves to reflect and reinforce the social meanings of the status represented by those symbols. The symbol embodies the status in the sense that it "gives it body" and this embodiment is equated with the symbolic object itself.

One of Searle's main examples of institutional facts is money. On a day to day basis we tend to equate the reality of money with the physical objects by which it is represented and yet when we stop and think about it we know that there is nothing inherent in the physicality of the pound in my pocket that gives it its status as money. The reality of money does not inhere in its materiality, but nor is it separable from its materiality, even if that is expressed merely in the form of digits on a screen. Thus the physical objects through which money is instantiated are constitutive symbols of a reality that only has meaning through the collective intentionality of human beings expressed in the form of social practices involving material objects. As Searle explains,

> The practice of using pieces of paper as dollar bills creates a class of entities that cannot exist without the practice. ... In order that the practice should exist people must be able to think the thought 'this piece of paper is a dollar bill' and that is a thought they cannot think without words or other symbols, even if the only symbol in question is the object itself.[6]

Searle designates this by a general formula for symbols whereby "X counts as Y in context C."[7] But if X is the symbol and Y is what is symbolized, how do we know what Y is except by reference to X? That is, if we want to know what money is, we need to refer to what *counts* as money, such as a dollar bill or the pound in my pocket. Without coins, paper, or digits with £ and $ signs in front of them, money has no existence—thus the symbol X constitutes the symbolized Y in the context of collective social agreement.

Searle shows how such institutional facts contrast with the "brute facts" of the natural world that exist independently of human activity.[8] By contrast, the symbols of human intentionality constitute the realities they represent. In Renfrew's example, there is a "brute fact" of heaviness to which the symbol of weight relates but heaviness is not a measurable weight any more than a piece of metal is inherently money. In both cases, the practice of using these material objects creates a class of entities that cannot exist without the practice and the practice cannot exist without symbols to think it with, even if the only symbols in question are the objects which are being symbolized (e.g., as money or weights). This gives the symbols of human intentional activity an *ontological* significance without which they could not exist, in contrast to the existence of "brute facts" which do not need symbolization in order to exist.

There is, however, a difference between things like money which exists *only* through human social activity and the concept of weight which is a socially derived transformation of a pre-existing ontological property of the material world. And it is the latter that I want to extend to the kind of things that Jung designated "archetypal" symbols, symbols which are characterized by their powerful affective charge ("numinosity") and the sense of special meaning and significance that attach to them. These symbols are emergent from affective responses that are transformed by being formulated as symbols *within a social context*, particularly the context of ritual. Hence the idea that symbolic imagination is *created* by symbols without which there is nothing to imagine with. If we were to look for the something which is symbolized by the Lion Man, for example, our point of reference would have to be the mammoth tusk carving itself. The material object *is* what it represents. The Lion Man (X) symbolizes Y in context C (e.g., Aurignacian rituals or beliefs) but Y only exists in and through the material object. And because the context in which it was created no longer exists, we can no longer decipher its meaning. For sure, we can recognize it *as* a symbolic object and give it other meanings in a different context, but, as with money, we cannot separate the meaning from either the object *or* the context.

With these considerations in mind, I will now return to the emergence of symbolic objects in the archaeological record in the form of shell beads. In my view, these objects are indicative of a crucial transition from a form of consciousness primarily concerned with managing the material world to one concerned with relating to the spirit world. And it is the latter that we see represented in the creative productions of the first *sapiens* of Europe, of which I have taken the Lion Man as emblematic.

Shell Beads as Constitutive Symbols

The use of shell beads is generally seen as having symbolized aspects of social status and identity. This implies a form of social organization that goes well beyond the small-scale shared intentionality that initiated language towards a form of collective intentionality operating at the level of the whole group. In Kuhn and Stiner's view,

> Body ornaments are most important for communicating to people 'in the middle distance' socially, individuals who are close enough to the wearer to understand the meaning of the ornaments he or she wears, but who do not know her or him personally.[9]

They propose that this marks a shift from the more local significance carried by the use of pigment such as red ochre as body-paint.

> We suggest that pigment-only decorative systems would have been oriented largely to increasing an individual's visual impact, and not media for conveying standardized social messages. Perhaps the use of pigments ... was basically a form of individual display ... rather than a medium for communicating about more constant, institutionalized relationships among individuals or groups of individuals.[10]

The latter implies the existence of some kind of social norms by which the symbolic communication can be understood, but, in turn, it suggests that the use of such material forms of symbolic communication *constitutes* those norms. The wearer enacts the meaning by selecting the shell and fashioning it into a bead, but the meaning is not simply attributed to the shell-become-bead, the object is itself an integral aspect of its meaning. The wearing of shells as beads thus constitutes the social distinctions they present. In this sense, the notion of representation is misleading since there is no cognition that exists separate and prior to the presentation of the shell-as-bead as a mark of identity. Identity is thus constituted by the wearing of the beads.

The use of material objects in this way constitutes a transition from forms of cognition that are primarily directed to transforming the environment to those that are directed towards transforming human consciousness itself. This is because symbolic objects enabled humans to conceptualize themselves and their own ways of relating to each other.

The formulation of social facts via material symbols provided a basis for thinking about the *non*-material world and therefore facilitated the development of consciousness, imagination, and a sense of there being a spiritual dimension to the world. In this way, material objects function as elements of the extended mind that provide "surrogates" for cognizing the immaterial, "thereby allowing human reason to reach out to that which is absent or distal or otherwise unavailable."[11] It is much easier to understand what status and identity mean in relation to their material instantiation in the form of shell bead necklaces than it would be to conceive of such intangible concepts entirely in our heads.

The more non-material the entities or states we are trying to realize, the more we need material artifacts to grasp them, get a handle on them, manipulate them—all metaphors derived from the physical, embodied activity of using our hands. This need may be especially acute in relation to the realm of the spirit, which is non-material by definition. In this context, Clark refers to Matthew Day who suggests that religious artifacts have played a major role in enabling brains like ours to explore the space of ideas concerning the supernatural.

> Day's claim is that 'the broad spectrum of rituals, music, relics, scriptures, statues, and buildings may represent central components of the relevant machinery of religious thought.' ... The way religious artifacts participate in the cognitive act is ... by creating tangible frameworks in which on-line cognition, safely coupled to anchoring real-world structures, can reach out towards the realm of the invisible.[12]

This suggests that before symbols can be imagined things, they are *actual* things—physical objects and images that function as tools every bit as much as a hand-axe or a bone harpoon. They are tools with which to think and imagine, tools which enable us to utilize resources that feed the mind just as the hand-axe and harpoon enabled us to use resources that feed our bodies. Shell beads are important not just because they are symbols but because symbols are tools—in this case, tools that made it possible to conceive of social distinctions. Such distinctions may well have been related to the division of labor required to make them, especially once they began to be produced on an industrial scale such as at Enkapune Ya Muto in Kenya and the Üçagizli caves in Turkey where thousands of fragments have been found.[13] Or, to emphasize the material agency of things, we might say that the process of making beads from shells introduced a division of labor that was then symbolized by their use as objects of display.

Iconic Features of Material Symbols

Material symbols of this kind are unlike the symbols of language in that they need to retain their concrete specificity in order to function as "surrogates." They make use of the same kind of associative similarities as metaphor but in a different way. Metaphor uses a source domain to illuminate features of a target domain. So, for example, a metaphorical expression such as "from little acorns, great oak trees grow" makes use of the transformation from small to great in the case of trees (source domain) to illustrate features of a target domain such as some human activity that starts small and slowly becomes much larger and more significant. In the case of metaphor, though, the material object which provides the metaphor is unchanged whereas with a material symbol, the source domain *becomes* the symbol whose meaning inheres in its concrete specificity. The source and target domains are fused and the source is transformed by its use as a symbol, just as a piece of paper is transformed by becoming a US dollar. Whereas metaphors simply *illuminate* meanings that already exist, material symbols *create* meanings that are inextricably located in the material object itself. So it is inadequate to suggest, for example, that the idea of psyche as breath is merely symbolic or that a particular animal represents a tribal god or totem as if the one could be separated from the other. There is an ontological dimension to material symbols such that, originally, breath/wind/air was not merely *like* the soul but *was* the soul. Psyche comes into being through being symbolized as breath.

Ironically, the importance of this iconic aspect of material symbols is brought out by philosopher Kim Sterelny who aims to deny that iconic images count as symbols at all. Like Deacon, he defines symbols in terms of their arbitrary, abstract qualities and this leads him to question whether symbols that serve as insignia of social place and identity are symbolic since they are neither arbitrary nor do they reference things which are temporally and spatially displaced.

> Ochre markings, face paintings, and features and masks worn in ritual and ceremony are not temporally displaced. The ornaments a person wears to signify membership and status are on him or her. Likewise, iconic elements almost certainly played a role in decoration and ornamentation— for example, in emphasizing or drawing attention to particular features. Nor is the significance of ornaments such as beads and ostrich shells merely conventional.[14]

Sterelny rightly concludes that shell beads do not meet the criteria for symbols *as defined in relation to verbal language* and that they are therefore better considered as icons. But this only points up the distinction between these two kinds of symbols. Constitutive symbols have a high degree of iconicity since they *are* what they represent. Thus, Sterelny compares shell beads with Ferraris as forms of "costly advertising" which act as conspicuous displays of wealth.

> Their rarity suggests that they are special, and so they are most plausibly seen as expensive signals of status, skill, or success. ... They are Middle Stone Age Ferraris. And the whole point of owning a Ferrari is that its meaning is not conventional or arbitrary; its genuine cost means that it is an honest signal of success.[15]

There are two points here. Firstly, Sterelny assumes a separation between the *concept* of social status and the means by which it is advertised (its "signals"), implying that the concept precedes the signal. But as the Boston Change Process Study Group (BCPSG) argued in relation to child development, interaction is primary and structure is secondary.[16] Thus one of the key means by which social status exists is through its material expression. So, if shell beads were expensive in terms of sourcing the materials and the time taken to produce them, then the wearing of them constituted that status—it did not merely represent it. And if the making and wearing of shell beads was part of a process whereby human groups were becoming more complex with a greater division of labor, then shell beads were constitutive of the very *idea* of social status—they were part of what social status *meant*. And even today, when we are all too familiar with notions of status and power, for those who value Ferraris, the car itself *is* the success as well as its signal. Once people begin to see their expensive car as merely a status symbol, they are already dissociating from it; their notions of what success really means have begun to move elsewhere, often a source of ongoing dissatisfaction.

The second point is that the symbolic significance of the Ferrari is located in its iconic specificity. It is different, for example, even from a Rolls Royce—both are very expensive cars but the messages of each are very different. The point is that material icons signal in very specific ways that are determined by the particular affordances of the material object utilized. The speed, power, shape, and even color of a Ferrari are part of its signaling in contrast to a Rolls Royce which suggests comfort, luxury, and being part of the Establishment. Typically, a Rolls Royce is white whereas a Ferrari is red—a red Rolls Royce would give a very different signal from a white one. In Jungian terms this has to do with "sticking to the image" rather than reading it as an arbitrary sign. The image does not *represent*, it embodies and enacts its meaning.

So it is precisely the non-arbitrariness of material symbols that constitutes their meaning. To illustrate this point, Malafouris quotes Bateson's comments about another kind of lion—the four emblematic lions of Trafalgar Square.

> The lions in Trafalgar Square could have been eagles or bulldogs and still have carried the same (or similar) messages about Empire and about the cultural premises of nineteenth century England. And yet, how different might their message have been had they been made of wood.[17]

So it is not only what is imaged that is relevant—it is also *how* it is imaged. The sensory qualities of the object are as significant as the content of the image—a stone lion is not the same as a stone eagle or a wooden lion. Although the lions of Trafalgar Square commemorate the factual event of the Battle of Waterloo, they do so in a form that elaborates the factual meaning into a symbolic icon of the British Empire, thus constituting part of the cognitive "institutional fact" through which the British Empire had facticity. The Empire has gone but the lions live on—unlike other representations of state power such as the statue of Saddam Hussein that acquired more iconic meaning in its fall than it ever had in its standing. Well might Malafouris conclude,

> Material signs do not represent; they enact. They do not stand for reality; they bring forth reality. ... Material signs

> are not simply message carriers in some pre-ordered social
> universe. Material signs are the actual physical forces that
> shape the social and cognitive universe.[18]

Malafouris applies this directly to the Aurignacian Lion Man in a paper on the origins of human religious intelligence where he writes, "The iconicity of the image does not simply reflect visual resemblances but rather establishes ontological ones. It is significant for what it does rather than what it refers to."[19] The figurine "brings forth" the symbolic reality of a "supernatural creature" by realizing it in material form.

Malafouris' emphasis on the physical specificity of the material sign echoes the Jungian emphasis on the particular qualities of the dream-image as well as Langer's distinction between discursive and non-discursive symbols:

> Things act most powerfully at the non-discursive level,
> incorporating qualities (such as color, texture, and smell)
> that affect human cognition in ways that are rarely explicitly
> conceptualized. These are properties not afforded by the
> nature of the linguistic sign. ... Language is linear and
> sequential. In contrast, material culture ... preserves no
> obvious point of commencement.[20]

Furthermore, the material sign is *prior* to the ideational image. That is, material signs are not the representation of imaginal images but the reverse; material signs bring forth the imagery which can then serve as the "furniture" of imagination. Thus material signs constitute the imagination through a process similar to Vygotsky's account of the process by which children acquire language. They first encounter language in the world around them and use it in social interaction; only gradually does it become appropriated for use as a means of private thought. Similarly, Vygotsky shows how imagination is scaffolded through the use of material objects as "pivots" which facilitate the development of an imaginative relation to the world—that is, the ability to imagine things and activities that are not directly presented to the senses, as well as non-sensory attributes and qualities of things that *are* present to the senses.[21]

This way of seeing things reverses the notion of projection in Jung's formulation that "unconscious contents appear first in projection." Rather than assuming that what is discovered in the world is simply a model for something that already exists unconsciously in the psyche, the notion of appropriation argues that it is only through

activity in the world with things and other people that we are able to
develop psychic lives at all. So before things can be "in" the psyche,
they have to exist in the world as concrete realities.

The significance of sensory qualities in material signification
indicates that there is no clear divide between different levels of
symbolic reference as Kuhn and Stiner assume when they distinguish
between "increasing an individual's visual impact" and "conveying
standardized social messages" since these sensory messages remain a
vital aspect of the symbol. Similarly, Paul Pettit distinguishes between
different levels of symbolic meaning from the simple to the complex.[22]
Chris Stringer elaborates:

> The most basic use might be purely decorative and reflect
> a personal preference ('I wear red because I like red'). Or
> the message could be one of enhancement of the signal ('I
> wear red as I know you will read it as a sign of my strength
> or be impressed by it'). A third level might reflect status or
> group identity ('I wear red as I know you will recognize
> it as the regalia of our clan, and infer from it that we are
> culturally the same'). A fourth and even more complex
> message might be 'I wear red as like you, I am a successful
> hunter and have killed an adult eland; it is my right to
> wear this color and I therefore command respect from all.'
> And, finally, the most complex, as part of an elaborate
> myth or cosmological belief might be 'I wear red only at
> this specific time of the year, marking when the ancestors
> created the land. This is a vital part of our beliefs, and by
> doing this I show that I am the bearer of this knowledge.'[23]

This is a helpful clarification of the different possible levels of
symbolic meaning and it may well be that the more simple levels acted
as scaffolding for the emergence of more complex ones. There is also
a process of codification and systematization involved as symbolic
meanings are taken up into more complex social institutional activities
such as kinship rules and religious rituals. Nevertheless, it is not
the case that the more complex levels supplant the earlier ones—
the simple levels continue to be operative in the most complex of
symbolic significations. As we have seen, the color red continues to
have an impact that is both sensory and metaphorical down to the
present day—and to that extent, the parallel between red ochre and red
Ferraris may be a useful one. Indeed, the choice of the brightest red
ochre, made brighter by scoring marks and lines into it, is thought to
be one of the evidential arguments for its symbolic, rather than merely

utilitarian, use in some of its earliest occurrences in the archaeological record. At the metaphorical level, the sensory qualities are gathered up into iconic parallels which form the basis for how metaphor works. That is, the iconic similarity between red as a pigment, red as the color of blood, red faces in the heat of passion, etc. enables red to be utilized in a range of overlapping metaphorical and symbolic contexts. Iconic similarity is a key feature of metaphor and metaphor is a building block for symbols. Material symbols may even be defined as metaphors with multiple iconic referents—e.g., I am strong like a lion; I am red like blood and full of fire and fury.

Here again there is a clear difference between discursive and non-discursive symbols since non-discursive symbols include a much wider range of referents to embody their meaning, including aesthetic, sensory, emotional, and iconic metaphorical referents. It is this which enables them to represent states of mind, including emotional and aesthetic experience, as well as factual states of the world. In this way, such inchoate states of mind can become formulated and available for thought; they become, as it were, realized. The hierarchy of iconic, indexical, and symbolic that Deacon takes from C. S. Pierce works quite differently in the non-discursive realm because non-discursive symbols remain concrete and specific whereas discursive symbols are abstract and general. On the other hand, concrete symbols have multiple referents while abstract discursive symbols are much more narrowly defined.

Value and the Sacred

The sensory and aesthetic features of personal ornamentation are linked to a further set of meanings that they enact and bring forth: the emergence of the concept of *value*. It is clear that shell beads must have been highly prized since they were often transported long distances from the coast and it is probable that they would have been selected for their aesthetic qualities. If, in addition, they were connected with social status, personal identity, and were used as a means of exchange and reciprocity (as they are used by some of the San peoples of South Africa today), then their aesthetic value would have reinforced their role as material anchors in the emergence of increasingly complex forms of social organization. Rather than being merely a conventional, arbitrary referent for status and value, the sensory and aesthetic element of such objects directly contributes to their meaning and significance; the power of desire takes on symbolic form which in turn shapes and transforms those desires in new ways. Thus, all those aspects of cognition that Jung designated as "functions"— feeling, thinking, sensing, and, perhaps, intuition as well—converge in relation to material symbols, contributing to a preconceptual sense that something has value at an emotional and visceral, as well as intellectual, level.

As a concept that has social as well as personal meaning, that is, as a concept that can become an institutional fact, value has to be constituted through symbolization in the same way as other originally bodily sensations, such as weight. Value is a particularly important concept, though, because of its many potential referents; it encompasses social, economic, emotional, and spiritual meanings and latterly includes the sense of having value as a person which is of central significance in moral, social, and political discourse in modern Western societies as well as having a major role in the theory and practice of psychotherapy. In all these aspects it is closely related to *meaning* since that which is meaningful has value and vice versa, that which is valuable gives life meaning and purpose. When value is lost, life can become "stale, flat, and unprofitable," a "quintessence of dust" as it was for Hamlet after his father died.[24]

Renfrew discusses the emergence of the concept of value in relation to gold, highlighting its powerful attraction as an object of desire. "A bar of gold has an allure that is almost physical. The image of the miser taking pleasure in counting the coins of gold that constitute his wealth is a familiar one."[25] Although gold has been a measure of value in many cultures throughout the world for thousands of years, before the early dynasties of Sumer and Egypt gold was accorded no significance whatever.[26] Of course, gold is not the only measure of value; in other cultures, jade had a similar significance and it seems probable that, in the Paleolithic era, marine shells played such a role. So it might be argued that material objects are merely variable images of value that all refer back to an archetypal core idea. Yet, if so, this would not be an idea in any recognizable sense but a bodily affective core of sensory desire (cf. the "pleasure" and "allure" referred to by Renfrew). It is only through its material representation as *symbols* of value that these bodily sensory-affective states can take the form of ideas. Like money, for which it used to form the material base, gold is a symbol of its own value.

For Freud, even desire could be further reduced back to the single source of *sexual* desire, but perhaps this only goes to show the pervasive fervor for reduction in theoretical models of the time. It seems evident that humans are not alone in having a much wider range of desires than can be encapsulated in any such instinctual model. For example, the desire for sensory pleasure, playfulness, and thrills is apparent in many other species. More broadly, as Damasio argues, organisms monitor their relation to the world via their emotional response and so attraction is a key element of intentionality. Simpler organisms are attracted to that which furthers their survival and development as described in Chapter 2 in relation to the bacteria being attracted to sucrose molecules. With the development of a sufficiently developed nervous system, emotion provides a powerful and highly differentiated means of relating to the environment. For humans, emotion is further differentiated through symbolization: basic emotional registers that are gathered up into conceptual systems of value that operate at a social-symbolic level. Freud referred to this as "sublimation," but for him this was a defense, a warding off of more "primitive" instinctual passions. Nevertheless, stripped of these connotations, the term is a useful one, not least because of its allusion to the sublime. This is not to suggest that the sublime is nothing but a defensive transformation of "base instinct" (or emotion) but to recognize that all thought has an emotional register that resonates at a bodily level. When desire is absent, so is meaning—then nothing has value and everything becomes stale, flat, and unprofitable, a tale told by an idiot and signifying nothing.[27] Indeed, as my late friend James Fisher argued, emotion may be considered to be the meaning of experience.[28]

Renfrew further suggests that symbols of value that evoke emotions of allure may have facilitated the emergence of the sacred through their embodiment of the notion of "supreme value," thus making such ineffable referents "thinkable." In this way, material objects of value would be the means by which sublimation occurs. In this context, Renfrew highlights the special significance accorded to religious relics.

> This can involve a veneration which again entails a factuality accorded to such material things as a tooth of the Buddha or a fragment of the True Cross. To the non-believer these things have no intrinsic worth, and the discussion may be related to that for gold, as outlined

above. Within a context of belief, however, such relics are
the source of miracles.[29]

Like gold, jade, or shell beads, religious objects do not have intrinsic
value as "brute facts," but their value to the believer gives them
factuality as social facts, as real as the value of a dollar bill. So gold
can be a measure of value in a context in which gold is believed to be
valuable; or a relic can manifest the sacred qualities of the god in a
suitable context of belief.

We should not assume that this requirement for symbolization
makes things *merely* psychic or imaginary. On the contrary, I am
arguing that material symbolization is necessary in order for the
imaginal world to be realized (i.e., made real). To return to Searle's
example of money: even though I know that at some level a £20
note only *represents* money, I should not be best pleased if someone
used my £20 note to light a fire on the basis that "it's just a piece of
paper." My likely emotional reaction indicates not only the affective
component of symbols but the way affect grounds symbolic reality in
forms of embodied engagement.[30]

And so it is with spiritual beings. As Renfrew indicates, spiritual
beings become real in the manner of institutional facts. In that sense
they are "believed" to be real, but once they are instantiated in a social
context, they become as factually real as a £20 note. And of course,
powerful as are the emotions evoked in relation to money, those that
can be evoked in relation to god-images are even stronger. Yet, like
any other form of value, these are rooted in bodily states that are
transmuted through complex symbolic realizations socially organized
as institutional facts, in contrast to the "brute facts" of the material
world. Symbols do not represent the gods, they *are* the gods. Or to put
it another way, there can be no gods without god-images.[31] The gods
are inherently symbolic beings.

This explains those perplexing conversations between people of
different faiths wishing to understand one another. Each party tries
to translate the other's reality into their own symbols, not realizing
that the symbols *are* the reality. Yet even though one does not share
the beliefs of the other, this does not mean that we necessarily *dispute*
those beliefs. Constitutive symbols thus give us some purchase on the
different realities that cannot be reduced to one another because the
reality is in the symbols that *present* that reality. To repeat, they do not
represent, they enact and bring forth reality.

The ontological facticity of the symbolic image is brought out in Brooke's critique of the Cartesian assumptions in Jung's approach to symbols. For Jung (and psychoanalysts in general), symbols are usually seen as external representations of psychic facts that exist in a separate realm of mind over and above their manifold representations as images. The latter are considered to be merely projections of a purely psychic reality, as mentioned previously. Brooke relates this to our "tendency to call something a symbol in order to account for our experience of its meaningfulness in what is assumed to be a homogenized, meaningless world."[32] Here he touches on the results of Descartes' despiritualization (de-animation) of the material world, a move that has resulted in the view that only that which is objectively real has ontological significance (hence Searle's "brute facts"). Meaning then becomes a human *attribution* to objects and situations that do not in themselves have meaning—a bead is just a shell, a lion-man is just a piece of ivory, a dollar bill is just a piece of paper. The same issue applies to synchronicity which is seen as a merely random coincidence to which humans attribute meaning.

Brooke's concern is that this way of regarding symbols as having only "internal" psychological meaning can destroy their meaningfulness as "the presencing of the world." He gives a revealing example:

> I once had a Xhosa graduate student who found Jung consistently disappointing. As we were talking, a bee flew through the open window into my office. He asked for a moment's respectful silence as the ancestors were present. We had our example, and he could state his problem. A Jungian interpretation seems to assume that the primary reality of the bee is its biological reality and that, in the student's ('primitive') mind, it symbolizes his ancestors and cultural commitments. This symbolic meaning is then projected onto the essentially biological bee, which is why it appears to be meaningful. Jung requires the concept of synchronicity to account for our experience of a meaningful lifeworld that is, for the phenomenologist, immediately given and available for description.[33]

However, Brooke goes on to show that this is not the only way of reading Jung.

> On the contrary, he writes of symbols binding the observer and the observed and combining all four functions, including perception. Symbols are *not* re-presentational

signs, but the presencing of a mystery in such a way that
psychic life is integrated and the person is transformed.[34]

As I have been arguing, though, it is not just at the personal level
that such transformation occurs. Rather it is only in the context of
a symbolic culture that the "raw material" of physically mediated
symbols is available for personal transformation. Before gold can be
an imaginal symbol of value—in a dream, for example—there has
to be a concept of value, and before there can be a concept of value
there has to be actual physical gold in the world to substantiate it.
The bee *is* the ancestor because the ancestor *is* the bee while at the
same time, the bee is a biological creature that lives and dies in the
material world in a way that is not co-terminous with its status as
ancestor. This double-vision is the manifestation, the bringing forth of
imagination not as something that is simply represented in images but
something that is actually created by those images. If the imagination
is a space in the mind, then it is one that is created by the contents of
that space. Of course, the notion of imagination as a space is itself
a metaphor—another example of the way material realities can be
utilized to metaphorically represent and thereby make thinkable the
intangible realities of the mind. Mind is emergent from the symbols we
use to imagine with; without symbols, there can *be* no imagination and
without imagination, there can *be* no human mind. Hence, imagination
makes us human.

CHAPTER SIX

THE EMERGENCE OF THE
SPIRIT WORLD

I f shell beads provide the earliest evidence for symbolizing the immaterial, the figurines and paintings left behind by the *sapiens* people of the Upper Paleolithic who arrived in Europe around 40,000 years ago are the first definite evidence of people who lived in a world with a *spiritual* dimension. By this I mean they had the capacity to imagine aspects of things that went beyond their utilitarian value for survival and had affective meaning and value beyond their material properties. This is not easy to define since the very notion of material properties has a Cartesian ring to it; indigenous people may not make such distinctions between the spiritual and the material so that what I refer to as imaginal may be entirely integrated with the ordinary world as a dimension of the sensory environment. Nevertheless, paintings and sculptures are clearly human creations which must have something to do with whatever we might mean by *imagination.*

As previously mentioned, early European "art" should not be taken as evidence of a "spiritual revolution"—the hard material remains we do have should not blind us to evidence that has not survived. Nor was rock painting unique to Europe in the Paleolithic era.[1] Although less spectacular, impressive rock art sites have been discovered in India at Bhimbetka dated to 30,000 years ago and in the Kimberly region of Northern Australia dated around 20,000 years ago ('Bradshaw' rock paintings). So it is highly probable that the spiritual beliefs and practices enacted by the European peoples of the Upper Paleolithic were by no means unique. Similar ritual practices may have been part of human life as far back as the first shell beads of 100,000 years ago, or even longer.

For example, reputedly the oldest skulls attributed to *Homo sapiens* are those discovered in 1997 at Herto in Ethiopia, dated to 160,000 years ago.[2] Two of these bore cut marks (indicating that they had been cut from the body) as well as patterned scratch marks. One of them—a child's skull—had been worn smooth by repeated handling. This suggests that it was used in some sort of mortuary ritual practice and may have been kept as a ritual trophy or even used as a drinking cup, as is certainly the case in more recent instances of the ritual use of skulls.[3] The use of skulls in this way may be compared with the prominent placing of a cave bear skull in the centre of a rock at the Chauvet caves, again suggesting it had an important role in whatever rites and rituals were practiced there. It could also be that ritual practices grew out of the role of the fireside hearth as a place of sharing and communal activity and a possible source for the development of collective intentionality. The hearth may have acted to draw people together and thus required them to develop ways of sharing social space and developing rules, rituals, and ways of communicating in order to do so successfully. If so, such developments would likely go back to the time of *Homo heidelbergensis* around 500,000 years ago or so since these people certainly used fire and are likely to have been developing the capacity for vocalized language as well.

So the reason for focusing on the peoples of France and Germany in the Upper Paleolithic is not to suggest they were unique in their practices and beliefs, let alone their mental capacities, but because the way they enacted those practices and beliefs was sufficiently special to leave behind awe-inspiring evidence of their work, although it is doubtful they would have considered their images as art or understood what *art* is supposed to be. Nevertheless, it seems reasonable to assume that the works they left behind had a meaning and significance that is best described as spiritual and that the people who made these images were engaged in expressing their intentional psychic states in material form in ways that are closely analogous to those of humans today.

This view has not always been universally accepted, to say the least. When the first cave paintings were discovered at Altamira in Spain in 1879, the idea that they were the work of Paleolithic peoples was fiercely resisted. Prehistoric humans, like the aboriginal peoples of the Americas, Africa, and Australasia were regarded as far too "primitive" to be capable of such artistic achievements.

Of course the term *primitive* is itself a prime example of one of the presuppositions that have obscured our understanding. When Europeans first encountered the native peoples of America, Africa, and Australasia, their assumptions about them were shaped not only by their relatively primitive technology and lack of what Europeans took to be the hallmarks of "civilization" but more fundamentally by their own imperialistic intentions. If they were going to colonize and exploit this new world for their own benefit, an ideology that guaranteed their inherent superiority and denied these native peoples even a shared humanity, suited their self-interest. Marx's claim that ideology serves the interests of the ruling class and legitimates their social position is hard to resist in this context. And since, as Marx also pointed out, "the traditions of the dead generations weighs like a nightmare on the brains of the living,"[4] it remains difficult to escape the vestiges of a colonial mind-set that treats non-Western ways of thinking as inferior.

The process by which these entrenched Western assumptions and prejudices have begun to shift and dissolve has been a slow and painful one, beginning with the controversy created by Darwin's *On the Origin of Species* in 1859 and continuing up to the present day—and all too frequently it is those aboriginal peoples, and their cultures, that have paid the heavy price of prejudice. Gradually we are beginning to recognize that while humans can live in entirely different ways due to their group-specific adaptability, everyone in the world today, as well as all those who lived far back into the ancestral past, are not only like us, they *are* us. Furthermore, as discussed in Chapter 3, there are many more overlaps with other species than was previously thought, from the problem-solving intelligence of crows, to the empathic social life of elephants and the capacity for "theory of mind" and rudimentary fantasy in chimpanzees. The more we recognize these commonalties, the more likely we are to understand how human beings could have emerged in the first place, and this may help us rediscover our commonality with the natural world from which Westerners have come to feel especially estranged.

This need to reconnect with our origins is no doubt part of the reason why Upper Paleolithic cave paintings are so revered. Nowadays, tourists flock to see the cave paintings at Lascaux (or at least the exact replica that preserves the originals from further deterioration). But wall painting is only half the story. In 2013, the British Museum staged a wonderful exhibition of Ice-Age Art which featured many of the carved images made by Upper Paleolithic peoples, including the Aurignacian Lion Man and the similarly aged Venus of Hohle-Fels which, in some ways, is an even more astonishing piece with its greatly enlarged buttocks and breasts. The presence of a ring in place of a head suggests that it was used as a pendant or was carried on the person in some other way (such as being attached to a waist-band like Japanese *netsuke*). The fact that such objects were worn on the body suggests that they may have functioned like a talisman, an object imbued with the power to "counteract or divert the effects of supernatural powers."[5] Similar objects are still used by many people today. Bar-Yosef Mayer and Porat detail ethnographic studies showing that in widespread contexts personal ornaments help people feel more open and confident as well as bring luck and strength.[6]

Today, the concrete thinking of belief in the talisman is usually regarded as inferior to symbolic thinking in which the object is merely a symbolic token for what it represents.[7] However valid this may be for modern Westerners, it is not an appropriate distinction to make in relation to those living in oral cultures for whom the entire sensory world is animated by symbolic imagination. Such people are unlikely to recognize the distinctions between the spiritual energy of a talisman, the symbolic token of a representation, or the aesthetic qualities of a work of art. Such distinctions belong only to cultures in which spiritual meaning has become cordoned off from practical activity resulting in such distinctions as secular or sacred, art or craft, ritual or sport.

Whatever their original purpose, these ancient objects of the Paleolithic have clearly been made with great skill, care, and investment of time and energy. The display of such objects as "art" at the Ice-Age Art exhibition was not intended to decontextualize their original purpose but to highlight their commonality with the kind of objects we regard as art today. They may have had a different significance or association with different beliefs and practices, but their outstanding aesthetic power resonates across the eons of time, stirring the feelings, senses, and emotions of the viewer in a way that must have at least some similarity with how they were experienced when first created. They were created by human beings like ourselves, yet living in an entirely different cultural world with ways of living, thinking, perceiving, and conceiving that we might struggle to grasp even were they still here to tell us about them.

Cave Art and Shamanic Visions

One of the most influential explanations of Upper Paleolithic cave painting in recent decades has come from ethnographic comparisons with the rock art practiced by hunter-gatherers today (or at least until quite recently). On the basis of his extensive knowledge of San rock art in South Africa and comparisons with North America, David Lewis-Williams has proposed that cave painting was associated with the induction of altered states of consciousness of the kind practiced by shamanic traditions throughout the world.[8]

In these altered states a parallel state of being or spirit world is experienced that is so memorable and emotionally charged that it has a factuality and life of its own.[9] As evidence of the link between cave painting and altered states of consciousness, Lewis-Williams points to the otherwise inexplicable presence of various geometric patterns that appear in all known forms of rock and cave painting. He connects these with similar "entopic" phenomena that occur in the early stages of altered states of consciousness induced in laboratory subjects, including those induced by psychotropic drugs. He quotes laboratory research that describes a typical series of stages that subjects pass through culminating in the occurrence of visions and hallucinations. Such states can also be achieved by sensory deprivation, prolonged dancing and/or rhythmic drumming, etc. He concludes that they are an inherent feature of the neurology of the human nervous system which explains other universal features of shamanic visionary experiences such as out of body experiences, flying, being underground, and the experience of the "vortex," a neurologically induced experience that is imaged as a tunnel or a hole.

On this basis, Lewis-Williams argues that cave paintings are a record of shamanic visions that would have been actually experienced in the caves. He argues that the animals painted on the walls of the caves were not physically real animals but spirit animals experienced in visionary states as emerging from the rock itself. As in other shamanic traditions, the caves would have been believed to be a passageway to the spirit world itself into which the shaman may go in trance-induced visions and out of which the spirits may come. Hence the way many paintings make use of features of the cave walls to depict animals as if they are emerging from the rock, believed to be a membrane between this world and the spirit world.

The shamanic hypothesis has become very influential in studies of rock art and cave painting but it has not gone unchallenged. A few critics are openly hostile, such as Paul Bahn who regards it as "the great leap backwards."[10] Bahn points to the evidence of careful planning and artistry involved in the execution of cave paintings which suggest they must be far more than simply "an accumulated record of images seen in a trance."[11] He also considers the great variation between large, open spaces and small, hidden spaces that are difficult to reach, as well as the fact that spaces with "the best acoustics [frequently] coincide with the richest decoration and the poorest with little or no decoration."[12] This suggests that the larger spaces were used for public ceremonies including music and dancing, implying a much wider involvement with the significance of the images than had they been entirely derived from the trance states of a special few. In this respect, Lewis-Williams' view implies a kind of shamanocracy in which the shamans created the imaginal symbology and mythology for the entire community, an internalist view that sees imagery as something that happens "in the head" rather than emergent from shared activity in the world. If the imagery and significance of animals was already part of the group's cultural world view and simply formed the means by which the trance images were construed, this begs the question as to whether its origins can be derived from the neurological "raw material" of trance states in the first place.

Even if altered states of consciousness are a universal feature of human consciousness, questions remain as to how and why some human cultures came to place such importance on these states of mind while others do not and, in the case of our own culture, positively dismiss them as mere hallucinations or delusions. Oddly, Lewis-Williams himself seems to take this view, claiming that "many Westerners today recognize the intensified trajectory *for what it is* and do not attach profound significance to its imagery."[13] [italics added] This is a curiously ethnocentric view for someone who has been so immersed in the consciousness of non-Western peoples who do not share the old imperialist view that the scientific mentality is more enlightened and gives greater access to the truth of things. Surely shamans across the world would make equal claims—that they too take the experience of the spirit world "for what it is" and attach profound significance to its imagery for that very reason.

Most critics of the shamanistic interpretation of rock painting do not deny the role of trance states but seek to place them in a broader context of the mythology and cosmology of the indigenous peoples who practiced rock painting in the recent past. They question whether the animal images can be read as metaphors of events taking place in trance states. For example, Anne Solomon argues that references to underwater, death, and drowning in rock art and mythology do not refer to sensations experienced in trance states that are metaphorically represented as "dying" but are references to real death and to beliefs about the places where the spirits of the dead reside.[14] So rather than deriving mythology from the raw material of trance states, she argues that

> mythology provides the material for understanding the trance experience. ... In other words, a trancer experiences and describes what he or she has been socialized to expect, in terms of cosmography and models of mortality and illness.[15]

In a different context, that of Coso sheep cults of Eastern California, Alan Garfinkel shows that the images of big horn sheep occur at optimally suited ambush and trap locations that allow for communal big game hunting.[16] This, together with the labor-intensive detail and effort of creating the images, argues strongly in favor of communal activities relating to actual hunting rather than the metaphorical record of individual vision quests as suggested by the shamanistic hypothesis. Here, too, "underground" may have been believed to be the location of the dead animal spirits. "Hence the rock pictures may manifest the animistic belief that a revered sky god or animal spirit helper would regularly 'recharge' the Coso hunting grounds afresh with a new supply of regenerated bighorns and other animals."[17] The potential application of this interpretation to underground European cave-act is obvious—it is at least as equally plausible as the shamanistic hypothesis.

Cartesian Assumptions in the Shamanistic Hypothesis

A more profound criticism draws attention to the implicit Cartesian bias in Lewis-Williams' work and that of some of his critics. It seeks to replace this with an understanding of how animic systems of belief do not divide up the world, as we do, into nature and culture or spiritual and material. There is then no significant separation between the ordinary activities of hunting and gathering, on the one hand, and the symbolic activities of trance and painting, on the other. All these activities are elements in an overall cosmology concerned with "the continued circulation of these vital life forces through the various activities that [constitute] human and non-human beings' identities."[18] This means that there can be no neat separation between what is metaphorical and what is actual.

As discussed in the previous chapter, concrete iconic symbols *are* what they represent; the imaginal element is intrinsically interwoven into their substance as the perception of energies, forces, powers, spirits, and the like. In cosmologies that do not divide up the world between animate and inanimate or material and spiritual, the world is alive with these forces. Painted images too have living force and significance. Here, anthropologist Tim Ingold distinguishes between *representations* and *depictions*. Totemic and animic depictions are not representational in the sense of reconstructing the material world they know; "their purpose is not to represent but to reveal, to penetrate beneath the surface of things so as to reach deeper levels of knowledge and understanding. It is at these levels that meaning is to be found."[19] Alternately, the terms might be reversed with the same meaning—thus I would prefer to say that totemic and animic images are not mere depictions of events, either real or imagined, but re-present them in their true (spiritual) guise as a way of revealing deeper meaning. They are not representations, however, in the sense of *mere* representations, and, in that sense, they might be better regarded as presences in their own right that, as previously discussed, enact and bring forth reality.

Dowson discusses this point in relation to "metaphorical" understandings of San rock art which assume that the images refer *either* to trance states *or* to the natural world of "real" elands as, for example, in the view of Parkington for whom the dying eland is a metaphor for the birth of the hunter rather than the death of the shaman.[20] Both interpretations make an unwarranted distinction between metaphor and reality in which the real physical eland is seen as a merely material (i.e., soulless) entity to be consumed as an object of food or meaning. As in Freud's distinction between manifest and latent content of dreams, there is no inherent connection between the metaphor and its meaning—it could just as well be something else— and the image can be discarded once its meaning has been elicited.[21] This is to read metaphor and symbol as arbitrary signs, on the model of a discursive alphabetic text in which the connection between the signs and their sensuous referents in the world has been severed.

But if, as I argued in the previous chapter, material symbols are what they represent, the dying eland *is* a real dying eland but it also has a spiritual meaning that may make it homologous (isomorphic) with the birth of the hunter and/or the death of the shaman. In other words, it is a *living symbol* with multiple indeterminate meanings. But it is not abstracted from a dead, material nature as if nature is only the "material" for the symbol or the eland is merely the meat that keeps the hunter alive. It is one and the same with the living being with which the hunter is in relation and there is no distinction to be made between literal and symbolic.

The same Cartesian presupposition is apparent in Lewis-Williams' reliance on neurology as an objective material "reality" (nature) subject to varying interpretations (culture). He sees these as merely "rationalization of experiences generated by the neurology of the human brain in altered states of consciousness."[22] These states are considered to be *"simply one of the raw materials* that society uses to construct itself" rather like the idea that animals are "raw material" for feeding humans or iron is the "raw material" of steel goods. [23] [italics added] There is an underlying psycho-cultural schema here of the material world (including our own brains!) as a commodity for humans to consume rather than being a sacred entity that is spiritually alive, as it is for oral indigenous peoples world-wide.

In the Cartesian cosmology, the material world, while soulless and dead, is seen as the only reality, thus creating the "problem of consciousness" as an anomaly to be explained in material terms. Such explanations make use of an implicit distinction between what *seems* to be the case and what is really the case, as I discussed in Chapter 1 in relation to the notion of behindology. In this context, neurocentrism, the view that human behavior can be explained in terms of brain functioning, shares much in common with the structuralist tradition in which Lewis-Williams explicitly places himself; both are behindological forms of explanation where what appears on the surface can be reduced to more fundamental structures that constitute the underlying reality. In the structuralist tradition, the mind is seen as an ontological, biologically fixed given that is reflected in the structure of the world it creates. Lewis-Williams traces this view back to Vico who argued that "the world is shaped by, and in the shape of, the human mind… . In performing this task of shaping the world, humanity created itself. This being so, there must be a universal 'language of the mind,' common to all communities."[24]

Despite the differences between them, this is the same tradition that includes Jung, Saussure, Chomsky, and Levi-Strauss, all of whom see the relation between the mind and the world as a one-way street in which, in Jung's language, the structure of the mind is "projected" onto the world. But if there is actually a two-way street (or even a multiplicity of directional influences) in which the structure of the mind is emergent from embodied engagement in a social and material environment, then there would be an *ontological* difference between, say, the visions of American students in a laboratory and those of Upper Paleolithic shamans, notwithstanding any common neurological base. The neurology of the brain neither explains nor creates the visions, it simply provides (part of) the possibility for them to occur.

Imagination in the World

If mind is extended via its cultural world and is therefore environmental as well as neurological, then imaginal phenomena *are* what they appear to be—there is no behindological thing in itself that can be taken for what they "really" are. We are not dealing with some kind of "spiritual elephant" that is seen from different perspectives according to cultural context; if mind is a product of brain, body, *and* environment then the thing itself is emergent within those contexts wherein it has its being. It cannot be reduced via abstraction to some other supposedly more "real" realm of being.

This is not simply a matter of relativism, as if any truth is as good as another. Rather it is to do with recognizing that the way things are is the result of being born into a cultural environment with particular ways of construing the world that are an inherent element of the way we learn to see the world. These ways of thinking constitute the models, schemas, or collective representations through which we experience our world. This is not to deny certain universals, such as the emotional responses I mentioned earlier in relation to ice-age art but to recognize that these are emergent within a particular cultural context.

Where Are Dreams?

So, for example, while dreaming is universal, the way dreams are thought about is not. Western culture makes the Cartesian assumption that dreams occur "in the head" and that imagination is to be sharply distinguished from the reality that exists "out there." Those that assume that altered states of consciousness are simply the result of the neurological oddities of the human brain are making the same assumption. Dreaming is particularly interesting here because it seems to contradict the phenomenological emphasis on mind as embodied engagement in the world, showing that experience can and does take place "in the head" in a way that is purely generated by the brain.

Yet we do not automatically experience our dreams in this way—we have to learn to do so via the responses of others. In our society this occurs when young children are told that their frightening night-time experiences are "just a dream" and that there are not "really" any monsters under the bed. So Western children are trained to regard dreams as "imaginary" and most people disregard them as insignificant and illusory. Many patients coming for analysis have to be re-trained to pay attention to their dreams as potential sources of meaning, and even then they are regarded as symbolic rather than real. Concrete thinking and symbolic equations are regarded as primitive and infantile along the lines of the same old devaluation of alternative ways of thinking and altered states of consciousness. Even amongst those who value the spiritual dimension of life, reports such as those who claim to have been visited by the dead are treated with a certain amount of skepticism—surely, we wonder to ourselves, this must have been a dream or a vision that only *felt* real? Yet, for example, one very practical, down to earth, no-nonsense friend of mine had several such visitations from a recently deceased loved one that overturned all her previous convictions: she *knew* that it was really *him*. Some powerful synchronistic experiences generate similar convictions. Even more ordinary is the experience of the kind of dream that lives with us all day (or longer) and takes mental effort to convince ourselves it was "just a dream."

So it seems to me that there is no ultimate reason for regarding dreams and visions as internal figments, especially since the phenomenological experience of dreaming is frequently otherwise. It is certainly difficult for most people who have become accustomed to thinking of dreams as "internal" to experience them as happenings in the "real world," but this confirms the point since it is bound to be similarly difficult for those who are accustomed to seeing them as information from the spirit world or the ancestors to be convinced that they are "really" fantasies that come from "the unconscious." Jung

attempts to deal with the problem by equating the one with the other.
In *Memories, Dreams, Reflections* he writes,

> The unconscious corresponds to the mythic land of the dead,
> the land of the ancestors. If, therefore, one has a fantasy
> of the soul vanishing, this means that it has withdrawn
> into the unconscious or into the land of the dead. There it
> produces a mysterious animation and gives visible forms to
> the ancestral traces, the collective unconscious.[25]

Now, although Jung does leave room for the idea of "the land of the
dead," there is an equivocal implication here that "the unconscious"
is the reality whereas the old idea of the ancestors is a symbolic myth
that *refers* to the unconscious. This is made more explicit in his view
of the Australian "Dreamtime":

> [T]he Australian word *aljira* means 'dream' as well as
> 'ghostland' and the 'time' in which the ancestors lived
> and still live. It is, as they say, the 'time when there was
> no time.' This looks like an obvious concretization and
> projection of the unconscious with all its characteristic
> qualities—its dream manifestations, its ancestral world of
> thought-forms, and its timelessness.[26]

Throughout his work, Jung interprets myths in terms of his
own theory of the collective unconscious, implying that this is not
merely a translation from one myth to another but an *explanation*, as
if, like Lewis-Williams' view of the "intensified trajectory," modern
psychology, takes myth for "what it is," albeit Jung does at least
recognize its profound significance. Nevertheless, this significance
is to be found by recognizing that the true location of myth is in a
Cartesian mind. Instead of taking things to be "outside," we must
"withdraw our projections" and recognize that they really belong to
"the inner world." And it is no coincidence that Jung is also wedded
to a structural behindological theory of the archetypes as the ultimate
generators of psychic reality.

An alternative way to view Jung's interpretation, though, would
be not as an *explanation* but as a translation. Jung is translating one
mythic language (the land of the ancestors) into another (the inner
world of the unconscious). Each is as mythic (or real) as the other.
So, if one were to try to explain the unconscious to a South African
sangoma, for example, we might well expect a reply along the lines of
"Oh, I see. This unconscious you speak about is where the ancestors
live." In practice, of course, it is not so easy because each idea is

embedded in its own cultural context and does not translate so easily into a different one.[27] Each is a valid myth that is the outcome of the human imagination at work in a specific cultural context.

Symbols as "Making Visible"

Rather than attempting to adjudicate which interpretation is the real one, we might look at the *activities* that are associated with concepts of the unconscious or the land of the dead. We might then notice that both traditions are concerned with making visible that which is hidden or in some way inaccessible to sensuous perception. And it is this, I want to argue, that is the function of symbols. The symbolic comprises that which is inaccessible to direct sensuous perception but can be brought forth in narrative, dream, and material representation. To the Western mind, this is the realm of imagination; for other cultures, it is the spirit realm or the world of the ancestors (the "land of the dead"); and for the Australian aborigines, it is the Dreamtime. Far from being "imaginary," the realm of symbolic imagination is a realm of eternal presence, but it requires the work of humans to maintain it. For Australian aboriginal peoples, considerable importance is attached to the practice of retouching paintings to keep the ancestral spirits alive since, if the paintings were to fade and disappear, so would the beings they depict, and with them would go the life-giving energy which they impart to the land.[28] Similar functions are accomplished by repeating the names and ancestral events associated with sacred sites as in the practice of those who go walkabout through the "songlines" of the land.[29] Thus, for the indigenous Australians, the land itself forms the imagery out of which symbolic imagination emerges; there is such an intimate relation between the two that neither one can continue to exist without the other. As Bruce Chatwin writes, "an unsung land is a dead land."[30]

For the peoples of the Eurasian North, as well as for the San people of South Africa, spiritual energy must be recirculated amongst living beings; humans need to behave in certain ways in order to ensure that they promote rather than detract from this natural order of things. Ingold describes the fundamental division in animic systems between "an interior, vital part that is the source of awareness, memory, intention, and feeling, and an exterior bodily covering that confers the powers that are necessary to conduct a particular form of life."[31]

In certain circumstances, animal and human coverings can be exchanged, thus manifesting the animal spirit in each (which, it should be noted, is *also* a concretely physical being—"spiritual" does not mean "immaterial" in these contexts). Should a traveler lose his way and find himself in the abode of an animal that is revealed in his inner being, he may never be able to return to the world of humankind, a predicament reminiscent of Celtic tales of becoming entrapped in the Otherworld of the spirits by eating their food. So here again there are motifs of a hidden other realm that humans may access but only in special and potentially dangerous circumstances.

While none of these cultures would regard their beliefs as symbolic or proceeding from imagination (or referring to an immaterial spirit), I contend that they depend on a particular mode of thought that is unique to humans. This goes beyond sensuous perception or, at least, perceives what is available to the senses in particular ways, and it this that I would characterize as symbolic imagination. Image-making has a crucial role to play in this process; it is not that images are made in order to represent symbols of the imagination, rather that image-making is an activity conducted for other purposes that could not exist without the faculty of human imagination. *Pari passu*, imagination could not exist without those activities. It is in this sense that images are a form of tool-use; more than tools to think with, they are *tools of revelation*, a means of simultaneously revealing and bringing forth the unseen world of spiritual reality.

Perhaps then, we might take the paintings of animals emerging from the spirit world in the caves of Chauvet and Lascaux as metaphors for the emergence of symbolic imagination into the world. This is not to suggest that this modern metaphor is any more real or "true" than how ever it might have been constituted by the image-makers of the distant past. It is simply to recognize that whether we speak of the imagination, the unconscious, or the spirit world, we are referring to a phenomenological domain that comes into being through material means beyond what is ordinarily visible in the material world.

This bringing forth and making visible that which is unseen is at the root of what we mean by *a symbol*. Here we might look at two etymological origins for the notion of a symbol. The more familiar one is that of the Greeks in which the sumbolon was a token divided in two halves by which one person might recognize the authenticity of a messenger carrying the other half. The word was derived from *sumballien* meaning to "throw together." So the concept of the symbol refers to the bringing together of two domains in a way that makes something apparent that otherwise cannot be known, as is also true of metaphor. The sumbolon token is literally a tool that reveals an otherwise hidden identity.

Victor Turner reports a similar idea amongst the Ndembu people.

> The symbol is the smallest unit of specific structure in Ndembu ritual. The vernacular term for it is *chinjikijilu*, from *ku-jikijia*, 'to blaze a trail,' by cutting marks on a tree ... to serve as guides back from the unknown bush to known paths. A symbol then, is a blaze or landmark, something that connects the unknown with the known. ... Furthermore, in discussing their symbols with Ndembu, one finds them constantly using the term *ku-solola*, 'to make visible' or 'to reveal.'[32]

Turner describes the derivation of this term from aspects of hunting concerned with the "making visible" of the game. It is applied in a variety of contexts such as fertility medicines to "make children visible" and other medicinal functions. Another derivative refers to "a place of revelation." These terms "refer to specially consecrated sites, used only in the final phases of important rituals, where esoteric rites are performed and secret matters are revealed to the initiated."[33]

Previously, I have referred to symbols as the clothing of affect in image, but I would now say that rather than the image being a mere outer covering, it is constitutive of what it brings forth.[34] The material beings re-envisaged as painted or carved images are elements of an extended mind through which psychic experience is distributed and becomes socially available as the factual realities of a particular culture. As Evan Thompson puts it, cognitive and emotional processes "extend throughout the body and loop through the material, social, and cultural environments in which the body is embedded."[35]

As I described in the previous chapter, the early use of symbolic objects and materials such as shell beads and red ochre paved the way for the capacity to imagine non-sensory aspects of experience that were not previously thinkable. Gradually, these material anchors extended the experiential possibilities for early humans by manifesting the world of the non-material in a way that made it real and alive via material presences. In this way, the activity of the Upper Paleolithic peoples (and/or those that came before them) was constitutive of the spiritual, psychic, and imaginal world in which we all now live. What we can now see in these great caves is the echo of the coming to birth of the spiritual world. For without a physical reality through which the sprit can be perceived, how can we know the spirit at all? This argument turns Berkeley's Idealism on its head: rather than the material world requiring a mind to perceive it, the mind requires a material world to symbolize it. Nor does this reduce the material world to a soulless materialism. On the contrary, it restores the world to an active aliveness since it is in and through the world that we are able to perceive the spirit. The living spirit is emergent from our imaginative engagement with the things of the material world. As the first materialist, Julien La Mettrie, put it so well, "through imagination … all inanimate objects come to life."[36] Roger Brooke makes a similar point in relation to the role of imagination in perception. "The psyche is truly realized in that imaginative perception which reveals the world's divinity."[37]

Lewis-Williams, too, emphasizes the materiality of the process by which visions were located in paint and pigment.

> The hallucinatory or spirit world together with its painted and engraved imagery, was thus invested with materiality and precisely situated cosmologically; it was not something that existed merely in people's thoughts and minds. The spiritual nether world was *there,* tangible and material … Moreover image-making did not merely take place in the spirit-world: it also shaped and incrementally created that world. *Every image made hidden presences visible.*[38] [italics added]

These spiritual presences, made manifest in visible images are the essence of what Jung meant by a "living symbol." Through the collective practices of a daily life enriched with imaginal meaning, the living symbol is repeatedly revealed in the timeless present of an eternal Now. Jerome Bernstein describes this in relation to his long-term involvement with Native American cultures. "In the Native American cultures with which I am familiar, particularly the Hopi and the Navajo, ritual is the enactment (not re-enactment) in the Now of specific components of their respective cosmological stories."[39]

Emotional Engagement and the Spiritual World

For Lewis-Williams the possibility of altered states of consciousness is enough to explain the imagery that occurs within those states since ultimately he regards them as illusory and lacking in any real significance. What is missing in his analysis is an explanation for why mystical experiences arise in the first place, why they take the form they do, and what aspects of human experience are enacted through cosmological stories, rituals, beliefs, and the daily practices informed by them. For this I think we need to consider the role of affect in our engagement with the world.

In sentient animals, the significance of environmental triggers is registered as emotion. Emotion fashions the *Umwelt* by registering those aspects of the environment that are significant to the organism. Hence the idea that emotion is the meaning of experience.[40] For human beings, it is not only the problem-solving aspects of cognition that have developed beyond those of any other species, it is also the intensity and complexity of our emotional repertoire. Yet there has been a consistent bias in the Western mind, especially since the Enlightenment, which over-emphasizes the rational as the defining feature of humanity at the expense of emotion. The latter is relegated to "base passions" of our animal nature, thus promulgating the split between the emotional body and the (supposedly) rational mind, as if only rationality is human and to be human is not to be animal (hence the designation that we are *Homo sapiens*—the humans who "know"). Similarly, the literature of the extended mind has focused almost entirely on intellectual problem-solving at the expense of the emotional aspects of cognition. It is these that find expression in the non-discursive symbols of metaphor and mysticism through which emotional cognition is extended and distributed by means of collective representations. These symbols are a way of representing that aspect of our experience that concerns not only our relation to the material world but also our relation to ourselves or, more precisely, the emotional experience of being engaged with the world. Symbols represent not so much the things they depict as the intentionality and emotional significance of our human relation towards those things. Through symbolization, our emotional states become available for reflection and manipulation. So the form that collective symbols take is a reflection of the objects and situations that have the greatest emotional significance for us.[41]

To understand the form taken by symbolic imagination as it began to emerge as a significant aspect of human cultural life, we therefore need to place its manifestations in the context of what was most emotionally meaningful to the people of that time. This may give us at least some indications of how the psyche "began" since I would argue that it is only through its symbolization in a cultural context that psychic life can emerge as a distinct domain of human experience. In this respect, psyche, imagination, spirit, and self-reflexive consciousness are all linked aspects of the same process. Symbolization not only enhances consciousness but also creates it or, as I would prefer to say, it brings it forth. In the process of being represented, emotional states are reformulated and thus constituted in a different, more reflexively conscious way.

Homo affectus: The Emotional Species

The need to represent emotional states must be related to the increased affectivity of the human species. Other species form attachment bonds but human attachment bonds have a much greater intensity associated with the intersubjective aspect of human relating which is embedded in, but goes beyond, the attachment system.[42] There are also many emotions amongst humans that have little or no resemblance to those of other species. For example, only humans can be offended, envious, or insulted, only humans can feel the complex bitter-sweet quality of something that is poignant and, with the possible exception of elephants, only humans can cry. It is possible that other animals may feel awe but, of course, only humans can take this further to wonder about the meaning of the universe in which they find themselves. Here, though, there is clearly a link with the level of conceptualization made possible by language.

It is not that we are the only animal with a rich emotional repertoire. For example, while writing this book, I have come across several examples of emotional warmth amongst chimpanzees. I referred to the caring and sharing amongst bonobos in Chapter 3 (pages 13–16); more recently, I came across a moving video of an orphaned, severely emaciated chimpanzee nursed back to health by Jane Goodall's team who hugs her with apparent gratitude as she is released back into the wild. It is unlikely, however, that the chimpanzee would understand the emotions of her caregivers as they watch her go, let alone the empathic response of those who watch and share the video.[43] Nor is it likely that chimpanzees would return the favor, even to one of their own kind, as also discussed in Chapter 3 in relation to the lack of concern for distressed infants amongst chimpanzees and baboons. There are no examples of long-term care of the sick amongst other animals as there are amongst early humans, such as those I referred to in Chapter 4.[44] Putting this and other evidence together, Penny Spikins argues that compassion emerged together with the greater level of collaboration amongst human groups that facilitated their survival and which, according to Tomasello, may also have fostered the emergence of language.[45] Social living thus intensifies human emotional life. Humans are not only capable of much greater love for each other but also levels of hatred not seen in other species; only humans react to conflict by seeking revenge. As Spikins puts it, we have a greater capacity for "spite."[46]

Our greater emotional investment in the world also becomes apparent in the value attributed to material objects, including the development of the aesthetic sensibility I referred to in connection with shell beads and red ochre. Similarly, the introduction of grave goods indicates not only a capacity to imagine an afterlife (or spiritual world) to which the dead may go but perhaps, more simply, an expression of feelings of loss and concern towards the dead. It is possible that placing objects such as a stone or the jaw-bone of an animal may originally have had more in the way of emotional significance than ritual meaning.[47] So it is possible that the rituals associated with burial and the objects buried with the dead have their origins in a greater capacity for emotional investment which requires some kind of materially invested activity as a way of managing the emotions involved. The symbolic meaning of objects associated with the dead would therefore emerge out of an emotional connection with the dead person that becomes extended to objects used by or meaningful to them.[48]

In a previous paper on mourning as a symbolic process I gave a personal example of the process by which a penknife on my father's desk became an important symbolic object in the hours immediately following his death.[49] My emotional feeling towards my father, deprived of his living being, found its way into this material object that he had inherited from his own father and used regularly as a paper knife. Through this emotional investment it became for me the symbol of my remembrance of him, a precious object that I would describe as less than a talisman but more than a token. Such objects are treated in a special way and deemed worthy of respect and even reverence; when objects that are invested with particular significance to individuals are treated without such respect, we refer to it as "sacrilege."[50]

Religion as Emotion in Action

The stronger the emotional investment in objects, the more they are likely to be experienced as having concrete power of their own, as with a talisman. When such objects have social as well as personal significance—that is, when they are emotionally invested by the whole social group—their emotional significance can shade over into a kind of awe that indicates the emotional intensity underlying the experience of the sacred. These are the objects felt to be invested with *mana*, a Polynesian word referring to a blend of fear, wonder, and attraction. *Mana* pervades many things:

> It is not confined to specific objects although certain things have more of it than others. The sorts of things that have *mana* include ritual objects, powerful or important individuals, special words, corpses, symbols, special places and locations, rocks, stones, trees, plants, animals. Things which possess *mana* are generally set apart from ordinary mundane things by the use of taboos.[51]

The concept of *mana*, first described by English priest and anthropologist Robert Codrington in the 1890s, greatly appealed to the anthropologists of the time.[52] In France, Marcel Mauss took it up as the principle underlying the primitive belief in magic while in England R. R. Marett saw in it the emotional experience that constitutes the original root of all religion.[53] Marett's stress on the emotional experience of religion was a reaction against his predecessor at Oxford, E. B. Tylor, who analyzed "primitive" religion in purely intellectual, rational terms. For Marett, emotion was at the heart of primitive religion. Tylor's conception of animism, the belief in personal souls that "animate" natural objects, was too ratiocinative for what Marett preferred to call "animatism," referring to a *feeling* that the inanimate world is pervaded with life and will.[54] Ideas and beliefs, such as the animistic belief in spiritual beings in Tylor's definition of religion are a subsequent development. According to Marett, "Savage religion is something not so much thought out as danced out."[55] By this he meant that it develops under conditions, both psychological and sociological, which favor emotional or motor processes rather than ideational ones. "Savages," he argued, should not be seen as "primitive philosophers" as in Tylor and Frazer's theories.[56]

One of the strengths of Marett's approach is that it includes bodily action as well as feeling (it is "danced out"). We have only to put back the ideation that he left out to see emotion as providing the link between act, image, and idea. Images and ideas arise in a context of emotional activity whether that activity is generated by emotion, such as in burial rituals, or itself generates emotion as is often the case in ritual dancing, drumming, chanting, etc.—the kind of activities that generate "altered states of consciousness." Similarly, what we *think* is often to do with what we feel; in states of heightened emotion our beliefs are often powerfully influenced in ways of which we are unaware—a daily occurrence in the psychotherapist's consulting room. For example, paranoid beliefs are often traceable to chronic states of fear and anger of which the patient is unaware. The same is true for the therapist who may make an apparently rational diagnosis of a patient that is over-positive or over-negative on the basis of unconscious counter-transference feelings. On the other hand, emotional states provide an important basis for many of our most valuable and "highest" thoughts. Poetry, as Wordsworth famously said, is "emotion recollected in tranquility," a further indication that the heart has reasons that require a different kind of symbolic language than reason alone.[57]

Marett has been criticized for neglecting the role that beliefs and ritual practices play in *evoking* emotion. According to critics, *mana* is not so much a spontaneous emotional response as an expression of cognitive beliefs. For example, a name or a place has *mana* because it is believed that it has certain powers or is the dwelling place of a spirit.[58] Marett's neglect of social factors was corrected to some extent by Malinowski who emphasized the public and social nature of rituals but nevertheless sought to explain them in terms of their cathartic functions, a means of strengthening social ties and containing otherwise disruptive emotional states.[59] This, however, still leaves unexplained the link between a specific form of emotion and a specific form of behavior.

Animal Spirits: Entering the World of the Other

So it may be that we need to look for the origin both of the *mana* emotion and the symbols that embody it, as well as the beliefs and the ritual practices that contextualize the emotional experience, in the specific activities which provide their origin. Religion is always a combination of experience, practice, and beliefs. Given the prevalence of animal representations in the Upper Paleolithic it seems highly likely that the central activity out of which their spiritual beliefs emerged was concerned with the activity of hunting. This is not to return to the discredited idea that the cave paintings were a form of sympathetic magic, but rather to recognize that the origin of the images that came out of the spirit world can be located in the practical activity of hunting in which the participants were deeply

emotionally invested. Of course, the other area that is most highly
emotionally charged for all humans is sexuality and procreation.
This also finds some expression in Paleolithic art, notably in the
"Venus figurines" found throughout Paleolithic Europe, especially
in the Gravettian period (30,000 to 22,000 years ago), most famously
in the Venus of Willendorf and the more recently discovered Venus
of Hohle-Fels from the earlier Aurignacian period. Depictions of
female pudenda reminiscent of this sculpture also turn up in the
Chauvet caves, the most renowned of which is painted on a hanging
pendant of rock at the furthest end of the caves, surrounded by
the looming figure of a bison superimposed on what might have
been the torso of a female figure.[60] Here the twin themes of spirit
animals and the power of female sexuality coalesce, although with
what meaning and purpose we can only speculate. A comparatively
recent analogy would be the Greek myth of Europa seduced by Zeus
in the form of the Bull, but, as with later images of lion-headed
men, we can only speculate as to how far there is a common referent
to their symbolic meaning.

Hunting and sexuality both involve heightened states of emotion
and potentially states of mind that blur the boundary between self and
other. This may be why the "gathering" side of hunter-gathering finds
less expression in religious practice and belief—it does not involve
heightened emotion and the relation to plants is not a social encounter
whereas hunters conceptualize their association to important animals
in relational terms that cut across the human/nature divide.[61] Successful
hunters need to think their way into the state of mind of the animal
they are hoping to kill in order to be able to predict its behavior. They
need to know the animals' favored habitats, how and when they travel
(especially if they are tracking game that is available at particular
seasons), how to chase and entice prey into particular locations, which
animals in a herd are the most likely targets, and how they will react
when feeling endangered.

Archaeologists often regard this as a matter of intelligence. For
Steven Mithen, it belongs in the "natural history" module that was
separate from the social module until the neurological merging of
the "chapels" in the modern human brain created the possibilities for
cognitive fluidity. So it was only then that animal-human associations
might be made and imaginative figures like the Lion Man could be
conceived.[62] This view of the matter neglects the key role of emotion

that would be especially heightened when hunting big game that could inflict severe injuries. And this was likely to have been even more the case for Neanderthals whose preferred style of hunting is believed to have involved confrontation at close quarters with handheld spear-thrusts rather than the projectile javelin throwing and bows and arrows utilized by *Homo sapiens*. But even where there are no obvious risks to the hunter, the activity of hunting is always emotionally invested and not only because it is a source of food that makes it ultimately a matter of survival. Hunters regularly form emotional bonds with the animals they hunt; they must respect and understand them if they are to be successful in killing them. So it is not unusual for hunter-gatherers to venerate the animals they kill.

There is a fine line here between the "emotional" and the "spiritual." In fact, I am suggesting that the transition from the one to the other comes about through making visible immaterial states of emotional engagement. In this way, emotional states are crystallized as ways of relating and systems of belief enacted through the rituals and material objects and forms (such as paintings) that accompany them. As they become distributed through a cultural group, the images and beliefs evoke the emotions as much as the original activities that inspired them. Over time, special practices that must be obeyed in relation to animals become institutionalized as collective representations that get passed on from one generation to another.

Images emerge in relation to actions that may often have been more important than the images themselves. This is evident in relation to the oldest ceramic figure in the world—the Venus of Dolní Věstonice. Many similar baked-clay figurines exploded in the hearth where they were fired. This is thought to suggest that they were used in a form of ritual performance wherein the act of making, baking, and perhaps even exploding the figures was more significant than the end result.[63] Paul Pettit considers that rock and cave art might be considered in the same way. Speaking about the only ice-age art found in Britain, at Church Hole in Nottinghamshire, he says, "These animals are critical to their survival. These are functioning, one assumes, as magical events and it may well be that it's not the image itself hanging there in perpetuity but the *act* of creating that image that was important." Drawing on the idea of the rock-face as a veil between this world and the spirit world he suggests that "the natural feature of the rock suggests a deer trying to come into this world. You help it and so you're helping in its birth. And perhaps only by bringing a deer into this world are you allowed to remove one from it."[64]

There is plenty of ethnographic evidence for the way hunter-gatherers strive to enter into the spirit of the animals they are about to hunt to maximize their potential success. Mathias Guenther provides a particularly vivid description of Bushmen's active identification with the animals of the hunt.

> Throughout the hunt the hunter would monitor his every thought, emotion and action, in order to sustain the bond of connectedness with the animal by which he felt he could steer the hunt towards an auspicious conclusion. … The bond of sympathy was something set up in the hours or days preceding the hunt, when the hunters would attune themselves spiritually to one animal species or another and, in the process, attempt to gather whatever presentiments they could about the impending hunt: the animals they might encounter, the direction they could come from, the likely dangers, the duration of the hunt. These presentiments … activated the hunter's entire body; they were felt at his ribs, his back, his calves, his face and eyes. His body would be astir with the "antelope sensation" at places on his body corresponding with those of the antelope's.[65]

Brian Morris reports similar practices amongst the hunters of Malawi.

> Attributing personhood to animals usually in the sense of seeing them as the embodiment of spiritual agencies only takes place in specific contexts. … Malawian hunters when out hunting engage more often in theriomorphic thinking, trying to imagine themselves as the hunted animal—to anticipate its movements and actions. … [W]hile out hunting or in their rituals, or even digging up mice, they do try to think like animals, for animals have subjective agency, consciousness and knowledge.[66]

This way of relating to the animal by entering into its otherness was precisely the way of thinking described so vividly by Joe Hutto in his account of living with turkeys. It was his life-long experience of being a hunter and, in particular, a turkey-hunter, that had enabled him to develop the requisite skills for his field work as a naturalist. As a hunter, he is no animal behaviorist; he relates to the animal's *experience* in and through his own and enhances his understanding through imaginative immersion in the way the animal behaves, not through observing it "objectively" but by actively relating to it and living with it. No wonder he has such a feeling for the living sacredness of the environment that is so much more than a "resource" to be exploited.[67] His work suggests that this traditional way of living and thinking is not such an anthropological relic as we might think, even if it is no longer surrounded by an entire cosmology.

At any rate, if we are to have any possibility of understanding how early humans first began to develop and use their imagination, we need to use our own in the attempt to enter into the world of the other as they may have been doing in entering "the Otherworld" of the spirits. This requires a radical re-thinking of many of our own presuppositions, particularly about the relation between humans, animals, and the material world. Tim Ingold emphasizes that so-called "animism" is not the imputation of life or spirit to things that are truly inert but a way of being in the world that is alive *to* the world. This is associated with a heightened sensitivity and responsiveness in perception and action to an environment that is always in flux, as can be seen in the way the Kalahari Bushmen go about hunting their prey.[68]

Ingold suggests that the relation of hunter-gatherers to animals is one of seeking to know not by amassing technical knowledge in the service of control but by a relation of trust. The knowledge they seek is more like the way we relate to other humans who are important to us and on whom we depend while being responsible for their care. In other words, they are our *kin*. "You get to know other human persons by sharing with them, that is by experiencing their companionship. And if you are a hunter, you get to know animals by hunting."[69] The hunter is thus seeking not control over animals but *revelation*.

Losey *et al.* point out how failure to recognize this can be very misleading when attempting to understand the meaning of archaeological remains.

> [F]aunal remains from virtually all contexts here have been interpreted from implicitly 'modern western' perspectives ... where animals are mindless food items, sources of tool materials, passive commodities, and status symbols that all are objects of cold calculations by their human counterparts. ... [T]he resulting portrayal of human engagements with the animal world is narrow and potentially misleading.[70]

Echoing Ingold and Hutto, they argue for interpretations that "should include humans who dwelt in worlds with meaning, where animals are more than mindless targets of human predation, and where landscapes are more than stages for foraging and human-centered political action."[71]

Hunter-gatherers in many parts of the world have complex beliefs and practices in relation to animals, many of which are seen as having spiritual forms or qualities that make them ontologically similar or equivalent to humans. Human and animal alike have souls that cycle through various cosmological levels and may return to new life or spirit forms. Just as I have described the way objects may become imbued with *mana*, the remains of animals may be felt to retain the living potency of the animals' spirits that can influence humans who engage with them.

Drawing on such ethnographic accounts (notably the perspectivism of Amerindians discussed by Viveiros de Castro), Chantal Conneller provides a remarkable interpretation of the use of antler-frontlets as "masks" at Star Carr, a Mesolithic site in North Yorkshire.[72] She argues that for the people of that time, human identities would have been much more fluid; there would not have been a sharp distinction between animal (nature) and human (culture). Like the hunter-gatherers of recent times, they would have lived in a shape-shifting world in which animals, humans, and spirits could each take on the form of the other. For those who wore the antler-frontlets, these animal body parts would have retained the living spirit of the animal; thus to wear part of the animal is to *become* the animal. Far more than a mere mask, then, these animal body parts acted as mediators between humans and animals, embodying the transformational quality with which each may become "spirits." Here it seems to me that *spirit* refers to something that does not exist merely in its everyday corporeal form but takes on a shape-shifting quality that in our current way of thinking we identify as *mind* and, in particular, *imagination*. Here, though, imagination takes material form and material form takes imaginative (spiritual) form; the boundaries between the two are blurred, just as the boundaries between human and animal are blurred. Thus Conneller argues that rather than disguising human bodies, the use of antler-frontlets revealed and transformed them into their spirit equivalents; they were a way of "becoming deer," perhaps to enhance their ability to hunt deer by assuming their qualities.[73] In this way, spirit is made manifest in material form as a living image that has actual existence in the world, yet is not *merely* material or, as we might say, not *reducible* to its materiality. Since it is most likely that the use of antler-frontlets was associated with some form of ritual, this transformative process would also be associated with heightened states of emotion in which "seeing is believing." The materiality of the performance promotes emotion and the emotional state promotes the sense of transformation—the transformation of a psychic state, albeit one that is taking place not in the head but in the world. This would then be an example of extended cognition although it might be more accurate to refer to it as extended affectivity.

Conneller suggests that this way of relating to animal body parts may have extended to the use of animal bones as tools, teeth as beads, and skin as clothes. This way of thinking is reminiscent of the emotional investment in material objects such as my father's penknife, something I would certainly describe as imbued with the spirit of my father. Whilst I regard this as a symbolic object, its symbolic qualities are certainly not detachable from its materiality. I would therefore consider that even though the antler-wearing people of Star Carr would not recognize the notion of a "symbolic" transformation, the processes involved have many commonalities. In both cases, materiality is a necessary component; in both cases the symbol has an actual existence in the world; in both cases it has that mysterious emotional quality so well conveyed by the notion of *mana*; and in both cases it is transformative of the psychic state of the person who uses it. The distinction between concrete and symbolic is therefore a misnomer that belongs to the outmoded notion of "primitive thought." A more useful contrast is between symbolic and literal. Animals are not *literally* spirits, nor humans *literally* animals—if so, the notion of a "spirit animal" would have no meaning. So I would suggest that the modern distinction between something that is symbolic and something that is not is mirrored in the distinction between animals (including humans) and their spirit forms which manifest only in special conditions.

Abram provides a useful illustration of this distinction. Every day his hosts in Bali left out bowls of rice for the household spirits. One day Abram realized that the rice was, in fact, being eaten by ants. At first, he was amused at his hosts' credulity but then it dawned on him that the ants *were* the household spirits! But, of course, they could not be identical with quotidian ants or else why would his hosts call them *spirits*? In some way the ants are transformed into spirits via the ritual of regular offering, while nevertheless still being ants.[74]

Jung comes close to this view in an unpublished manuscript in which he discusses the distinction made by Pueblo Indians between an "ordinary coyote" and a "doctor coyote" (which presumably would be a spirit animal). While this distinction would be meaningless for "us," he says, for whom "all coyotes are ordinary coyotes, what we failed to realize was that the difference was not to be seen outwardly, but inwardly."[75] Jung speculated whether a white man might be able to see the difference by allowing himself to be "psychically altered," a recognition of one's embeddedness in a cultural tradition and the need to allow oneself to be transformed by what one is trying to study. This is just the process Abram describes as a result of the year he spent in Bali not only absorbing the culture and learning from the local sorcerers, but becoming immersed in the sensory environment and living in an entirely different way than we live in the urbanized, literate West. So the "psychic alteration" that Jung wondered about is not only cultural but also sensory and affective. Insofar as our perceptions loop through the physical and cultural environment as well as our own bodies, the alteration is not, strictly speaking, a "subjective factor" as Jung describes it, nor is the difference between ordinary coyote and spirit coyote seen "inwardly" (except perhaps in relation to the inner nature of the coyote itself). It is true enough to say that the psychic state of the Swiss psychiatrist is different from that of the New Mexican Pueblo Elder but that is as much a way of living as a way of thinking and feeling. We might therefore say that the difference between spirit animal and ordinary animal is an emergent function of embodied social engagement in shared activities, their associated affective states and the beliefs to which they give rise.

The widespread veneration of bears amongst hunter-gatherers of the North provides further ethnographic evidence of the spiritual qualities that inhere in animal bodies after they have been killed. These beliefs and practices seem to have been widespread throughout the North dating back to the time of the Upper Paleolithic.[76] Losey *et al.* describe one of the most spectacular hunter-gatherer cemeteries in Eurasia, dating mainly to the early Neolithic period (8,000 to 7,000 years ago) at Shamanka in Eastern Siberia. As well as human remains, this cemetery included thousands of tools and animal remains within the graves. Special attention seems to have been given to the burial of bear-parts, particularly the head, teeth, and penis bone suggesting that these were felt to retain living spiritual qualities that required careful and respectful treatment after death.

> Bears' deaths, like those of humans, were gradual processes, and their souls and the potencies of their bodies lingered on

after what we would consider the time of death. Mortuary
rites were held for the bears, in part to help them regenerate,
but also as a means of showing them respect and to prevent
their retaliation against the living.[77]

Their article also refers to a film showing the practices and beliefs
of the Koyukon of Alaska in relation to bears.[78] For example, after a
bear has been killed, its eyes are carefully cut out so that it will not
observe any transgressions that the hunters may inadvertently make
towards it. Since the flesh of bears remained alive and potent after
death, eating some body portions could be dangerous. For example,
everyone was prohibited from eating meat from around the atlas
vertebrae because it would cause one to move slowly—in the same
slow manner in which a bear moves its head. Consuming bears' brains
would cause a person to become angry.

These beliefs and practices all show a way of thinking that
we would now regard as metaphorical: aspects of one domain are
transferred to another by a principle of likeness and association.
Therefore we would regard practices such as cutting out the eyes as
symbolic—it is *as if* the bear could see potential transgressions and
so a symbolic ritual is performed.[79] It is clearly not literal since it is
hardly likely that a living bear would approve of having its eyes cut
out to say nothing of being dismembered and eaten. So these beliefs
and practices must have something to do with how the human agents
felt about the bears they killed, that is, the quality of their affective
engagement with these important animals.

This is illustrated in the BBC documentary *The Human Planet*,
in which one of the last hunters of the Kalahari Desert is shown
instructing an apprentice. After waiting for six days, the young
apprentice shoots his first kudu with a poisoned arrow. At this point
both hunters are cock-a-hoop and behave like back-slapping males the
world over. , Later, though, after tracking the weakened animal for a
day or so (by looking at the landscape through the eyes of their prey)
and delivering the final spear-thrust that brings the hunted animal to
the moment of its death, their mood is quite different. They look on
with a quiet, somber, and respectful gaze, perhaps even sorrowful in
the face of the mysteries of death. Like the hunters of the North, these
animals are of great importance to them—the dead kudu will feed
their families for a week. So, there is undoubtedly a bond between
hunter and hunted.

Perhaps then, the Koyukon remove the eyes of bears because of their disturbed feeling of being observed, a sense of guilt towards a loved and revered animal they have killed. No wonder such an animal is felt to continue to live for a long time after its physical death and its body to remain potent for an extended period; it is the imaginative *feeling* for the animal that continues, just as we feel for our human companions when we conduct burial rites and treat the belongings of the dead person as having special significance. This shows that even modern humans feel that the spirit of the dead remains alive for some time after death, and not only for humans—pets are often accorded the same treatment in some cultures. It is simply that the circle of those animals with which we maintain emotional bonds has been sharply reduced in comparison with hunter-gatherers.

Here, then, is an example of religious or spiritual activity consisting of emotional experience, social practices, and beliefs, all of which arise out of ordinary activity that we would now regard as secular: the practice of hunting. In addition, the intense involvement with the animal world is likely to be reflected in dreams and waking visions, such as the eidetic replays that often occur at the end of a period of being intensely focused on a particular activity. I have in mind here a rather ordinary personal experience of hunting for crabs in rock pools. When I closed my eyes at night, I saw vivid images of crabs moving in the sunlit water. This was not simply a memory; it expressed my concentrated effort to "think like a crab" as a way of knowing where to find them and how to catch them. As with dreams, we have become used to thinking of such "visions" as occurring "in our heads," but, as previously discussed, there is no fundamental reason why this should be the case. It is a cultural belief that structures the phenomenology of our experience in certain ways. But what if the neurological events that give rise to dreams, visions, and eidetic images are, experientially, structured otherwise? That is, the brain processes that make it possible to envisage something as a mental image do not come labeled with any particular information as to how these images *should* be construed. So, phenomenologically, such images are neutral and are not necessarily experienced as internal *or* external. As Wittgenstein supposedly said in his critique of an internal/external world differentiation, "External to what?"[80] They can only be considered external in relation to a concept of *internality*. Without this, they are simply phenomena. But this does not mean that they are experienced as being the same kind of phenomena as those that occur when seeing the world through our eyes—i.e., material phenomena. For one thing, they usually occur with the eyes closed. One way of categorizing them, then, is that they are "spirit" phenomena, which, given that they are not material, seems perfectly reasonable.

In fact, this is far from a new idea—it was put forward by one of the very first social anthropologists to consider the beliefs of what were then thought of as primitive peoples, Herbert Spencer. Spencer argued that for our primitive ancestors dreaming must have been like living in a separate reality "not governed by the same limiting forces and laws of everyday existence."[81] This led to ideas of a dream self or soul and therefore the belief that all things have a soul or spirit, a view also taken up by Tylor. Evans-Pritchard criticized Spencer (and Tylor) for attempting to place himself mentally in the position of a human being living during the early period of the evolution of the species and trying to imagine how it would have been and how one would have thought.[82] Evans-Pritchard referred to such a procedure as the "if I were a horse" fallacy of the introspectionist psychologist, assuming that he can simply imagine how evolution must have proceeded on the basis of his own imagined psychological processes.[83] According to Max Gluckman, the "if I were a horse" argument "refers to a story of a Middle West farmer whose horse strayed out of its paddock. The farmer went into the middle of the paddock, chewed some grass, and asked himself: 'Now if I were a horse, where would I go?'"[84]

Ironically, it turns out that this is what hunters actually do except that they don't need to eat the grass; they are perfectly capable of using their imagination, albeit they do mimic the movements of the animal as an imaginative aid. So the problem with the imaginative identifications of Spencer, Tylor, and Frazer was that they assumed that horses would think like themselves. Instead of entering into the world of the other, as in "if I were a *horse*," they attempted to accommodate the horse to themselves, as in "if *I* were a horse." If they had really tried to think like a horse, they may have realized that there was nothing false about primitive beliefs and that they were not based on limited knowledge but on a very different *kind* of knowledge, the knowledge of feeling and imagination that is expressed in concrete symbolism.

We have already seen that "thinking like the animal" is a very effective way of hunting and something that a good hunter in any era is likely to do. For our ancestors though, it may have provided the active, material basis for a much more extensive way of entering into the world of the other. That is, I am suggesting that the activity of hunting provided part of the evolutionary basis for the development of imagination in the context of a much greater participatory involvement with the "more than human world" than most of us have today.[85] Social imagination in relation to other people must have been important too, going back to the origins of shared intentionality and gestural communication. If, as I have proposed, humans began to symbolize their social relations via the use of personal ornamentation, then the use of ritual objects and the development of painted images would have furthered this process, becoming a means of symbolizing *spiritual* relations, a means of embodying emotionally invested imagination. Thus early religious practices too would have involved thinking oneself into the mind of the other and the other into the mind of oneself, not with the disembodied concept of mind we have today but as an embodied mind in which mutual identity between creatures is a form of inhabiting and being inhabited by the other via an imaginative identification conceptualized as a spirit realm.

The Lion Man Revisited

With all this in mind, we may be able to understand a little more about the enigmatic and emblematic figure of the Aurignacian Lion Man with which I began my story of the origins of symbolic imagination. While many aspects of its meaning must remain forever mysterious to us, it has at least become less opaque through this exploration of the context of thought in which it may have been created. One particularly apposite example occurs in Lienhardt's report of the Dinka people of Sudan who believed that "some men are really lions and can change into lions—they suppose that the outward form changes, but the essential nature remains the same. A person human in outward appearance may therefore be *in his nature* an animal of some kind."[86]

Jonathan Z. Smith refers to Lienhardt's account as "neither contradiction nor metaphor but rather a mode of expression between the figurative and the literal" which seems close to what I mean by a concrete symbol.[87] These beliefs evidence a world view in which the distinctions between humans and animals and the nature of personal identity are much more fluid than those we have come to take for granted. The animal-spirit-human hybrid proposed in Conneller's account of "becoming deer" is particularly suggestive in this respect.

Perhaps the Aurignacians used lions' heads in the way the Star Carr people used deer-antlers and many peoples of the North use the head and skins of bears, particularly in shamanic practices. However, there does not seem to be any fossil evidence of lions' heads that might support this hypothesis so it is more likely that the carving is an imaginative realization of a lion-man spirit.

Lions were certainly important animals for the Aurignacians, though, since they are often featured in Upper Paleolithic cave paintings, especially at Chauvet. One suggestion is that, since they were the dominant predator, a spirit identification with a lion would have been a way of becoming imbued with their hunting prowess. The dominance of lions is still an important aspect of their symbolic meaning today—they are the "king of beasts," hence their symbolic association with kings and empires from ancient Egypt to the British Empire. There is no need to look for any archetypal meaning here that is extraneous to the material affordances provided by actual lions. That is, their spirit qualities inhere in the living qualities of lions in the world; the psychological element is provided by the commonalities between human qualities, emotions, and aspirations—dominance, power, fearlessness, etc.—and the animals who embody and epitomize these qualities. So the Lion Man must be an animal-spirit in human form and/or a human spirit in animal form. The imagination that fashioned the material icon may then have been a way of bringing that spirit into the world.

Certainly it is likely that the qualities of the image were felt to concretely inhere in the materiality of the image. The life of the image is in the material from which it is made as much as it is in the mind and skill of the human who fashions it. It is, then, most probable that this was some kind of talismanic figure whose spiritual significance was embodied and brought forth in its material form.

Even though the Lion Man may have partaken of lion-like qualities which we still recognize today, we should remain cautious. Thousands of years of lion images and symbols have themselves created meanings that may not have been there before and these meanings exist in cultural contexts that are very different from the hunter-gatherers of the Upper Paleolithic. We can recognize our common humanity in our response to this figure, but there is no pre-existent form which is manifested by it or which can be appealed to as its source. It is a work of symbolic imagination and, as such, remains uniquely itself in all its materiality and mystery. It is no mere image of a lion-man, it is the thing itself. Kant's "thing-in-itself" to which Jung appealed as a correlative to archetypes is not to be found elsewhere in some unknown realm but is repeatedly expressed in the material activity of embodied human beings making sense of the world in which they find themselves. We do this by means of symbols which both create and are created by an imagination that is made possible by the capacities of our brains but whose contents are not reducible to the brain. In short, symbolic imagination is an emergent feature of human being in the world.

CHAPTER SEVEN

TWO KINDS OF THINKING

The discussion in the previous chapter makes plain that symbolic imagination involves a mode of thinking very different from the tradition of logical thought that has been developed and exported from Europe since the time of Plato and Aristotle. The dominance of the latter mode of thought, especially since Descartes and the Enlightenment, created enormous difficulties for early anthropologists attempting to understand the very different ways of living and thinking of the indigenous peoples they encountered in Africa, Australasia, and the Americas, and was hardly helped by the ideology of colonization in which this occurred. The overriding assumption was that these were "savages" who were at an earlier, more primitive stage of evolutionary development. So the only thing that Europeans might hope to learn from them was about their own prehistory, now happily superseded by the advances of civilization.

The recent resurgence of interest in animistic ways of relating to the world amongst anthropologists such as Tim Ingold, Philippe Descola, and Eduardo Viveiros de Castro, cultural ecologists such as David Abram, and philosophers such as Bruno Latour has an entirely different ethos. Inspired by the effort to overcome Cartesian habits of thought, anthropology is not simply in a better position to understand the life and thought of pre-modern cultures but also to learn from them. Belatedly, and in most cases tragically so, we are turning to indigenous people not for what we can teach them but for what they can teach us. It is not that we are likely to adopt their ways of thinking, let alone their practices and beliefs, since our cultural and environmental circumstances are obviously entirely different. It is more that learning to see the world as they see it helps free us from the shackles of rationality and Cartesian dualism in which our own culture otherwise encapsulates us.

Psychoanalysis stands in an awkward position in relation to these currents of thought. In one way, it has been in the vanguard of the challenge to rationality, undercutting the presumptions of belief in rational thinking by revealing deeper unconscious motivations that concern bodily and emotional desires unacceptable to consciousness. The study of dreams and, in Jung's case, visionary fantasy has revealed the importance of non-discursive modes of symbolism and the links between these and mythology, fairy tales, and the beliefs of non-Western cultures. In many ways, Jung strove to emphasize the value of these deeper currents of thought, to warn of the dangers of becoming cut off from them, and to encourage his patients and modern Western culture at large to reconnect with these sources of spiritual meaning. Yet there is another side to all this. Not only does psychoanalysis remain dominated by Cartesian modes of thought that regard the psyche as "internal" and our emotional relation to the world and sometimes even to other people as "projection," it has also retained the old idea of this "other" mode of thought as primitive and therefore inferior, now transposed to the unconscious mind. The aim of psychoanalytic therapy, Jungian and Freudian alike, has been to make the unconscious conscious, to integrate more primitive modes of thought within conscious rationality—an expansion of consciousness to be sure, but one that leaves the dominance of Cartesian rationality unchallenged. Arguably, the psychoanalytic model of the mind transposes colonial hegemony to the psyche: "where id was, there shall ego be" could, with a little poetic license, be translated as "where the savage instinctual life of the primitive was, there shall the civilizing forces of enlightened consciousness prevail." Consciousness might therefore expropriate the valuable resources of the unconscious in a similar way that Westerners expropriate indigenous culture: aping their fashions, art, culture, and even their religious practices in a bohemian, New Age potpourri of dilettante romanticism.

Modern anthropologists might well wonder why psychoanalysts spend so much time wallowing about in the stagnant pools of nineteenth century anthropological traditions (I include myself here). For them, the idea of the primitive is long gone and few of them give much attention to the debates concerning "common mental endowment"

(Boas) or Lévy-Bruhl's conception of pre-logical participation.[1] Yet these debates remain alive and relevant for psychoanalysis for two reasons. Firstly, psychoanalysis retains a strong universalizing tendency, claiming to have identified common psychological features that can be discerned, as Boas put it in 1909, "not in the outward similarities of ethnic phenomena but in the similarity of psychological processes so far as these can be observed or inferred."[2] Secondly, as I have indicated, the idea of the primitive remains alive in psychoanalysis in its trajectory of individual psychological development from a state of primitive unconsciousness to a more socialized consciousness. While no psychoanalyst today would associate themselves with the idea of the primitive as a racial or cultural notion, it remains deeply embedded in psychoanalytic thought and, in this way, is likely to subtly entrench out-of-awareness racist attitudes amongst the psychoanalytic community. Perhaps this is one of the reasons why our record on diversity is so poor.

My aim in this chapter is not to explore the socio-political issues of diversity in the analytic profession, important as they are, but to explore the biases and prejudices that still cling to the notion of what Jung aptly called "Two Kinds of Thinking." I want to argue against the notion that what I have referred to in previous chapters as concrete or iconic symbols and what might be called the "animated" way of thinking in which they occur is primitive, inferior or associated with infantile states of mind, psychosis, or the unconscious. Rather, I would suggest that, following Jung's more enlightened intentions, this other way of thinking is an invaluable component of all thought, for it is the language of emotion, spirituality, and embodied meaning. If it has been suppressed and relegated to early childhood, madness, and the so-called unconscious, it is only because it is so undeveloped in our culture due to our rational, Cartesian, and Enlightenment modes of thought. That Enlightenment rationality has yielded enormous results in the transformation of the material environment through science and technology is not in doubt. As one aboriginal Australian reacted when a naïve tourist asked if they still hunted in the traditional way, "Why would we use bows and arrows when we can use rifles?"[3] Yet the cost has been high—in the loss of connection to the land and the life that teems within it, the spiritual uncertainty, anxiety, alienation and isolation of modern Western societies, and the devastation of the environment and indigenous peoples. So I think it is fairly safe to conclude that an important difference between ourselves and oral-indigenous cultures is that they have (or had) a much more sophisticated awareness of and language for their connectedness to the physical world that includes an affective and spiritual relatedness to the environment. By contrast, in the post-industrial world of Western societies, such states of mind are, at best, separated off into reservations such as religion and psychotherapy.

While psychoanalytic thinking regards this mode of thought as a more or less innate distinguishing feature of the unconscious, the second aim of this chapter and the next is to show that all forms of symbolic imagination are socially mediated by collective representations, a term introduced by Durkheim and taken up by Lévy-Bruhl in his discussion of *participation mystique* as a social rather than a psychological phenomenon. In psychoanalytic thinking, conscious rationality, the sunlit world of the ego, is held to be public, social, and objective, whereas the dark lunar world of dream and fantasy is held to be private, individual, and subjective, the province of the so-called "inner" world of the unconscious, another Cartesian division. By contrast, I want to show that this other way of thinking is equally social and equally organized by socially agreed rules that constitute the world in terms of a particular symbolic vision. The symbols of dream and fantasy are imagined things that are as socially constituted as the value of gold, jade, or shell beads.

Jung: Directed Thinking and Fantasy-Thinking

I begin my discussion of these different ways of thinking with Jung's contrast between directed and undirected thinking made at the outset of the ground-breaking book that marked the parting of the ways between Jung and Freud in 1912, *Wandlungen and Symbole der Libido*.[4]

Jung defines directed thinking as carried out more or less in word form and directed wholly to the outside world. It is therefore reality-thinking "which adjusts itself to actual conditions,"[5] the language of practical activity and communication with our fellows.[6] Non-directed thinking proceeds by means of trains of images and spontaneous reverie; it leads away from reality into fantasies of the past and future and (with a nod to Freud's theory of wish-fulfillment) it arranges things as one would like them to be. Thus, it is typified by dreaming. In sum,

> The former operates with speech elements for the purpose
> of communication, and is difficult and exhausting; the
> latter is effortless, working as it were spontaneously, with
> the contents ready to hand, and guided by unconscious
> motives. The one produces innovations and adaptations,
> copies reality, and tries to act upon it; the other turns away
> from reality, sets free subjective tendencies, and, as regards
> adaptation, is unproductive.[7]

Jung equates directed thinking with scientific thinking by
which he means modern, post-Renaissance science. Echoing Boas'
distinction between a universal "mental endowment" and variable
"mental characteristics," he argues that although people in the past
were just as energetic and intelligent as us, it is only in the modern era
that we have directed our intelligence to "material knowledge." To the
classical mind, everything was still saturated with mythology.[8] Thus,
non-directed thinking is the language of myth, symbol, and dream.

Unfortunately, Jung's own thinking was saturated with the
presuppositions of his time and his characterization of the two modes
of thought is biased towards the notion that directed thinking is the
mark of "progress" and therefore somehow superior. Fantasy-thinking
is seen as "primitive" thinking in which are included not only the
indigenous hunter-gatherers of Africa, Australia, and the Americas but
the classical world of the "ancients," all of which are equated with
children via the formula that ontogeny recapitulates phylogeny; thus
the childhood of the species is repeated in the childhood of modern
individuals. Drawing on the example of mythological depictions of the
sun with wings or little feet, Jung opines, "It needs no very elaborate
proof to show that children think in much the same way. They too
animate their dolls and toys, and with imaginative children it is easy
to see that they inhabit a world of marvels."[9]

Although Jung revised this hurriedly-written work in 1950,[10]
it is surprising to see how much of what he had written forty years
earlier he allowed to stand. In relation to the psychoanalytic view that
fantasy-thinking, including the great myths of classical civilization is
"a fragment of the superseded infantile psychic life of the race,"[11] he
makes only one qualification:

> One must certainly put a large question mark after the
> assertion that myths spring from the 'infantile' psychic
> life of the race. They are, on the contrary, the most mature
> product of that young humanity. ... Myth is certainly

not an infantile phantasm but one of the most important
requisites of primitive life.[12]

Despite this, the model of undirected fantasy-thinking which turns
away from reality as opposed to directed rational thinking which is
directed outwards is left unrevised, as is the concept of "primitive life."

One other addition he made in 1950 attempts to qualify the
apparently pathological tone with which he had described fantasy-
thinking in 1912. Then he had described it as bound to produce an
"overwhelmingly subjective and distorted picture of the world" if not
constantly corrected by adapted thinking. Now, he adds that "the inner
motive that guides these fantasy-processes is ... itself an objective
fact" rooted in the instinctual, archaic basis of the mind.[13] Yet this
shows that he is still wedded to an evolutionist outlook for he continues,
"Just as the body has its evolutionary history and shows clear traces
of the various evolutionary stages, so too does the psyche," and, for
further elaboration, he refers his readers to his major 1947 paper "On
the Nature of the Psyche."[14]

In his efforts to rescue undirected thinking from the pathologically-
tinged notion of being overwhelmingly subjective and distorted he
has to resort to claiming that "subjective fantasy" is derived from
"an objective fact" which risks making the subjective/objective
distinction meaningless. The contradiction can be avoided by showing
that the two kinds of thinking refer to different aspects of reality,
neither of which can be encompassed by the division between inner-
subjective and outer-objective. It is only because Jung still thinks that
reality has to be objective to be real that he needs to insist on the
objectivity of the psyche. By locating symbolic forms of thinking
(fantasy-thinking) in an internal Cartesian mind rather than in our
engagement in socially organized worlds of collective intentionality,
Jung risks blurring the boundaries between "mental endowment"
and "mental characteristics." That is, the "archaic" forms of fantasy-
thinking become part of our inherited human endowment while
directed thinking becomes a "mental characteristic" possessed only
by modern civilization.

The alternative is to recognize that *both* forms of thinking are
constituted by what Wittgenstein called "forms of life," referring to
the social contexts in which language is used, and that these are public
forms that have to be appropriated by the individual to be meaningful.
Dream and fantasy images don't come from "the unconscious"; they

come from the socially mediated world of constitutive meanings. Similarly, Wittgenstein famously denied the possibility of a private language, not only because language exists for the purposes of communication but because the criteria by which meaning is established are public and shared and therefore cannot exist as a purely private and subjective enterprise. It is only by talking to each other and appropriating language that it becomes possible to structure our own thoughts *as* thoughts. No matter how abstract/rational or concrete/affective, all symbols arise from humans communicating, acting, and thinking together about their shared worlds.

It is only when fantasy loses connection with a symbolic system that it becomes "overwhelmingly distorted." As Winnicott said, "Should an adult make claims on us for our acceptance of the objectivity of his subjective phenomena we discern or diagnose madness."[15] The psychotic does not live in a world of private "subjective" meaning; they live in a world of *no* meaning. I learnt this many years ago when I worked on a psychiatric ward. I was fascinated by a woman who could not sit down because she had teeth in her vagina and was all set to interpret the meaning of this classic symbol of the *vagina dentata*. My supervisor had to carefully explain that this was not *symbolic* for the patient—it had no symbolic meaning because it was, to the patient, literally true. So here again we see the distinction between the concrete symbolism of animism and totemism in which symbols are living presences replete with spiritual meaning and the literalism of psychosis in which they are dead objects with no meaning at all.

Part of the difficulty in which Jung finds himself is that his definition of "directed thinking" is so narrow that it applies only to the most recent version of the modern mind, that of Cartesian science and industrial technology. This results in a somewhat bizarre characterization of "the ancients," by which he means the classical civilizations of Greece and Rome, as being capable only of undirected fantasy-thinking. In order to be fair to Jung, it is worth quoting the relevant passage in its entirety.

> Directed thinking or, as we might also call it, *thinking in words*, is manifestly an instrument of culture and we shall not be wrong in saying that the tremendous work of education which past centuries have devoted to directed thinking, thereby *forcing it to develop from the subjective, individual sphere to the objective, social sphere*, has produced a readjustment of the human mind to which

we owe our modern empiricism and technics. These are absolutely new developments in the history of the world and were unknown to earlier ages. Inquiring minds have often wrestled with the question of why the first-rate knowledge which the ancients undoubtedly had of mathematics, mechanics, and physics, coupled with their matchless craftsmanship, was never applied to developing the rudimentary techniques already known to them (e.g., the principles of simple machines) into a real technology in the modern sense of the word, and why they never got beyond the stage of inventing amusing curiosities. There is only one answer to this: the ancients, with a few illustrious exceptions, entirely *lacked the capacity to concentrate their interest on the transformations of inanimate matter* and to reproduce the natural process artificially, by which means alone they could have gained control of the forces of nature. What they lacked was training in directed thinking. The secret of cultural development is the *mobility and disposability of psychic energy.* Directed thinking, as we know it today, is a more or less modern acquisition which earlier ages lacked.[16] [italics added]

Jung seems so mesmerized by modern technology here that he fails to see that "transformations of inanimate matter" are definitive of human activity as far back as the first stone tools.[17] It is what makes us *Homo faber*. For example, the use of fire is a uniquely human transformation of inanimate matter which we now know dates back almost a million years. Recent discoveries have shown that both the European (Neanderthal) and African (Sapiens) descendents of *Homo heidelbergensis* were making complex composite tools as far back as 300,000 years ago involving the use of plant gum and red ochre. These required the use of heating, "implying a high level of knowledge, planning and thought."[18] In relation to tools dating from the Middle Stone Age in Africa (approximately 50,000 year ago and more), Lynn Wadley has shown

[s]ome cognitive executive steps cannot be taken without drawing on mental abilities such as abstraction, recursion, multilevel thought and cognitive fluidity. ... The entire process was intricate and demanded full attention, requiring the manufacturer to hold many things in mind simultaneously.[19]

It is hard to see how that could *not* be directed thinking. Perhaps, though, there is a clue to Jung's drastic limitation of directed thinking in a hypothetical interpretation mooted in Wadley's article that "creating compound adhesive from disparate ingredients may have been regarded as symbolic in the past." Here, the Jungian reader may be reminded of the transformations of alchemy that so interested Jung. So, what Jung is really referring to is that it is only in the modern era that directed thinking has become *separated* from undirected thinking, just as physics and chemistry have become separated from the symbolic transformations of alchemy. It is not that thinking has been forced out of the subjective sphere toward the objective, social sphere, it is that a great divide has rent the one from the other. What Jung must mean by "a real technology" is the technology of creating machines to carry out work previously done by humans—that is, creating machines in the image of humans, and, in turn, this has only become possible through seeing the whole of nature (including humans) as mechanical. The more we have created machines that operate like humans, the more we have come to see humans as operating like machines. All this has been achieved by the radical innovation of separating out the soul from Nature and placing it firmly "inside" the human mind. Jung has things exactly the wrong way round; it is not that thinking has been forced out of the subjective, individual sphere, it is that the soul has been forced *into* the subjective, individual sphere. In my view, this has little or nothing to do with the "mobility and disposability of psychic energy." Rather, it cries out for a socio-historical explanation of the cultural development of mind rather than a Cartesian psychology that restricts directed thinking to the treatment of the material world as soulless and inanimate (the so-called "objective world") and relegates all other forms of thinking to a dislocated "subjective" mind.

The Supposed Inferiority of Fantasy-Thinking: Historical Influences

Jung's characterization of the two modes of thought was influenced by three trends of thought which all conspired towards a view of fantasy-thinking as inferior to rational directed thinking: the enlightenment valorization of reason; the evolutionist assumptions of nineteenth-century anthropology; and Freud's theory of dreams as a regression to infantile memories and ways of thought.

1. The Enlightenment and the Romantics

If the findings of seventeenth-century science drove a wedge between science and religion then the eighteenth-century Enlightenment secured that division by relegating fantasy, myth, and superstition to a benighted medieval past now surpassed by the progressive triumph of reason. One area where this view was highlighted was in relation to the meaning and significance of dreams. Ever since Locke, philosophers had taken a "subtractive" view of dreaming according to which it lacked some element that waking thought possessed. In the eighteenth century, philosophers had contrasted the objective associations of waking thought which proceeded according to reason with the subjective associations of dreaming in which associations were made according to laws of similarity and analogy in place of the real relations between things.[20]

Such views were contested by the positive valuation of dream, imagination, and the "sublime" in Romanticism, a movement that emerged at the end of the eighteenth century, especially in England and Germany, in reaction to the excessive claims for reason made by the Enlightenment. Romanticism invoked imagination in terms rather similar to the unconscious and regarded dreaming as a source of inspiration for poetry, spectacularly illustrated by Coleridge's *Kubla Khan*, the product of a dream whose conclusion was lost when the inspired reverie in which Coleridge wrote out the poem was interrupted by a visitor. For the Romantics, *Kubla Khan* was evidence that there was "no real abandonment of intellectual action" in the sleeping mind.[21] Rather than seeing the dream as a lower, derivative condition of waking consciousness, it was viewed as a higher state, "more appropriate to the language of the soul than natural language and infinitely more expressive."[22]

While both Jung and Freud were influenced by German Romanticism, they were trained as natural scientists in the period when Darwin's theory of evolution was taking hold. For Jung, the conflict between these two modes of thought echoed through his entire opus as he attempted to give due weight to both sides. Freud maintained a much less ambivalent allegiance to positivist science but managed to achieve an apparently seamless and subtle integration between the two trends, often switching from scientific to poetic modes at difficult points of his argument.[23] The art of his considerable rhetorical gifts enabled him to create an apparently scientific narrative that was simultaneously a work of literature, winning him the Goethe Prize for literature in 1930. Hence the homage paid to him by novelists such as D. M. Thomas in literary narratives written as Freudian case-histories.[24]

2. Evolutionism in Biology and Anthropology

One of Freud's important early influences was the neurologist Hughlings Jackson who conceived the human mind in terms of a hierarchical series of functional levels with "higher" voluntary functions overlaying and keeping down the more involuntary "lower" ones that had been superseded in the course of evolution.[25] In 1876, Jackson's teacher, Thomas Laycock had argued that, in dreams, we reverted beyond our immediate ancestors to a "substrate of the race acquired during savage life in long-distant ages."[26] This view was echoed by Nietzsche and quoted by Jung in "Two Kinds of Thinking."

> As man now reasons in dreams, so humanity also reasoned for many thousands of years when awake; the first cause which occurred to the mind as an explanation of anything that required explanation was sufficient and passed for truth ... it is the foundation upon which the higher reason developed.[27]

Thus waking thought was considered to be an evolutionary development of dream-thought which was seen as a relic of the primitive thought still practiced today by the savage races. By studying these phylogenetic remnants it should be possible to construct the evolutionary history of thought towards its highest level of development: modern science.

These were the assumptions underlying the work of nineteenth-century anthropological theorists such as Frazer who outlined a progression of stages of thought in which magic was superseded by religion which was now being superseded by science. Tylor, who coined the term *animism*, thought that belief in magic and spirits was the result of a misapplication of the association of ideas so that (as in dreaming) mental subjective associations are taken to be real. These beliefs operated on the principle of likeness (analogy) and association. Thus, in magical thought, things which resemble each other are believed to be causally connected with each other. Implicitly, then, thought based on analogy and association (which must include metaphor and symbol) is characterized as inferior or, perhaps, is only allowable as modern if there is a clear recognition that such thought is *merely* metaphorical, clearly prefaced by an *as if*.

In 1904, Lévy-Bruhl proposed a rather different model, albeit with the same assumptions that primitive thought was inferior to modern thought. Tylor and Frazer regarded the thinking of native peoples as primitive in the sense of rudimentary, in the same way that their tools were rudimentary; they made the best use they could of logical thought based on cause and effect but arrived at the wrong conclusions through lack of knowledge and experience. Lévy-Bruhl proposed that the difference was not one of degree but one of kind. Primitive peoples thought in a qualitatively different way because they were "pre-logical," which he later clarified to mean that their way of thinking was informed by entirely different principles than those of logic. These principles were those of mystical participation. And even though he thought that this was a "lower" form of thought that had since evolved into "higher types," he admitted that "our most familiar concepts nearly always retain some vestige of the corresponding collective representation in pre-logical mentality."[28]

While Jung made considerable use of the concept of *participation mystique*, he carried over from Lévy-Bruhl its evolutionist baggage and invariably regarded it as a primitive state of mind associated with the (erroneous) projection of psychic contents onto the world. His notion of psychological individuation therefore maintained the same evolutionist assumptions of development to a "higher type" of thought in which projections are reclaimed and returned to the psyche where they really belong.

3. Freud and the Primary Process

The third influence on Jung's "two kinds of thinking" was Freud's distinction between the primary process of the unconscious, observable in dreams, and the secondary process of conscious waking thought. Freud's study of dreams led him to conclude that unconscious thinking proceeds in a way that abrogates the logic of conscious thought. The unconscious consists of instinctual desires (wishful impulses) that seek immediate satisfaction independently of each other and without any regard for logic. They are exempt from mutual contradiction so that in the unconscious there is no negation, no doubt, no degrees of certainty.[29] As Strachey explains,

> Similarities are treated as identities, negatives are equated with positives. ... The objects to which the conative trends are attached in the unconscious are extraordinarily changeable—one may be replaced by another along a whole chain of associations that have no rational basis.[30]

It is easy to see the similarity between Freud's description of unconscious thinking and Lévy-Bruhl's description of pre-logical thought in which one thing could be identified with another in complete disregard of logic and contradiction. So, to take an example quoted by Jung, when two women are discovered to have been eaten by a crocodile, it is believed that this was the work of a witch or sorcerer that was *identical* with the crocodile, while at the same time being distinct.[31] The same way of thinking is apparent in the Dinka belief that men can transform themselves into lions and that there are lions existing in the form of men. Lévy-Bruhl's most famous example of this kind of pre-logical identity was derived from an anthropological report of the Bororo people, a South American tribe whose members claimed to be parrots—not that the parrot symbolized their identity or that they would become parrots after death but that here and now they were both human and parrot at the same time.[32]

These identities are examples of condensation and displacement, the major mechanisms identified by Freud in the construction of dream images. So just as many disparate images or thoughts can be condensed into a single image, the same thought or idea can be displaced into a series of different images, all referring back to the same thing.

Freud's discoveries seemed to offer empirical validation to the speculations of Laycock, Jackson, and Nietzsche. Yet, while both Jung and Ernest Jones drew on Freud's remarks concerning the connection between the psychology of individual childhood and the childhood of the species, Freud himself was rather more circumspect.[33] He preferred to stick to his own data gleaned mainly from the analysis of adults and only rarely made forays into anthropological speculations such as *Totem and Taboo* (which he later dismissed as "something I dreamed up one rainy Sunday afternoon.")[34] In *The Interpretation of Dreams* Freud tentatively suggests a "probable" development in the history of thought from symbolic *identity* to symbolic *connection*. "Things that are symbolically connected today were probably united in prehistoric times by conceptual and linguistic identity. The symbolic relation seems to be a relic and a mark of a former identity."[35]

Some years later, in the *Introductory Lectures*, he suggests that the history of the development of thought may be seen in reverse through the process by which the dream work "submits thoughts to a regressive treatment and undoes their development."[36] The earliest stage would have been sensory images to which words were attached and the words eventually became thoughts. The dream "harks back to states of intellectual development which have long been superseded—to picture language, to symbolic connections, to conditions, perhaps, which existed before our thought-language had developed."[37]

It is interesting that Freud does not speculate as to when this development may have occurred and he certainly does not link it to any humans existing today. Given his views about the "primitive horde" as the original social organization of humans, an idea he took from Darwin, it seems more likely that he was thinking in terms of the distant origin of the species from a common ape-like ancestor rather than the more commonplace equation between primitive thought and that of people living today (or even our Paleolithic ancestors). He certainly accepted the notion that ontogeny recapitulates phylogeny and expressed the hope that it might be possible to penetrate into the phylogenetic prehistory of the human race as well as the individual prehistory of childhood through the study of the dream-work; however, he was scrupulously careful not to equate the two, something which would only be possible if psychoanalysis were able to distinguish "which portion of the latent mental processes is derived from the individual prehistoric period and which portion from the phylogenetic one."[38]

This was an attractive proposition, indicative of the excitement that accompanied the early years of psychoanalysis. The investigation of the unconscious seemed to open up a vast uncharted territory with the promise of hitherto unsuspected discoveries. Even though Freud was more cautious than his followers, he too seems not to have noticed a potential flaw in his reasoning that would vitiate these hopes—the assumption that the latent processes of the unconscious mind can be equated with the phylogenetic past. Why should it be that only the conscious, rational part of the mind had evolved rather than the entirety of human mental functioning? This is where the implicit influence of Hughlings Jackson remains apparent—the notion that the higher voluntary functions of the mind "keep down" lower functions belonging to our evolutionary past. Yet this assumes that those lower, unconscious functions continue to exist unchanged, as if only one part of the mind evolved while the other primary, or primitive, part of the mind continued unchanged in its original phylogenetic aspect. At best, if the ontogeny-recapitulates-phylogeny motto were true (and it is has now been more or less abandoned), this would only apply to certain elements of development; it would still be necessary to already know what the phylogenetic ancestor looked like to recognize which elements were the remnants of the past.

Recent Reformulations

Freud's account of unconscious mental functioning has remained a fertile source for later psychoanalytic theorists, as has Jung's account of two kinds of thinking. Yet it has been difficult to shake off the hierarchical, evolutionist origins that imply that one form of thinking is "higher" than another. Freud was explicit that scientific thinking was the highest, most developed form of thinking possible and, while much of Jung's writing celebrates fantasy-thinking and the value of mythological thought, he continued to associate these modes of thought with notions of the "primitive." An alternative way of differentiating "two kinds of thinking" would be to distinguish between different modes of thought that are culturally variable in their emphasis but aspects of which can be found in all human cultures. Cultural anthropologist Clifford Geertz pointed out that it was absurd to imagine that *any* group of people could live in a world composed entirely of mystical encounters, as Lévy-Bruhl seemed to say, any more than they could live in a world composed entirely of practical action, as Malinowski seemed to say.

> The movement back and forth between the religious perspective and the common-sense perspective is actually one of the more obvious empirical occurrences on the social scene, though, again, one of the most neglected by social anthropologists, virtually all of whom have seen it happen countless times.[39]

Here I want to consider two recent reformulations of these different modes of thinking that avoid hierarchical polarization and show how different cultures may lay more emphasis on one than the other: Iain McGilchrist's account of the differences between right and left brain functioning and Michael Robbins' reformulation of Freud's primary process as "primordial mental activity."

1. The Master and His Emissary

Iain McGilchrist delineates two characteristic modes of thought that are closely associated with the neurological differences between right and left brain functioning. He reviews a vast array of neurological literature and the picture he demonstrates is necessarily complex.[40] Nevertheless, there are a number of striking resonances with the "two kinds of thinking" model. For example, there is evidence of left-hemisphere dominance for local, narrowly focused attention and right-hemisphere dominance for broad, global, and flexible attention;[41] the left brain registers abstract categories, while the right brain registers gestalt wholes and individual elements.[42] The right brain has an affinity with the bodily experience of emotion, is concerned with the relations *between* things, and is crucially involved in symbol formation since "it appears to be essential for the integration of two seemingly unrelated concepts into a meaningful metaphorical expression."[43] On the other hand, the left brain is dominant in dealing with abstraction; its "superiority for language stems from its nature as the hemisphere of *representation*, in which signs are substituted for experience."[44]

Although it is obviously the case that *both* modes of functioning must be active in everyone at all times, McGilchrist argues that some people and some cultures lean more heavily on one mode of functioning than the other. McGilchrist has a rather misleading tendency to "anthropomorphize" the brain, writing as if the hemispheres are themselves thinking agents or homunculi. For example, he says, "the right brain sees the whole" or "the left brain … tends towards a slavish following of the internal logic of the situation."[45] This form of expression endorses an internalist, Cartesian view of the mind that is in danger of equating mind with brain. Yet this is not, I think, his intention. He is not simply equating modes of thought with the neurology of the brain since he is also concerned with cultural styles; the second half of his book turns to art and literature to show how what he calls "left brain functioning" has become over-dominant in modernist culture. His argument is that once certain modes of thought become dominant, they are likely to carry neurological consequences. If, for example, a particular individual or culture over-relies on mental faculties whose neurological correlates are primarily in the left brain, then it is likely that will engender further consequences due to the overall biases in each hemisphere's functioning. So, for example, certain styles of thought that heavily utilize logical, discriminatory thinking are likely to entail emotional detachment and an inability to attend to the wider picture. Ways of thinking are not caused or explained by the brain but they can only function according to the brain's neurological architecture which may carry with it certain limitations, a sort of side-effect.

One of the advantages of McGilchrist's model is that it is entirely free of the old hierarchical assumptions that have dogged psychoanalysis. If anything, he reverses them since he considers that, because of its overall integration, the right brain should be "the master" while the left brain acts as its "emissary." But if there is a ground of being here, it is to be found not in the brain nor deeper in the unconscious realm of instinct or archetype but in the manner that we relate to the world in which we find ourselves. The brain is simply one vital element in the emergence of mind.

Allowing for the metaphorical anthropomorphism I have already mentioned, McGilchrist's summary echoes many of the distinctions I have been discussing between mechanistic and animistic approaches to the world.

> I believe the essential difference between the right hemisphere and the left hemisphere is that the right hemisphere pays attention to the Other, whatever it is that exists apart from ourselves, with which it sees itself in profound relation. It is deeply attracted to, and given life by, the relationship, the betweenness, that exists with this Other. By contrast, the left hemisphere pays attention to the virtual world that it has created, which is self-consistent, but self-contained, ultimately disconnected from the Other, making it powerful but ultimately only able to operate on, and to know, itself.[46]

The left-brain tendency towards a narrow focus of attention and the registration of separate elements make it very difficult for patients with right-brain damage to perceive things as a whole. Murray Stein's reformulation of Jung's directed and non-directed thinking as solar and lunar consciousness makes a similar distinction. The imaginative mind (of lunar consciousness) "is able to grasp symbols and work with them whereas the analytic mind stands helpless and puzzled before them and often tries to make sense of them by dividing and subdividing, by cutting them to pieces."[47]

This difference is passionately expressed by Patricia Vinnicombe in Peter Amman's film about South African San rock art, *The Spirits of the Rocks*. Vinnicombe was a white South African who had been fascinated by rock art since she was a child. As an adult, she wrote a seminal text on rock art, *The People of the Eland*, and later moved to Australia where she spent the rest of her life living and working with and on behalf of aboriginal peoples. Here she reflects on the restricting limitations of white people's atomistic division of the world and ourselves.

> This whole concept of what is material, what is real, what is
> actual and what is spiritual is so enmeshed in both peoples—
> both Australian aboriginal and the indigenous peoples
> here. We separate these aspects off so readily in our culture
> and our educational background. Our upbringing is to keep
> things in boxes and keep them separate; and something that
> we could all learn from is to try and abolish the boundaries
> that we have created, abolish the boxes and think wider,
> think deeper, think taller and enjoy all the senses that they
> enjoy: rhythm, smell, you know, they just are combining
> everything in order to *draw* on this power. It's not just one
> aspect or one tangent that they're connecting with. They
> are sensing and feeling and thinking really widely and this,
> this is a great, a great example to have before us.[48]

2. Primordial Mental Activity

American psychoanalyst, Michael Robbins, has made an interesting
attempt to explain these attractive features of what he calls "spiritual
cultures" by suggesting that they are more able to integrate what he
calls "primordial mental activity" (PMA).[49] His definition of PMA
is like Freud's primary process but he contrasts this with thought
in a way that is unlike Freud's ethnocentric definition of secondary
process. He allows for different modes of thought which are more or
less in touch with PMA. Robbins considers that the mental capacities
of PMA are already fully functional at birth and continue throughout
life as a core process without being transformed into thought, albeit
they are a continual underpinning to thought occurring during waking
life as well as in sleep and dreaming. PMA is the body's mind. It
is driven by raw affect and is sensory-perceptual; it is concrete and
holistic and does not observe logical distinctions involving time,
space, and causality.[50] Things experienced in PMA are experienced
as an actual happening rather than as a mental event, and its concrete
sensory-perceptual-somatic-motor expressive quality distinguishes
it from the reflective subjective experience of representational
thought. Robbins thus seems to be describing a state of unreflective
consciousness that we share with other animals: awareness prior to
any form of thought at all.

Echoing Abram and McGilchrist, he argues that Western modes
of thought tend to suppress PMA whereas spiritual cultures use a
mode of thought that is better able to integrate it. In Western cultures,
phenomena such as hearing voices, having visions, or out-of-body

experiences and the like are regarded as signs of psychosis and, for the past two hundred years or so, persons having these kinds of experiences have been locked away and shunned either physically in institutions or, more recently, psychically, by the use of psychotropic drugs. In spiritual cultures, these are understood in an entirely different way.

> Such cultures integrate PMA with thought in a dialectical way that provides controlled access to it ... and utilize the result in the service of establishing and maintaining cohesion and harmony in the collective community. ... While the kinds of mental activities that are called psychotic in western culture are not so labeled in spiritual cultures, such cultures do identify persons who are out of harmony with the community, nature and the ancestral world, and attempt to heal them.[51]

Anecdotal evidence suggests at least some of those diagnosed as schizophrenic in our culture do much better in shamanic cultures. Often their illness is regarded as a sign that they are potential healers themselves and being treated as such provides a means of making sense of their disturbing experiences.[52] African methods of healing are likely to make use of communal and bodily activities such as drumming and dancing and these are likely to be integrated into ritual practices expressing beliefs about the spirit world.

One of the most important elements of Robbins' argument is that the appreciation and utilization of those aspects of the mind he calls PMA depends on processes of cultural acclimatization. Children in indigenous spiritual communities are inducted into certain modes of thought that make more sense of PMA whereas Western children are taught to ignore and disregard it, as I suggested earlier in relation to how children learn to think of their dreams as imaginary phenomena occurring in their heads. Psychoanalytic therapy often involves a kind of re-education in which patients learn to relate to their dreams, their emotions, and their bodily experience in a different way that makes them available for symbolic meaning. The form of meaning is, of course, quite different from that practiced by African healers, not least because psychoanalysis takes place within an entirely different milieu. Nevertheless, all cultures require some kind of symbolic system into which PMA can be integrated. This way of looking at the matter explains why different theoretical models within psychoanalysis can be equally effective. It is not this or that interpretation that matters—it is the art of formulating the bodily, affective states in which PMA is rooted as modes of thought. We might call this a training in symbolic imagination, and, if McGilchrist is right, this is a mode of thought that draws more heavily on neurological functions associated with the right brain than the left.

This is not simply about interpretation in the sense that the "raw material" is the same. We are not merely trained to understand our dreams in a particular way; the interpretation constitutes the form and content of the dreams themselves. We do not just *think* differently; our thinking constitutes the kind of experiences we have as well as what we make of them. For this, the term interpretation is too narrow; it would be more appropriate to think in terms of socially generated schemas or models that construct our individual experience in particular cultural ways.

Formulating Affective States

The creation of meaning is an important theme in the developmental models proposed by the British psychoanalysts Winnicott and Bion in the 1950s and 1960s. Both models describe processes whereby bodily, affective states are transformed through infant-mother interaction. Winnicott locates the origin of the symbolic world of cultural experience in the intermediate area of shared experience between mother and infant, initially via transitional phenomena that are neither created (imagined) nor found (already existing).[53] In the light of emergence theory we can now recognize that Winnicott was referring to something *emergent*, just as grasping and conversational turn-taking are emergent (see Chapter 1). Winnicott shows that symbolic meaning too has to be scaffolded by the mother's recognition of the infant's gesture, enabling the infant to enter a world of meaning, initially via meaning something to another. Without sufficient early attunement, the child may become unable to make meaningful sense either of affective states (their own and other people's) or the shared symbolic world of culture. Winnicott insists that, in relation to the child's use of transitional objects, it is forbidden to ask "did you create it or did you find it?"[54] Space must be left for something which is neither subjective nor objective, indicating his intuitive sense of the limitations of Cartesian dualism in the area of symbolic imagination. His delineation of a world of cultural experience that is exempt from the requirements of "objective reality" implies a distinction similar to those of Jung, Langer, and McGilchrist, between directed discursive thinking, subject to the criteria of analytic discrimination (e.g., "did you create it or did you find it?"), and the non-directed, non-discursive thinking that occurs in relation to culture, the arts, and religion.

Bion's theory of thinking also relies on the role played by the mother in enabling the infant to make sense of their own experience.[55] He designates the contents of "raw experience" as "beta elements" which the mother's "alpha function" transforms into meaningful "alpha elements" suitable for thinking, including dreaming. Bion regards beta elements as a kind of proto-thought without a thinker; only through the containment provided by the mother does it become possible to think one's own thoughts which, most fundamentally, consist of affective states that require alpha function to become thinkable. This suggests that thinking is an emergent process, somewhere between the early emergent patterns of action discussed by Hogenson and Hendriks-Jansen and the more sophisticated appropriation of language discussed by Vygotsky. There might also be a link with Knox's image schemas here. Knox does view these as patterns of relational interaction although she does not make explicit the influence the mother's own image schemas must have in the way the infant comes to conceptualize their world. In this sense, formulating experience is more than thinking since it involves bodily action as well—the way we use (and do not use) our bodies in relation to how others use their bodies in relation to us.

Bion proposes that if beta elements are unable to find a container they cannot become thoughts and so are suitable only for evacuation. In Chapter 3, I discussed an example of this state of mind in relation to the man who dreamed of fucking a cathedral. Inevitably this makes it difficult to adapt to the demands of living since it is not possible to tolerate emotional states, let alone think about them. Such a person becomes, in Clifford Geertz' vivid phrase a "formless monster."

> The extreme generality, diffuseness, and variability of man's innate (that is, genetically programmed) response capacities means that without the assistance of cultural patterns he would be functionally incomplete, not merely a talented ape who had, like some underprivileged child, unfortunately been prevented from realizing his full potentialities, but a kind of formless monster with neither sense of direction nor power of self-control, a chaos of spasmodic impulses and vague emotions. Man depends upon symbols and symbol systems with a dependence so great as to be decisive for his creatural viability.[56]

Geertz's social perspective as a cultural anthropologist is very different from the individual perspective of the psychoanalysts and yet there are close similarities in their views. What Bion formulates in terms of one-to-one emotional containment by a responsive mother, Geertz formulates in terms of the need for socio-cultural meaning systems and rituals, but the implication is the same— humans cannot develop to maturity without a socio-cultural context within which meaning can be formulated. This implies that symbols come from the world, not from the mind or, rather, that a human mind without a symbolic world would hardly constitute a human mind at all. An additional strength of Winnicott and Bion's models is that they are culturally neutral; the particular form to be taken by the infant's induction into meaning is not specified. There is a great deal of leeway for different cultural patterns to be fashioned out of these simple gestures and beta elements as long as this occurs in a context of maternal attunement. This interplay between styles of child-rearing and cultural patterns adapted to environmental circumstances was extensively demonstrated by Erik Erikson in relation to different Native American societies, Nazi Germany, and mid-twentieth-century America.[57]

Symbolic Use of Cultural Images: An Example

Symbolic images play a key role in enabling the child to formulate their own and others' affective states. These are provided by the surrounding culture and therefore induct the child into specific cultural ways of thinking. In this example, taken from an infant observation, a three-year-old little girl was sitting on her mother's lap while she leafed through a magazine. On one page, there was an article about the film *Amadeus* with a large picture of the poster image for the film, featuring the menacing figure of Mozart's nemesis Salieri, shown entirely in black except for his eyes, with arms outstretched as if enticing someone to their doom. The little girl pointed at the picture and said, "Mummy looks like that sometimes." Mummy, to her credit, was unfazed by this unflattering comparison and simply remarked, "Yes, I suppose I do."

Now on the face of it, this figure does not look like anyone's Mummy but what the child was seeing was not a physical correspondence but an emotional one—an image that corresponded with her emotional sense of a generally loving mother subject to bouts of depression, rage, and distress, especially with the demands of two young children. The little girl was able to communicate her fear of her mother (enticing and threatening) who was able to accept and thereby contain this emotional communication for which the *Amadeus* image provided a form of symbolization; a complex intersubjective affective state could become encapsulated in an image. In Bion's terms, a beta element was transformed into an alpha element through the mother's alpha function ("I suppose I do.") and thereby became an element suitable for use as a dream thought. Similarly, children frequently dream of witches but how could they do so if there were no witch narratives and witch images to furnish the substance of the dream?

Now a Jungian archetypal interpretation of this situation would point to an underlying archetype behind the image—the terrible devouring mother perhaps. Witches, dragons, enticing black magicians—these are merely images, representations of the thing-in-itself. But what is this thing-in-itself other than the unformulated affective experience which the image gathers together into a thinkable symbolic form? That is, the image constituting the archetype is emergent from an interpersonal affective situation. Interaction is primary, structure is secondary, as the Boston Change Process Study Group (BCPSG) argues.[58]

Nor, of course, are these images merely symbols in the sense of *as if*. No one was ever frightened by an as-if witch; the witch is frightening because she is real. In that sense she is a presence rather than a representation. The witch's power may be depotentiated by means of a device like "it's only a story," a repeated ritual in which the spell cast by the frightening witch is dissolved by being reduced to an image. In other words, turning affectively charged presences into symbols is a culturally specific means of containing affective states, possibly one that makes most sense in literate cultures in which the differentiation between representations and things is a familiar one. At any rate, culture provides the means that makes this possible and thus scaffolds basic affective states into forms of affective cognition that are extended and distributed across the social and material world. In this example, a material object (the two-dimensional picture) is mediated by a social interaction which creates a local habitation and a name for what, until that point, has been an unformulated experience, an element of the unthought known.[59]

Matte Blanco: The Symmetry of Affect

Perhaps then, if there is something fundamental that might constitute an archetype, it is to be found in the affects themselves. Richard Carvalho proposes that archetypes consist of "affective dispositional cores" that he links with the Chilean psychoanalyst Matte Blanco's model of the "unrepressed unconscious."[60] Matte Blanco describes the five characteristics of the unrepressed unconscious in the now familiar terms of Freud's primary process: *displacement* and *condensation* (whereby all contents of the psyche are ultimately interchangeable), *absence of negation* (contradictions are not registered), *timelessness* and the *absence of space* (the lack of distinction between inner fantasy and outer reality). The common trait amongst all these characteristics is that they unite or unify things which for ordinary thinking are distinct and separate.[61] Matte Blanco argues that these characteristics of the unconscious constitute a *symmetrical* form of logic in which, ultimately, everything is the same as everything else, in contrast to the *asymmetrical logic* of what he regards as ordinary conscious thought. Matte Blanco does not simply propose two kinds of thinking but speaks of a series of *strata* in the mind ranging from pure asymmetry to pure symmetry, thus allowing for a range of differing degrees to which things are equated with each other (symmetry) or discriminated from each other (asymmetry). Furthermore, one of the key elements in symmetry is *affect*; more intense affect creates higher levels of symmetry and tends towards infinity—an example of which is the feeling that *everything* is wonderful/terrible and always has been/will be, depending on one's mood. When we speak of being "flooded" with affect, this implies that our capacity to distinguish and discriminate one thing from another is overwhelmed, the distinctions being dissolved in the undifferentiated flood.

Matte Blanco describes numerous examples which are highly redolent of some of the features of thought associated with concrete symbolism and *participation mystique*. Simply put, at stratum one, where asymmetry is highest, there is a difference between a man and a lion; at stratum two, a man may be like a lion; but at stratum three, where affect is more intense, feeling *like* a lion may become indistinguishable from *being* a lion. At an even deeper stratum, I may become identical with a lion or, in this illustration from Rodney Bomford, a wolf.

> In the fourth stratum emotional intensity becomes so great that it results in chaos and the almost complete destruction of rational thought. It would be expressed by somebody running on all fours and howling like a wolf. The metaphoric identity of the third stratum here becomes absolute without any accompanying sense of distinction. This fourth stratum is perhaps most clearly expressed in extreme psychotic disturbance, but it is important to realize that this stratum is within us all.[62]

Here we can see some of the difficulties that can arise from the apparent similarity between "the destruction of rational thought" and those modes of thinking, feeling, and being that are perfectly normal amongst indigenous hunter-gatherers. For example, the process of "becoming deer" discussed in the last chapter could be seen as an example of symmetrical logic not dissimilar to "howling like a wolf," as could totemic identifications such as "I am a parrot," the symmetry between men and lions amongst the Dinka, and a host of similar examples adduced by Lévy-Bruhl as examples of *mystical participation*. There is certainly an important similarity in that these identifications are often associated with high levels of affect but there is also a crucial difference: they are highly structured by forms of socially organized beliefs and activities that Durkheim called collective representations. In the case of psychotic disturbance these are entirely missing, hence the chaotic and psychotic form in which highly symmetrical mental states appear. This may be in part because the collective representations of Western society are overwhelmingly *asymmetrical* to the point where this has become seen as the norm; Aristotelian logic then becomes the yardstick by which all thought is to be evaluated. There is nothing inherent in Matte Blanco's model that requires this since he considers that all psychic phenomena manifest a combination of symmetrical and asymmetrical elements in differing mixtures that he calls "bi-logic." So if we are to apply Matte Blanco's bi-logic more widely, we need to make some adjustments that take account of the biases inherent within Western modes of thought.

It is noticeable that Rayner and Tuckett frequently refer to asymmetrical thought as "ordinary thought." This may be true for "us" but that is because the forms of thought characteristic of modern Western societies are unusually high in asymmetry due to the influence of scientific rationalism. That is, the mode of thought necessary for the scientific method dominates the way of thinking in our culture to such an extent that other equally ordinary modes of thought become sidelined with a taint of the supposed inferiority of being "irrational," somewhat akin to the way "received English" used to be seen as the correct form of speech despite the fact that most people did not speak like that. In our ordinary lives, we use symmetrical thinking all the time for the obvious reason that we are highly emotional beings, yet emotional thinking has been banished from the hegemony of what our collective representations tell us that "ordinary" thinking is. So, given that psychoanalytic practitioners recognize the limitations of rational thinking only too well, it seems odd that they should nevertheless use this as the yardstick of "ordinary" thinking.

I would therefore question whether it is the case that symmetry is *necessarily* associated with unconsciousness and asymmetry with consciousness since that may well depend on the different forms taken by consciousness. It may be true, as Carvalho says, that "the logic of the unconscious is, in practical terms, indistinguishable from the logic of affect since they are effectively indistinguishable";[63] however, that does not mean that symmetry (or affect) is restricted to the unconscious. Put simply (and asymmetrically!), while the unconscious may be symmetrical, symmetry is not necessarily unconscious.[64] Clearly, the balance is rather different in cultures whose "ordinary" thought regularly disregards Aristotelian logic and makes use of higher levels of non-discursive symbolism. The link that Matte Blanco makes between affect and these more symmetrical modes of thought reinforces my argument that the spiritual beliefs and practices of indigenous peoples are ways of symbolizing affect. It also follows that cultures who utilize this alternative logic in their modes of thought are bound to be closer to emotions, sensations, and the body. As Vinnicombe says, they think *wider* and enjoy all the senses because they have the conceptual means of doing so.

As Carvalho shows in his clinical examples, this is very much what he enables his patients to do through using his own psychoanalytically derived language to make sense of their emotional states. In that respect, the sense that psychoanalytic theories make of affective experience can be transformative, not through the colonization of the id by the ego, but through an increased, more flexible symbolic capacity in the ego itself that enables affective states to be apprehended and enriched by the multi-dimensionality of symbolic form. Whether this means that they are more conscious or simply conscious in a different, more self-reflexive way is another matter.

In this respect, it is interesting that Matte Blanco came to think of the fundamental antimony as symmetry/asymmetry rather than unconscious/conscious and to suggest that the concept of the unconscious was misleading.[65] In my view, that is because it is difficult to escape the spatial metaphor of the unconscious as a "place" in the mind rather than simply a *mode*, as Matte-Blanco refers to it. There are similar difficulties with the distinction between "internal" and "external" reality since, as I have been at pains to show, there is nothing inherent in dreams, for example, to suggest that they are "inside" the mind (or that the mind *has* an inside!). Nevertheless, this does not mean that in cultures where dreams are real and include traffic between the spirit world and the human world there is no difference between dreams and waking life, as Lévy-Bruhl points out.[66] So it remains the case that in order to make sense of more highly symmetrical phenomena (e.g., where lions and men are equivalent), an asymmetrical structure of difference is *also* required.[67] As Carvalho explains, "the logic of symmetry can *only* be expressed asymmetrically, that is bi-logically" (personal communication, January 12, 2015).

Although bi-logic is culturally neutral, it is also, in a sense, culturally blind. That is, the role of culture in formulating thought in different ways is not considered. While bi-logic is a valuable tool for analyzing ways of thinking, it does not reveal how thought originally emerges. In evolutionary terms, this cannot, of course, be a simple development from more symmetrical/affective modes to more asymmetrical/logical ones since it is obvious that *all* organisms make distinctions between phenomena on the basis of what is meaningful to them and, in the case of champion problem solvers like crows and our own hominid relatives, many features of asymmetrical logic, such as cause and effect, must be highly developed, though not necessarily consciously so. The animal does not think "if I do this, then that will happen" but clearly *behaves* on the basis of such distinctions. Similarly, emotion is a primary means of registering difference in all animals so it cannot automatically be equated with symmetry.

There may be something in Robbins' suggestion that primordial mental activity is present at birth, and this would certainly be highly symmetrical, being derived, like Matte Blanco's much more sophisticated model, from Freud's primary process. But if so, this would be a peculiarly human form of mental activity, associated with our exceptionally long period of post-natal development and the opportunities for socially mediated learning this creates. Perhaps then, given that humans are the most emotional species and exceptionally immature at birth, bi-logic emerges from the symbolically mediated emotionality indicated by Bion and Winnicott.

Emotion and symbolic thought go hand in hand since our higher levels of emotion require robust forms of thought to contain them while symbolic thought also *promotes* a greater range and depth of emotional sensitivity, especially in relation to other humans. Hence, the association between symmetrical unconsciousness and affect in humans is in dynamic tension with the association between reflexive consciousness and symbolic (bi-logical) thought. It is only for a *symbolic* species that emotions can be associated with the loss of distinctions between one thing and another since biologically they are normally a means of registering what is meaningful and discriminating it as desirable/undesirable. As a symbolic species, we are necessarily a cultural species and it is culture that provides the means of expressing unformulated affective states in the symbolic forms of bi-logic.

Clifford Geertz argues that our high levels of emotionality requires us to maintain a fairly high degree of emotional activation without becoming overwhelmed by uncontrollable feeling; he describes the cultural means by which this is achieved through forms of extended affectivity.

> [T]he existence of cultural resources, of an adequate system of public symbols, is just as essential to this sort of process as it is to that of directive reasoning. And therefore, the development, maintenance, and dissolution of "moods," "attitudes," "sentiments," and so on—which are "feelings" in the sense of states or conditions ... —constitute no more a basically private activity in human beings than does directive "thinking." ... We acquire the ability to design flying planes in wind tunnels; we develop the capacity to feel true awe in church. A child counts on his fingers before he counts "in his head"; he feels love on his skin before he feels it "in his heart." *Not only ideas, but emotions too, are cultural artifacts in man.*[68] [italics added]

That is, it is impossible to detach affective states from the social (and cultural) context in which they arise and are given form.

Psychoanalysis as Distributed Affective Cognition

Here I would like to illustrate this by means of one of Richard Carvalho's clinical examples which shows how not only the analyst's understanding but his emotional responses (counter-transference) are structured by the system of public symbols that constitute psychoanalytic knowledge. The example concerns a remarkable instance of synchronicity that occurred between him and a patient.

> *One morning while awaiting a patient I had been seeing five times a week for some time, I was gripped by a powerful pain due to a muscle spasm in my anal sphincter, known as proctalgia fugax. Fortunately, by the time my patient arrived, I had recovered. To my astonishment, she described having had exactly the same symptom earlier that morning. Some time later, I was considering using the event for a conference paper about the basic matrix. The night before the deadline I was awakened by excruciating proctalgia so intense I feared I might pass out. Thinking felt impossible, yet I forced myself to free associate. My associations included fantasizing about being comforted like a baby, falling into nothingness, a waitress in a café that made me think of the breast and having been weaned at the age of six months. I then realized that the pain felt as if it were a clench around a small dense object, the size perhaps of a large pea, or then a nipple.*[69]

Now these associations may be free but they are by no means random. They are highly structured by the context of psychoanalysis, consisting in the disciplined use of a detailed, complex symbolic system of interlocking metaphorical and symbolic references in which Carvalho is a seasoned and gifted adept. Without this established cultural system of thought, it is highly unlikely that he would have had such a series of thoughts and associations (babies, falling into nothing, the breast, the nipple, etc.). There is a bodily experience of unmediated panic issuing in a visceral response (the muscle spasm in the anal sphincter) but this can only become thinkable by means of the system of collective representations called "psychoanalysis."[70] Here psychoanalysis is functioning as a form of *distributed cognition* in just the way Shaun Gallagher describes the way lawyers' knowledge operates within the distributed structure of the legal system (see Chapter 2).

The same could be said of the disciplined practices of spiritual cultures. They too are using a complex and subtle non-discursive symbolic system within which to think about and enact their affective experiences. Both are culturally organized systems of thought that are the expression of forms of life. In this respect, it makes little difference that one considers itself to be trading in the symbolic while the other insists that its presences are real and not symbolic. Nor does it matter much that I would designate both systems as "imaginal," whereas members of indigenous spiritual cultures would insist that the presence of spirits, for example, are real. It makes little difference because I would say that imagination is also spiritual and real. So there is at least a rough equivalence between the reality of the spirit and the reality of the imagination. In both cases, forms of thought that are contextualized within a particular system of meaning are experienced by the practitioners as actual. Carvalho's associations include some of the most profound emotional events of his life (events that turned out to correspond remarkably with his patient—hence the synchronicity) but these emotional events are nevertheless being structured in a particular way that, ultimately, is socially given. That is, they are collective representations.

And this brings me back to Lévy-Bruhl. Carvalho acknowledges the similarity between symmetrical states of shared affect and *participation mystique* but he is misled by the way Jung locates this form of thinking in the archetypal collective unconscious as a purely psychological function. This was not what Lévy-Bruhl originally meant. For Lévy-Bruhl, as for Durkheim, collective representations did not belong to the unconscious but to the social world. Primitive peoples think as they do, not because they live in unconsciousness, as Jung believed, but because they live in a society that structures thought in a different way, according to different criteria in which highly charged affective experiences are particularly important. So rather than *participation mystique* referring to a primary (unconscious) state of non-differentiation, Lévy-Bruhl uses it to refer to the socially organized perceptions, practices, and beliefs that are formulated and impressed on the mind in affectively charged conditions. And in a very different way this is what analysts do too. *Participation mystique* refers not only to experiences of extended affectivity but to a socially structured way of formulating those experiences that gives them meaning and fosters their socially structured occurrences. This is the theme of the next chapter.

CHAPTER EIGHT

PARTICIPATION MYSTIQUE REVISITED
(THINKING THE SPIRIT)

In this chapter, I want to use a revised account of Lévy-Bruhl's conception of mystical participation (*participation mystique*) as a way of gathering together several of the themes I have been exploring in this book. I began my discussion by arguing that archetypes do not provide a satisfactory explanation for the products of symbolic imagination, especially once the archetypal hypothesis has been reconfigured as emergent rather than pre-existent. George Hogenson's work in this area provided a starting point for an exploration of the mind as contextual, extended, enactive, and distributed via symbolic forms. After a brief foray through the possible evolutionary trajectories of the human species towards the emergence of a symbolic culture, including language, I focused on the nature of constitutive symbols that bring into being that which they represent in the context of the development of collective intentionality amongst human groups. The attempt to understand the earliest evidence of symbolic imagination in the paintings and figurines of the European Upper Paleolithic led me to recognize that this required entering into the very different modes of thought of hunter-gatherer societies, and this in turn led to a discussion of a variety of psychological approaches to two kinds of thinking, mainly stemming from or closely related to Freud's delineation of the "primary process." These latter themes stressed the intensity and complexity of human emotional life. This too is a central feature of the extended mind that I have referred to as extended affectivity.

I have already indicated how closely the primary process appears to mirror the characteristics of Lévy-Bruhl's description of the "pre-logical" thought of "primitive" peoples. I now want to show how

Lévy-Bruhl's discussion also provides a model for a mind that is extended, distributed, and affective, all of which are given form and meaning through the constitutive symbols that Lévy-Bruhl, following Durkheim, refers to as collective representations. *Participation mystique* thus provides a model for the emergence of symbolic imagination as a collective, social phenomenon before it can be a psychological one that is "internalized" or, to avoid the Cartesian metaphor, appropriated by individuals.

Of course, it is first necessary to strip away Lévy-Bruhl's evolutionist assumptions of "lower" and "higher" forms of thought. As I have shown, these assumptions cling to almost all the models of two kinds of thinking discussed in the previous chapter in the implicit hierarchy model that locates primary, symmetrical, non-directed fantasy thinking in the "unconscious" implicitly conceived as "below," and directed, secondary, scientific thinking in the "ordinary" mind of consciousness. This is apparent even in Matte Blanco's model in the way he locates a hypothetical pure symmetry in the unconscious and argues that the more symmetrical the thinking, the closer to this proposed unconscious. The very notion of "strata" of thought implies that one is built upon the other—the geological metaphor entails the notion of "lower" strata that are older than "higher" ones. Jung's well known dream of a multi-storied house in which the upper levels represent consciousness while the lower levels represent the historically archaic layers of the unconscious utilizes the same metaphor.[1]

The only model that entirely escapes this presupposition is McGilchrist's discussion of right and left brain functions. McGilchrist argues that these different modes of processing information are inherent to the human brain and therefore occur at all times in all people. He also argues that variations in the emphasis given to the different modes of thinking arising from these brain functions are cultural. Despite this, McGilchrist's approach is tied to the internalist presuppositions of a Cartesian mind by its neurological underpinnings.

By contrast, Lévy-Bruhl provides the link to a non-Cartesian formulation of mind in several ways: his notion of "participation" shows the way we do not experience ourselves as divided from the external world but feel that we are in participation with it as an active, living force, a view that Lévy-Bruhl designates as "mystical." Secondly, by rooting *participation mystique* in collective representations, Lévy-Bruhl shows the social origins of thought and thereby reveals how psyche and the social world are part and parcel of one another and come into being together through the emergence of constitutive symbols. Thirdly, Lévy-Bruhl emphasizes the affective and sensuous nature of "pre-logical" thought, thus including the body in the thinking process which in turn breaks down the Cartesian divide between mind and matter. The more we can see the way thinking is situated in the activities from which collective representations arise, the more we can see that the supposedly "ordinary" mode of Cartesian scientific thinking that dominates Western culture is just as much informed by collective representations as any other. The difference is that these are collective representations from which affect, the body, and our intuitive sense of participation have been deliberately and carefully screened out. Very useful for physics, no doubt, but inevitably limited for the study of psychology in which affect, the body, and participation in the world are basic elements of our psychic lives.

Collective Representations

Essentially, a collective representation is "a symbol that articulates and embodies the collective beliefs, sentiments, and values of a social group."[2] Furthermore, collective representations do not merely represent but actively form the way individuals think and feel. Durkheim argues that all thought is structured by collective representations so that even apparently "given" concepts such as time and space are collective representations that structure the way the individuals view and relate to their world. Collective symbols of this kind are expressions of humans' active engagement in shaping their own *Umwelt*—like Winnicott's transitional objects, they are both created and found. They are not, however, created by individuals but arise from the collective activity of social groups, transmitted from one generation to another as the symbolic matrix in which individuals are located.

Durkheim believed that what lay behind collective representations was the structure of society itself. So in the case of religious beliefs, that which a society represented as sacred was formed on the model of the group's social structure. Put simplistically, "God" is a representation of society, and religious rites and beliefs are ways of expressing and reinforcing the social realities of a particular society.

> Religious representations are collective representations
> which express collective realities; the rites are a manner of
> acting which take rise in the midst of the assembled groups
> and which are destined to excite, maintain, or recreate
> certain mental states in these groups.[3]

A modern example of this can be found in sports such as football. Football fans experience intense emotional states of excitement and euphoria on an alternating knife edge with desolation, despair, and humiliation. There is a high level of participation between the members of the crowd and the players on the pitch such that individual differences are eclipsed in the emotion of the moment. Since the game is focused entirely on winning or losing, it expresses and reinforces the values, norms, and beliefs of a society organized around achievement, social mobility, and competition and allows participants to experience the highs and lows of success or failure. It is thus a collective representation of group solidarity in a competitive environment, closely mirroring the social world and values of corporate capitalism of which it has become so inextricably linked over the past few decades. This example indicates that *participation mystique* in modern society is rather more than the "vestige" Lévy-Bruhl suggests.[4]

While Lévy-Bruhl took the idea of collective representations from Durkheim, he was less concerned with their sociological aspect than their role in creating modes of thought. For him, the important element of collective rituals was their affective aspect. He argued that it was because the objects of "primitive" representations were discerned in states of high affectivity, such as initiation, that they had a lasting impact, becoming cherished, formidable, and really *sacred* to the initiated.[5] This is somewhat similar to Terrence Deacon's argument for the establishment of symbolic language through ritual repetition except that, for Lévy-Bruhl, it is primarily affective intensity which impresses conceptions of the world on the mind rather than their repetition, although the fact of repeatedly participating in rituals must also have a significant effect. Since the rituals induce and contain intense emotional states, there is an incentive to repeat them; the affect itself becomes an important element of the social glue as well as becoming cognitively formulated through the constitutive power of social symbols.

Mystical Presences

The role of affect also indicates the "mystical" nature of "pre-logical" thought which is perhaps rather better rendered in Susanne Langer's terms as non-discursive symbolic thought or presentational symbolism. For example, the football game does not so much "represent" competitive social aspirations as "present" them; its participants do not think about the game symbolically but have a direct emotional experience of the highs of success and the lows of failure. In a very different way, I have argued that many of the beliefs and practices of indigenous peoples with regard to the animals they hunt, the plants they gather, and the land in which they live can be understood in terms of an affective engagement that presents its meaning rather than representing it. The meaning is expressed in the carrying out of the actions themselves rather than being thought of as separate from them in the way we usually think of symbolic meanings as being separate from the forms by which they are represented.

Lévy-Bruhl defines what he means by *mystical* as "the belief in forces and influences and actions which, though imperceptible to sense, are nevertheless real."[6] I would argue that these forces are primarily affective without being merely affective. I am not suggesting that "God" is a representation of affect in the way that Durkheim argues that God represents society. That would fail to take account of the constitutive role of (collective) symbols. Thus, belief in spiritual forces is an expression of affective states that have become symbolized via collective representations and thereby transformed, which includes taking on a social aspect.

This can be compared with Langer's view of the function of art. For Langer "art is the creation of forms symbolic of human feeling"[7] which makes

> the obscure or elusive [feeling] conceivable.[8] ... [A]rt fulfils a cognitive function that imparts knowledge, insight into the world of feeling *which would otherwise remain hidden*. Art achieves this aim by a process of *formulation*, i.e., by inventing forms which transform "felt activity (in) to perceptual quality."[9] [italics added]

There is a strong echo of this view in Lewis-Williams' reference to the images in cave painting making hidden presences visible, although Lewis-Williams does not reference Langer directly. Langer was particularly interested in music, and in our society music has become the art form which most closely resembles ritual in that the powerful emotional states it evokes are often expressed in the communal bodily activity of dancing.

In his later work, Lévy-Bruhl responded to his critics by dropping the term "pre-logical" and making a stronger connection between the mystical and the affective, as Mousalamis explains:

> Now affective, participation could be more easily explained both in its derivation and in its persistence. It derived from the mystical experience. The mystical was affective: the experience was 'the feeling ... of the presence, and often of the action of an invisible power.'[10] This experience involved two perceptions simultaneously: the sensory perception of physical things and the affective perception of the invisible power. The two perceptions 'intertwined and interlaced.' They intermixed continuously, and this intermixing was the experience of participation. It felt the mystical (the affections) to be in the physical world.[11]

Perhaps, though, this is because the mystical *is* in the physical world precisely because affects are physically experienced in the body but not confined to the body; they extend into the physical world where they are aroused and felt.

Mystical experience can sometimes be overwhelming in its affective power. As a schoolboy, I was fortunate to have an unusually inspiring religious education teacher who taught his classes about this quality of religious experience using literary and artistic analogies. One of these I have never forgotten came from *The Wind in the Willows*. In this scene, Rat and Mole encounter a vision of Pan, presaged to Rat in a song-dream. Both are overcome with a sense of *Awe*, described in vividly emotional and bodily terms.

> Breathless and transfixed the Mole stopped rowing as the liquid run of that glad piping broke on him like a wave, caught him up, and possessed him utterly. He saw the tears on his comrade's cheeks, and bowed his head and understood.
>
> Then suddenly the Mole felt a great Awe fall upon him, an awe that turned his muscles to water, bowed his head, and rooted his feet to the ground. It was no panic terror—indeed he felt wonderfully at peace and happy—but it was an awe that smote and held him and, without seeing, he knew it could only mean that some august Presence was very, very near. With difficulty he turned to look for his friend and saw him at his side cowed, stricken, and trembling violently.[12]

It is fascinating to see that this account of religious experience is centered on the encounter with a spirit animal (who also functions as a helper, enabling Rat and Mole to find a lost companion) and features a premonitory dream. Perhaps Kenneth Grahame had read some of the ethnographic accounts of the time or perhaps this came directly from the Greek mythology of Pan; either way, there is no hint of condescension towards the "primitive" here, and he is surely writing out of his own experience. Nor is there any split between matter and spirit or mind and body. Grahame's description is striking for its detailed references to the bodily aspect of the intense emotional state which the vision evokes: Mole is breathless, his muscles turn to water, he bows his head, his feet are rooted to the ground, and he sees that his companion is violently trembling.

Participation

Participation is not always so obviously affective though and is much more of a feature of ordinary modern life than Lévy-Bruhl allows. The "law of participation" refers to the way persons or objects are felt to be connected with one another in a "mystical" way that defies the logic of cause and effect. Dowson gives a concise illustration of what Lévy-Bruhl describes at length. Speaking of Kalahari Bushmen, he says, "Supernatural potency is thought to be everywhere, from healing dances and puberty rituals, animals and plants, swarming bees and the rain, to the vapor trail of a jet plane, tape recorders and travelling in a truck at high speed."[13]

While this is hardly the case in a Cartesian society that has de-souled the material world, it is not entirely absent either, not least in the relatively common experience of synchronicity, which I have previously described as "the feeling that the universe is alive."[14] Following Bruno Latour's claim, "We have never been modern,"[15] Alf Hornborg points out that animism is still alive and well in modern society:

> The notion that the world of objects and the world of subjects are separable, in any other than an analytical sense, has been an illusion from the start. ... [H]uman beings everywhere impute personhood and agency to entities which according to official modernist doctrine ought to be classified as objects (think of our favourite trees, houses, cars, teddy bears).[16]

Or, as the call-center worker at my car insurance company explained when I had to wait for her to update my policy, "My computer isn't liking me today." Although this is partially a joke, it implicitly relies on the sense that she and her computer are in participation in just the way that the theory of the extended mind suggests. And being engaged together in a shared activity, it makes sense for her to relate to her computer as having an affective agency ("not liking me") that flows together with her own frustration at the delay ("I am not liking the computer.") So here we see an implicitly symmetrical way of thinking expressing a muted affective experience in which "I don't like the computer" is equivalent to "the computer doesn't like me."

The notion of *participation mystique* captures this much more successfully than projective identification which starts from the notion that worker and computer are wholly separate and restricts the mind to an internal "space" in the worker's head; rather, this example reveals a field of activity and meaning in which there is no dividing line between psyche and world.

An equally common experience of participation occurs in the extension of the body boundary to include technological aids. Merleau-Ponty's description of the tip of the blind-man's stick being an extension of his sensory perception has become the most famous exemplar of this.[17] The same applies to the bodily extension that occurs when driving a car. While I am in the car my sense of my physical boundaries extends outwards to the boundary of the vehicle: if another car comes too close, I may flinch as if about to be hit. And if an accident occurs I am likely to say that "someone went into the back of me." Once we take the idea of an extended mind seriously, we begin to recognize that participation is in fact the normal state of affairs and it is only the peculiarity of our Cartesian world-view that blinds us to this. It is then no longer the "primitive" whose beliefs are strange and incomprehensible—it is *us*. We are the ones who are caught in an illusion of being separate from the world we inhabit. For the reality is that we are always in participation with whatever we are engaged with. As David Abram says: "We always retain the ability to alter or suspend any particular instance of participation. Yet we can never suspend the flux of participation itself."[18]

Mystical participation also refers to the apparently impossible states of identity that so perplexed Lévy-Bruhl whereby "things can be themselves and something other than themselves."[19] Arguably this is true of the car that is both itself and its driver in a way that is no more troubling than Lévy-Bruhl's most famous or infamous example, the South American Bororo tribe that claim to be parrots. In another example, Lévy-Bruhl regards it as inexplicable that the Huichol Indians treat corn, deer, and hikuli (a sacred plant) as one and the same thing. They are regarded not as *symbols* of one another but as actually identical. Lévy-Bruhl explains this as an affective state which is "felt by them" by virtue of their collective representations.[20] A clue may be found in the relation between the part and the whole:

> It is by virtue of participation that the eagle's feather possesses the same mystic qualities as the eagle itself, and the whole body of the deer the same as those in its tail, and it is by virtue of participation too that the deer becomes identified with the eagle's plume or the hikuli plant.[21]

Here we can see that the "logic" operating in these identities is one that is closely related to the formation of metaphor and symbol: metonymy. For Matte Blanco these are examples of the principle of symmetry which ignores any differentiating feature so that anything can be interchangeable with anything else.[22] It utilizes the same kind of associative links that we see in metaphors and symbols but in a different way. The condensation or symmetry is occurring at the level of language and classificatory thinking, driven by the same cross-modal fluidity that drives metaphor.

As a form of language, such condensations are quite familiar. Thus, we have no difficulty in understanding Flaubert's claim that "Madame Bovary, c'est moi." We understand that Flaubert is saying much more than he is *like* Madame Bovary or that she is "based on him." We understand perfectly well that Flaubert is saying that the character he had created is an expression of his life and character and, as such, she is in some sense identical with him. The same is true of Hazlitt's remark, "It is we who are Hamlet."[23] So it is not really incomprehensible that things can be both themselves and something other than themselves at the same time. This is in fact, the *sine qua non* of any dramatic performance when an actor *plays* Madame Bovary or Hamlet. The difference is that a Western audience has to "suspend disbelief" or make an implicit distinction between a metaphorical identification ("C'est moi") and a literal one, whereas the Bororo—and many other peoples—do not. This is an example of the way in which the two modes of thought are less separated in other cultures, and therefore special situations like the theatre do not require a special explanation.

Later anthropologists such as Evans-Pritchard and Lienhardt suggested that the way of speaking and thinking that Lévy-Bruhl had regarded as "pre-logical" referred to different aspects or points of view that could co-exist and that the identification had to do with "a special revelation of the Spirit."[24] This could be described as having to do with something that occurs "in imagination" as long as it is understood that the imagination is a special dimension of reality. It is for such truths that we still visit the theatre, watch films, or go to an art gallery. We regard the matters portrayed as fiction and yet they reveal to us aspects of our world that we cannot discover in any other way, and this brings the truth of art into close relation with the truths of religion.[25] These too can only be discovered through special means of revelation, often through the use of material artifacts, as argued by Matthew Day.[26]

A more glaring example of *participation mystique* in Western religion, on which Lévy-Bruhl was conspicuously silent, was the consubstantiality between man and God in Christianity. Jesus of Nazareth was simultaneously an ordinary human being and the Son of God. Later God, Son, and Holy Ghost became the Three in One of the Trinity. And, at least for Catholics, the Mass is not representationally symbolic but concretely, or presentationally, symbolic: the bread and wine *are* the body and blood of Christ.

So it turns out that *participation mystique*, supposedly a primitive mode of thought is characteristic of mythic, religious, dramatic, and artistic thought and is also the state of mind to which the fullest appreciation of music aspires—the capacity to lose oneself in the music and become "one" with it.

Jungian Views of *Participation Mystique*

This potential value in Lévy-Bruhl's approach was only partially grasped by Jung who followed Lévy-Bruhl in seeing *participation mystique* as primarily a primitive state of mind in which

> the subject cannot clearly distinguish himself from the object but is bound to it by a direct relationship which amounts to partial identity. This identity results from an *a priori* oneness of subject and object. *Participation mystique* is a vestige of this primitive condition.[27]

Jung must have taken this directly from Lévy-Bruhl who also uses the term *vestige* to describe the way "our most familiar concepts, nearly always retain some vestiges of the corresponding collective representations in pre-logical mentality."[28] For Jung this is something to be outgrown in the process of individuation. "The aim of individuation is nothing less than to divest the self of the false wrappings of the persona on the one hand, and of the suggestive power of primordial images on the other."[29]

Subsequently, many Jungians have related *participation mystique* to the psychoanalytic concept of projective identification, again as something that needs to be analyzed, enabling the patient to become more separate, an essential aspect of individuation. Some Jungians, though, have taken a more positive view, linking *participation mystique* with experiences of mystical union that, far from being primitive vestiges to be outgrown, are life-affirming, profound, and unforgettable experiences that are treasured for life. Mark Winborn's recent collection of papers on *participation mystique* indicates this more positive aspect even in the book's title, *Shared Realities*. He begins the book with one such memorable experience of his own in which he experienced a timeless communion with a falling leaf:

> After a few moments, which seemed to exist as an eternity ... the enchantment slowly dissolved. The leaf once again became just another leaf. However, the feeling of communion I shared with that singular leaf has now persisted over a number of years and I continue to experience the sensation that the leaf 'spoke' to me in that moment and invited me to participate in its journey.[30]

Having reviewed the generally negative views of *participation mystique* in Jungian psychology, Winborn links the concept with more recent analytic thinking in areas such as intersubjectivity, empathy, and reverie. He concludes his review with a discussion of Neumann's view of a unitary reality, the identity and sympathy of all things whose aliveness and significance is primarily experienced through feelings and intuition.[31] Neumann's views are strikingly in accord with the phenomenological critique of the isolated mind. He argues that inner and outer are merely categories of a conscious knowledge system, not reality, which has an underlying unity. He links *participation mystique* with a special type of knowledge he calls "knowledge of the field" which encompasses interactions between human beings, between human beings and animals, between human beings and things, and between animals and their environment.[32] This wide-ranging conception references several of the areas I have discussed including sociality based on cooperation and compassion, material engagement, and the interchangeable relations between humans and spirit animals. The notion of the field tallies closely with Ingold's reconfiguration of animism as an appreciation of

> the dynamic, transformative potential of the entire field of relations within which beings of all kinds, more or less person-like or thing-like, continually and reciprocally bring one another into existence. The animacy of the lifeworld, in short, is not the result of an infusion of spirit into substance, or of agency into materiality, but is rather ontologically prior to their differentiation.[33]

Several chapters in Winborn's collection of papers touch on this view of *participation mystique*, notably Deborah Bryon's account of her apprenticeship with Peruvian shamans.[34] Her use of the concept of *participation mystique* is poles apart from the undifferentiated primitive state of unconsciousness in Jung's usual use of the concept. Her description of the Q'ero medicine people's concept of living in *ayni* is more reminiscent of the Chinese concept of *Tao*; Jung would probably have seen this as referring to experiences of the Self. "The attachment that develops in a state of *ayni* is to the numinosity and vitality of the actual experience itself—the movement and exchange of sharing energy as part of being in the totality of *one world* in nature."[35] This is referred to both as a state of ecstasy and one of living in right relation to *Pachamama* (Mother Earth).[36]

Bryon emphasizes that the *p'aqos* are eminently practical people who eschew abstract concepts because they "can't grow corn with it." Rather they perceive and experience the world through their senses using a "heart-centered focus." For the *p'aqos*, a heart-centered focus literally means "attuning to what they are experiencing in their hearts, and sensing from that physical place with awareness."[37] The experience of *ayni* is essentially one of *feeling* in which affect is conjoined with collective representation. "[S]tates of *participation mystique* develop among members in groups that identify with a collective belief system, which fosters feelings of togetherness."[38]

What are we to make of such wide-ranging uses of the concept of *participation mystique*? Clearly, states of "oneness" are not all the same. Consider for example the distressing experience reported by a borderline patient who complained that on some days she felt as if she had lost all her boundaries and was unable to distinguish herself from the sky. Contrast this with the mystic who, after many years of meditative practice, has an experience that, while beyond words, is best described as being "one with the universe." Or, to take a third example, the ersatz version of mysticism that can be experienced by the use of hallucinogenic drugs, something which might be compared with the difference between climbing a mountain on foot and taking the cable car—the view may be the same but the experience is entirely different. Obviously, the difference is that the mystic has engaged in a disciplined practice in a communal context of collective meaning, as is the case with the Q'ero shamans. In Jungian terms, this could be described as the difference between training the ego to become open to the Self and a weak or non-existent ego being overwhelmed and flooded to the extent that there is a complete loss of differentiation. Any such training relies on a context of collective social meanings and beliefs that places the ego within a socially extended network of distributed cognition. Mystical traditions provide many such systems; the various schools of psychoanalysis provide several others. In this way, chaotic unformulated states of non-differentiation are structured by collective representations that offer ways of seeing the world that cannot be expressed in discursive logic—hence their apparently illogical aspect. The point I want to stress is that this cannot be described in purely psychological terms as a movement from primary process to secondary process or different strata of the mind; the difference is to do with participation in the symbolic forms of collective representations. This involves entering a structured social system that provides distributed cognition of potentially overwhelming affective experiences that extends far beyond what individuals alone can do. We should not forget the vast resources of Jung's library on which he drew for his apparently individual visions.

Socially Structured Meanings

Unfortunately, Jung ignored this due to the way he "psychologizes" *participation mystique*, severing the crucially important link with the social origin of collective representations that is fundamental to both Durkheim and Lévy-Bruhl. This was a serious loss that separated *psyche* from the social world and obliterated the social and material dimension of emotional experience. As Robert Segal puts it, "Where for Lévy-Bruhl 'primitive' thinking is to be explained sociologically, for Jung it is to be explained psychologically. 'Primitive' peoples think as they do not because they live in society but because they live in unconsciousness."[39]

Jung replaces the social group with "the collective psyche" and loses the sense of human participation in the group which is reduced to "unconsciousness." He desocializes collective representations so that they become merely "psychic contents."[40] In Jung's view, "the primitive" is unable to distinguish between the inner world and the outer world and so "psychic happenings take place outside him in an objective way" by means of "projection."[41] Furthermore, via mythological motifs, Jung equates collective representations with his own concept of the archetype.[42] In this way, he confuses the emotional processes which inform *participation mystique* with their public, symbolic representations so that he ends up putting the symbolic representations back "inside" the psyche as "pre-existent forms." This reduces social being to an internally located Cartesian psyche, thus losing the possibility of seeing how collective representations structure affective states. For it is only through engagement within a social-symbolic world that psychological/affective states can become represented and therefore structured and thinkable. Collective representations and their social mediation are, in Bion's language, the alpha function that transforms beta elements into usable thoughts, albeit here "thought" is to be understood not simply as intellectual thought but in a wider sense that includes being able to recognize affective states as meaningful and thinkable. This would include those mystical experiences that cannot be put into words but are nevertheless contained within an organized meaning-structure of myth, tradition, and disciplined practice.

Jung turned his back on all this in his enthusiasm for exploring the "inner world" of the psyche which he claimed was capable of coming up with representations entirely independently of human engagement in the social and material worlds. Indeed his argument for archetypes depended on this to refute the alternative explanations of cultural diffusion and cryptomnesia. Jung insisted that the potential forms for symbolic representation were located not in the collective world of social and material living but in the mysterious realm of the collective unconscious. External circumstances merely "constellated" these pre-existent forms rather than generating and structuring them through the extended engagement of the affective mind in the lived body of a shared world.

Lévy-Bruhl's emphasis on the affective origin of "primitive beliefs" suggests that collective representations are social means not only of *representing* affect but of organizing the way affects are experienced—they shape perception as well as conception. This is saying more than simply "we see what we expect to see" as if the things that are seen are "not really there." Rather it is a recognition that without public meanings, most of our perceptions would make no sense at all. Bringing something into being in this sense has to do with bringing it into the form of a symbolic language through which it can enter the domain of meaning. All symbolic language utilizes existing collective representations even if it adapts them to its own purposes and thereby contributes to the development of new forms of life. As Winnicott wrote, "It is not possible to be original except on the basis of tradition."[43] Meaning is always public and shared since, as Wittgenstein argued, there is no such thing as a private language. Without culture, there can be no meanings because there can be no thoughts. Or, as Clifford Geertz puts it "culture is public because meaning is."[44] In other words, meanings are created and made manifest through their public cultural enactment.This is what it means to be a human animal. We cannot rely on instinct alone to find our way in the world, especially a world where perception involves imagination as well as sensation, that is to say, our perception of intangible realities.

Even if there is, as Jung claims, a religious "instinct," the novitiate has to be inducted into the particular symbolic forms of a culturally located spiritual tradition to be able to participate in its mysteries. So, for example, when the Sioux Indian, Siyaka, wished to embark on a vision quest, he sought out a medicine man who gave him detailed instructions of the rituals he needed to follow involving offerings of well-tanned robes and tobacco and told him about his own "dream" in order to give the novitiate "an idea of what a dream was like."[45] Similar examples can be found in any meditative spiritual tradition and the same is true for the trainee in the mysterious arts of psychoanalysis. The novitiate reads the clinical accounts in the literature and is instructed by their supervisor as to what transference, archetypes, Oedipal material, projective identification, etc., etc., look like in the clinical situation and what to do when they occur. The novitiate then brings their "material" to the supervisor who reveals to them the hidden significance of what they have seen and what to do the next time such phenomena appear.

I am not questioning the veracity of either psychoanalytic interpretations or vision quests here but wishing to locate them in the context of the ritualized practice of symbolic imagination. Their veracity is not to be found in their content but in the methodology whereby imaginal realities are brought to being by the practice of a symbolic discipline. The training of novitiates consists of an induction into a "form of life" constituted by a set of collective representations. I also wish to emphasize that I use the term "brought to being" rather than "brought to consciousness" advisedly since the idea of "bringing to consciousness" implies that these realities already exist someplace else like the unconscious and are simply "discovered" rather than created. Not that they are created entirely anew out of whole cloth. Siyaka is given his instructions but he embarks on his vision quest alone, and the experiences he has and the feats he is able to perform as a result constitute a personal process of development or, perhaps, individuation. As I have written elsewhere, in the context of psychotherapeutic practice, "We can only be the analyst our particular personality allows us to be" notwithstanding that no-one could be an analyst in any other historical time than the present and almost entirely within Western cultures.[46]

Rangda and Barong:
Emotional Containment via *Participation Mystique*

I now want to give a detailed example of the containment of emotional states through symbolic enactment taken from Clifford Geertz's paper on "Religion as a Cultural System."[47] This example brings together many of the themes I have been considering, including *participation mystique*, extended affectivity, collective representations, and constitutive symbols. While this example could be seen as the expression of archetypes—in this case the witch and the clown/fool—I want to show how these symbolic forms are emergent rather than pre-given and can be related back to the emotional states they present and thereby represent. In traditional cultures where mythological motifs remain a living reality, these collective representations are not experienced as existing "in the mind" since that which we now call the psyche is indistinguishable from the world. They do, however, occupy the special socio-spiritual space of ceremony and ritual. As Geertz puts it, "in a ritual, the world as lived and the world as imagined, fused under the agency of a single set of symbolic forms, turn out to be the same world."[48] Imagination is made real by being enacted; act becomes image.

The example comes from Bali where Geertz conducted ethnological research in the late 1950s and concerns the ritual enactment of the combat between a terrible witch called Rangda and an endearing monster called Barong.[49] Geertz describes it as a "theatrical cultural performance" that is somewhere between religious ritual and theatre, being also a form of ceremony presented on the occasion of a death temple celebration.[50] Geertz' stock in trade is "thick description" by which he means that interpretative understanding requires closely observed, specific detail of the kind that is needed to distinguish between, say, a twitch of the eye and a deliberate wink.[51] In other words, actions only make sense when we grasp their intentional context and this requires as full an immersion in the world of the other as it is possible to achieve. So, it is not easy to provide a condensed account of Geertz's colorful description of the performance without losing the evocative detail that brings it to life.

> The drama consists of a masked dance in which the witch—depicted as a wasted old widow, prostitute, and eater of infants—comes to spread plague and death upon the land and is opposed by the monster—depicted as a kind of cross between a clumsy bear, a silly puppy, and a strutting Chinese dragon.[52]

As the comedic Barong attempts to defeat the terrifying and horrific Rangda he is assisted by various helpers and entranced members of the "audience." Geertz explains, "[T]he drama is, for the Balinese, not merely a spectacle to be watched but a ritual to be enacted. There is no aesthetic distance here separating actors from audience and placing the depicted events in an unenterable world of illusion."[53]

There is no standard form to the performance but various related mythic scenes are usually enacted before the battle begins. Barong succeeds in driving Rangda back towards the temple but is unable to defeat her. At length, it appears that Rangda will prevail but then a number of entranced men rush to support Barong only to be attacked by Rangda before she collapses and retreats to the temple. Having been revived by Barong, the helpers realize Rangda has disappeared and "sheer pandemonium breaks out" amongst them before they too collapse in coma. The great battle ends, as ever, in a "complete stand-off. Rangda has not been conquered but neither has she conquered."[54]

The key features of the performance are the physical appearance of the main characters, the entranced state of the participants, and the emotional conflict that is being dramatized between "horror and hilarity."[55] Geertz's description of the appearance of Rangda and Barong needs to be given in full to appreciate its impact:

> Rangda, danced by a single male, is a hideous figure. Her eyes bulge from her forehead like swollen boils. Her teeth become tusks curving up over her cheeks and fangs protruding down over her chin. Her yellowed hair falls down around her in a matted tangle. Her breasts are dry and pendulous dugs edged with hair, between which hang, like so many sausages, strings of colored entrails. Her long red tongue is a stream of fire. And as she dances she splays her dead-white hands, from which protrude ten-inch clawlike fingernails, out in front of her and utters unnerving shrieks of metallic laughter. Barong, danced by two men fore-and-aft in vaudeville horse fashion, is another matter. His shaggy sheepdog coat is hung with gold and mica ornaments that glitter in the half-light. He is adorned with flowers, sashes, feathers, mirrors, and a comical beard made from human hair. And though a demon too, his eyes also pop and he snaps his fanged jaws with seemly fierceness when faced with Rangda or other affronts to his dignity; the cluster of tinkling bells which hang from his absurdly arching tail somehow contrives to take most of the edge off his fearfulness. If Rangda is a satanic image, Barong is a farcical one, and their clash is a clash (an inconclusive one) between the malignant and the ludicrous.[56]

That this is no "imaginary" theatrical event to be observed and reflected upon with a suspension of disbelief is made abundantly plain by the state of the participants. Rangda seems "insane with fear and hatred" and her entry provokes near-panic in which many may go amok, running frantically about in total confusion. Those who perform Rangda may become permanently deranged by their experiences. By the end of the performance, a majority, often nearly all, of the members of the group sponsoring it will have become caught up in it not just imaginatively but bodily. Frenzy, panic, and running amok are the order of the day.

> Mass trance, spreading like a panic, projects the individual Balinese out of the commonplace world in which he usually lives into that most uncommonplace one in which Rangda and Barong live. To become entranced is, for

the Balinese, to cross a threshold into another order of existence—the word for trance is *nadi*, from *dadi*, often translated 'to become' but which might be even more simply rendered as 'to be.'[57]

Here, the separation between "imagination" and "reality" is almost entirely eclipsed but not quite. Although the mass trance teeters on the brink of getting entirely out of control, it is almost always possible to enable the entranced to return to the "commonplace" world. There is no "as if" to this form of imagination and it is experienced as entirely real. Yet Rangda and Barong are symbolic presences nevertheless that evoke a powerful enactment of the emotional conflict they embody. The whole village may be said to be more or less in a state of *participation mystique*. We are used to a rather more sedate form of emotional involvement, whether in ritual or drama, but the basic mechanisms are the same: at the height of the drama, the distinctions are dissolved and we *live through* the imaginal world in a way that transforms our experience, sometimes permanently.

Rangda and Barong are symbols not because they are imaginary "as if" figures—on the contrary, they are experienced as powerfully real—but precisely because it is not possible to state with any clear certainty what it is they represent. As Geertz says, "they are ... not representations ... but *presences*."[58] [italics added] The performance enacts a range of myths, tales, and beliefs, but these are various and variable. Like the figures in a dream, they are subject to numerous possible interpretations but nothing can replace or substitute their vivid, embodied, and powerfully emotional selves. And it is this which makes them symbols, for, like all non-discursive symbols, their meanings are multiple, indeterminate and irreducible. Their power is in their concrete presence that embodies the emotional states they both evoke and depict.

Yet, physically real as they are, they are also collective representations—the story is well known, frequently repeated, and part of the collective mythology of the participants. It is this which enables it to provide a containing structure for the intense, volatile emotionality that is aroused by the performance. Such extreme states of enactment are not unfamiliar to the practicing psychoanalyst; they are not everyday occurrences, but most analysts who engage at depth with their patients will have had experiences where the boundaries between "transference" and "reality" become blurred to the point of non-existence and will recognize the enormous struggle it can be to return to the commonplace world. In these encounters the joy and longings of love, the violence of hatred and betrayal, the pain and anguish of guilt, fear, shame, and despair are experienced not as symbolic "as if" states of transference and counter-transference but as powerful realities for both analyst and patient. Out of such a crucible in which the analyst knows not whether he is the alchemist stoking the flames or the salamander in the fire, both parties are indeed transformed.[59]

Whether this process occurs in the intersubjective exchanges between analyst and patient, at a theatrical event, or in a religious ritual, it consists of providing form and substance for the intangible fluidity of our affective relation to the world. We symbolize our affects in the act of experiencing them in relation to socially organized collective representations. The more these are experienced as concrete presences rather than psychological symbols, the more powerfully we "get the message"; we are taken out of ourselves in order to be returned to ourselves transformed, as symbolic beings. That, in my view, is the becoming the Balinese are referring to when they call their trance state a state of being. Thus Rangda and Barong may be regarded as constitutive symbols that bring into being the unthought, affective states they present. They make something tangible through a form of affective cognition that is clearly extended—no way is this simply going on "in the head." These are bodily affective events in which the whole community is engaged and which constitute them *as* a community with shared experiences of conflict and cooperation.

Co-Evolution of Emotion, Ritual, and Symbol

Of course, I have no idea whether the rituals conducted by our ancestors of the Upper Paleolithic were anything like this, although it is virtually certain that whatever they were like, they were experienced in this concrete way as living realities. But what I think Rangda and Barong do illustrate so well is the engagement, containment, and symbolization of emotional states via collective representations and *participation mystique*. In this reconfiguration, *participation mystique* is not simply a feature of "primitive" thought but a feature of the extended mind primarily related to the experience and cognition of emotional states. These states of mind do not occur individually but are always in relation to the social and material world—they are, as Damasio put it, the feeling of what happens. For humans, emotional cognition is socially distributed and organized through shared image-making activities that, in modern terms, would be classified as religion, the arts, and, perhaps increasingly, forms of sport like football in which the spectators are active participants. As I have suggested, psychotherapy too shares many of these features.

Wherever Rangda and Barong "came from," the form in which they appear must have evolved over time, over many generations or even centuries through a gradual process of accretion and creative innovation by countless individuals. In these presences, the collective activity of a whole society is embodied and presented. Just as Siyaka the Sioux was told how to dream, the Balinese learn how to become entranced, not by instruction but through participatory involvement in a shared activity that gives collective form to otherwise terrifying and vagrant emotions. Victor Turner referred to this as "a set of evocative devices for rousing, channeling, and domesticating powerful emotions"[60] which sounds a bit reminiscent of Freud's view of taming the Id. Geertz puts it more strongly and is more reminiscent of Jung in referring to the role of symbols in the creation of meaning. He indicates the constitutive power of religious symbols to "provide a cosmic guarantee not only for their ability to comprehend the world, but also, comprehending it, to give a precision to their feeling, a definition to their emotions which enables them, morosely or joyfully, grimly or cavalierly, to endure it."[61]

This means that symbolic imagination needs to be seen as a feature of a culturally shared world rather than a process occurring inside the head of individuals. The same is true of language: as Vygotsky showed, we learn to think in our heads after we have learned to use the language available to us by a process of appropriation. Similarly, we can only imagine via the imaginal language available to us in our culture; only then are we able to reconfigure what is found by what we make—the process of human creativity. Symbolic imagination is, therefore, a way of thinking (and feeling) suited to the expression and representation of emotional aspects of experience. It is related to the use of non-discursive symbolism in dream, myth, ritual, art, and religion as well being closely connected with intuition and other non-rational forms of apprehension such as synchronicity. When the necessary cultural resources are available for symbolization, experiences of this kind can be transformative, just as the mother's mediation of the infant's beta elements transforms them into usable alpha elements fit for dreaming.

In making this comparison between the containment provided by ritual and similar processes occurring in infancy, I am not suggesting that ritual is a "re-enactment" of infancy but, if anything, the opposite. For the question I have been posing is how symbolic imagination emerged in the first place, and it seems to me this is a very likely route. At some point in prehistory, adults who had only a rudimentary capacity for symbolic imagination would have needed some means of creating this other world of symbolic imagination as a way of making meaning of their heightened levels of affectivity which, in turn, derived from the increased importance of collective social living and the intersubjective aspects of attachment.

Deacon suggests that ritual would have been the means of providing a scaffolding for language itself. In my view, this puts ritual rather too early in hominin development. As I discussed in Chapter 3, I think Tomasello's model of the development of cooperation and Levinson's "interaction engine" are more promising models for the origin of language, with symbolic imagination emerging a considerable time later. Even if *Homo erectus* had some capacity for language (given the evidence of their capacity for compassionate co-operation), it is not until the use of symbolic objects, such as shell beads by early *Homo sapiens*, that we see evidence of concrete symbolism and representation of the intangible. So it seems to me more likely that ritual is concurrent with the emergence of the less tangible symbols of religion, art, and social status: the constitutive non-discursive symbols that bring imagination into being.

The evolutionary need for this would have been due to the gradual increase in emotionality as a distinctive feature of human social life. This view makes sense of the correlation between the processes of containment that occur in infancy and in the symbolic rituals of art and religion: rather than one being consequent upon the other, it makes sense to think of them as *co-evolving*, along the lines proposed by Deacon for language, tool-use, and the brain. The more humans lived in social groups, the more developed their emotional lives became and the more symbolic language was needed both to reflect this and to organize it. Human emotionality would have increased together with intersubjective sophistication, making humans more emotionally responsive and more able to discriminate different emotional states but also more vulnerable to being overwhelmed by their volatility and intensity. The longer periods of infancy in recent human species would have provided both the opportunity and the need for emotional containment in the sense that human infants became more dependent on being inducted into the human community of symbolic meaning. At the same time, these emotional states needed containment at a social level, a pressure that could be met by collective rituals out of which collective symbolic presences might emerge, including the emergence of special individuals with heightened emotional sensitivity and imaginative capacity who might mediate the symbolic world—shamans, priests, visionaries, or whatever. And, of course, one would support the other—just as those infants who had been able to develop a more sophisticated "emotional vocabulary" would be more able to engage in the symbolic rituals that ensured the group's cohesion, so the need to engage in such rituals would require more emotionally developed individuals capable of engaging in an affective way in rituals that could therefore *mean* something to them.

The implication of this proposed evolutionary trajectory is that the notion that non-rational modes of thought are more "primary" than rational modes of thought is a misreading of our evolutionary past and the nature of mind. The archaeological evidence I outlined in Chapters 3, 4, and 5 indicates that humans had been developing a theory of mind and problem-solving abilities they inherited from the common ape ancestor for several million years. They had been adding to this with technological, social, and linguistic innovations for over a million years and beginning to develop complex technologies requiring forethought and planning for as much as the past 500,000 years. Yet the first material evidence of symbols dates back only as far as 100,000 years and it is not until the Upper Paleolithic that there is clear evidence of symbolic ritual and "art." Notwithstanding that symbolic rituals were probably being practiced for some time before this, it is nevertheless the case that practical reasoning is far older than symbolic imagination. Some other animals are even better problem-solvers than we are (crows and parrots being the most outstanding examples), but no other animal ever wondered about the meaning of the universe or the purpose of life, or constructed a mythology. It is imagination, not reason, which makes us human, for other animals can reason but only humans can imagine a world beyond the phenomenal world of our senses.

It is true that the rules of logical reasoning were formulated much more recently and the scientific method developed even more recently than that. Practical reason, though, is far older than this, as is language; evolutionist notions about "secondary process" and the like made the ethnocentric error of confusing rational thought in general with a highly specialized mode of thinking used in science and philosophy which was then seen as the *sine qua non* of "civilized man." This was the confusion apparent in Jung's claim that directed thinking was a modern invention of only the past few hundred years as well as Freud's relegation of symbolic thinking to the supposedly archaic pre-history of the species.

If we consider rational thought on the broader canvas of problem-solving capacities, technological innovation, social cooperation, and language, it becomes apparent that the perception and conceptualization of spiritual states of being in the world must be *subsequent* to rational, technological, and linguistic modes of thought. We had to have language and a publically shared culture in which intangible realities could be represented in material form before this kind of thinking could become possible.

Since the "other" world, whether conceived as a "spiritual" world, a "psychic" world or simply a special quality of the sensuous world itself, consists of different "stuff" from the "ordinary" world, it requires a different mode of thought both to perceive it and to conceptualize it. Despite its original evolutionist baggage, the concept of *participation mystique* remains a useful way of describing both the state of mind and the mode of thought of this "other" world: it is collectively shared, it is affective, it takes us out of the world of the common-sense perspective, and it utilizes the language of non-discursive symbolism in which the logic antimonies of modern rational thought do not apply.

As humans found ways to conceive of this other intangible world be it known as spirit, psyche or imagination, their capacity to *perceive* it increased along with the techniques and rituals with which to do so. This is where socially generated collective representations are so important in providing the means to formulate symbolic images that constitute experiences in particular ways. In some way, this must be what was going on in the caves of Upper Paleolithic Europe. Rather than these images being representations of pre-existing archetypes, I have argued that it is only through the production of collective imagery that typical, even universal, images can coalesce and become instantiated as psychic realities. In this way, symbolic imagination constitutes our world. The point is well made by Roger Brooke:

> Existence can only be historical because it is also imaginative. Without imagination our world would not be a world but merely an environmental *umwelt*, like the concrete and tightly circumscribed 'worlds' of our animal cousins. Our imaginations do not belong to us any more than do language and cultural history. When I speak of 'my' imagination, it is not my possession any more than is my language, English. Imagination, language and temporality, each inconceivable without the others, are what constitute that psychic gathering we call the world.[62]

Images or Archetypes?

When I began this investigation, I saw the Lion Man image as simply the earliest example of this imaginative process, as if from the two materially present elements of *lion* and *man* someone had simply dreamed up a composite image, a creative innovation. I now see that the creative process is much more complicated than that: the Lion Man is emergent from the complex of collective spiritual experiences, beliefs, and practices in which it was embedded. It is neither the creation of a single individual nor a manifestation of putative archetype. There is simply no need for an archetype to explain the emergence of such an image, notwithstanding that similar images may have emerged on numerous other occasions through human history and prehistory. They may be similar, but they are not necessarily the same.

The archetype idea is at the other extreme to Geertz's thick description. Where Geertz embeds images and practices in specific contexts and emphasizes the manifold differences between cultures, Jung's comparative method *strips away* differences in favor of a conceptual abstraction which is then identified as the archetype, existing independently and over and above the embodied engagement of humans acting together to create "that psychic gathering we call the world." At the same time, Jung uses associative thinking to justify his hypothesis, collapsing the metaphorical congruence between one idea and another into a purported conceptual identity. In this way, we might see Rangda and Barong as representative symbols of "the terrible mother" in her incarnation as "the witch," and "the archetype of humor" which would be associated with the clown, the fool, and the trickster (one archetype or three?). I would argue, however, that these images are ultimately *themselves* and their significance lies precisely in the multiple, indeterminate meanings they evoke. We might also draw the parallel between Rangda and my previous example of the child looking at the shadowy image of Salieri from *Amadeus*. Here too is an image of fear and evil. But while there is a commonality, there are also innumerable differences. We can certainly say that fear is a universal human experience and we might add that mothers are often likely to arouse it due to the power they have over their infants and the highly charged emotional states of both parties. But there is more to fear and evil than the terrible mother and perhaps more to the witch than fear and evil, especially once we embark on an analysis of the demonization of women in the Middle Ages, to take another example of a specific social context.

Oddly, despite the abstractive reductive thinking involved in the formulation of archetypes, when it came to working with symbolic images, Jung too counseled "sticking to the image" albeit still in terms of using the comparative method in which social, cultural, and historical contexts can be ignored in the free play of active imagination and amplification.[63] To do this as a means of fostering imaginative connections and vitalizing a capacity for symbolic meaning is one thing; we are at liberty to *play* with these images symbolically and make our own imaginative use of them. We do not have the same liberty to claim that these imaginative activities justify objective transcultural statements that ride roughshod over the context and texture of the images themselves. To do so is to confuse the two kinds of thinking, using fantasy-thinking to reach conclusions that are then presented as directed thinking, and the modern kind of objectively verifiable scientific thinking at that. In this investigation I have attempted to do the opposite: to use directed thinking to construct a material basis for the existence of the non-material fantasy-thinking of symbolic imagination.

CHAPTER NOTES

INTRODUCTION

1. C. G. Jung, *Symbols of Transformation*, vol. 5, *The Collected Works of C. G. Jung*, trans. R. F. C. Hull (London: Routledge and Kegan Paul, 1956), p. xxiii.

2. The term *hominid* is now used to refer to all currently existing and ancestral great apes, including humans and their ancestors. *Hominin* is a more specific term comprising modern humans, extinct human species, and their immediate ancestors, including the earliest upright walking apes, the *australopithecines*.

3. Michael Tomasello, *Origins of Human Communication* (Cambridge, MA: MIT Press, 2008); and Stephen Levinson, "Interactional Biases in Human Thinking," in ed. Esther N. Goody, *Social Intelligence and Interaction: Expressions and Implications of the Social Bias in Human Intelligence* (Cambridge: Cambridge University Press, 1995).

PROLOGUE

1. Jill Cook, *Ice-Age Art: The Arrival of the Modern Mind* (London: British Museum Press, 2013), p. 30.

2. *Ibid.* The German, *Löwenmensch*, has the advantage that the word "mensch" has connotations of "person" or "human," thus avoiding the controversy as to whether the figure represents a male or female; however, Elisabeth Schmid's claim that the figure may originally have had female breasts has not been upheld. Cook argues that the overall physical stance of the figure suggests masculinity and points out that the absence of a mane is not significant since no depictions of cave lions show this characteristic. In any event, the gender of the figure is of less significance than the combination of human and animal features.

3. *Ibid.*, pp. 28–9.

4. *Ibid.*, p. 32.

5. *Ibid.*, p. 34.

6. David Lewis-Williams, *The Mind in the Cave* (London: Thames & Hudson, 2002).

7. C. G. Jung, *The Red Book*, ed. Sonu Shamdasani (New York: W. W. Norton & Co., 2009), p. 252 and n. 211; and C. G. Jung, *Aion* (1951), in *The Collected Works of C. G. Jung*, vol. 9ii, trans. R. F. C. Hull, 2nd ed. (London: Routledge and Kegan Paul, 1968).

8. "Seeing in front" may also refer to the fact that predators tend to have eyes that face directly forward, such as hawks and cats, while prey animals, like rabbits, have eyes to the sides of their heads (George Hogenson, personal e-mail communication, Dec. 6, 2014). Rather than being an alternative explanation this may suggest the way that abstract concepts such as time were originally embedded in the imagery of the living world. See David Abram, *The Spell of the Sensuous: Perception and Language in a More-Than-Human World* (New York: Vintage Books, 1997).

9. C. G. Jung, "Instinct and the Unconscious" (1919), in *The Collected Works of C. G. Jung*, vol. 8, trans. R. F. C. Hull, 2nd ed. (London: Routledge and Kegan Paul, 1969), § 270.

10. C. G. Jung, "The Psychology of the Transference" (1946), in *The Collected Works of C. G. Jung*, vol. 16, trans. R. F. C. Hull, 2nd ed. (London: Routledge and Kegan Paul, 1966), § 354.

11. Jung, "The Structure of Psyche" (1927/1931), CW 8, § 339.

12. New York Times, Oct. 4, 1936. Reprinted in W. McGuire and R. F. C. Hull, eds., *C. G. Jung Speaking: Interviews and Encounters* (London: Picador, 1980), p. 100.

13. See Warren Colman, "Theory as Metaphor: Clinical Knowledge and Its Communication," *Journal of Analytical Psychology* 54 (2, 2009): 199–215.

14. McGuire and Hull, *C. G. Jung Speaking*, p. 100.

15. C. G. Jung, "Man's Immortal Mind," *London Observer*, Oct. 6, 1935, in McGuire and Hull, *C. G. Jung Speaking*, pp. 96–7.

16. Chris Stringer, *The Origin of Our Species* (London: Allen Lane, 2011), p. 9.

17. *Ibid.*, p. 14.

18. *Ibid.*, p. 35.

19. Richard Klein and Blake Edgar, *The Dawn of Human Culture* (New York: John Wiley & Sons, 2002), p. 89.

20. The origins and development of language are extremely hard to track as it leaves no direct evidence in the archaeological record. Some possible scenarios are explored in Chapter 3, suggesting that the earliest forms of language may have originated as gestural communication during the time of *Homo erectus.*

21. Mauricio Cortina and Giovanni Liotti, "Attachment Is about Safety and Protection, Intersubjectivity Is about Sharing and Social Understanding: The Relationships between Attachment and Intersubjectivity," *Psychoanalytic Psychology* 27 (4, 2010): 410–41.

22. Jung, "Structure of Psyche," CW 8, §§ 321–22.

23. C. G. Jung, "The Structure of the Unconscious" (1916), in *The Collected Works of C. G. Jung*, vol. 7, trans. R. F. C. Hull, 2nd ed. (London: Routledge and Kegan Paul, 1966), §§ 455–56.

24. Anthony Stevens, *The Two Million-Year-Old Self* (College Station, TX: Texas A&M Press, 1993).

25. *Ibid.*, pp. 3–4.

26. As Stevens himself points out, his work was never of any interest to followers of James Hillman who deliberately eschewed any attempt to root his psychology in any other discipline. Stevens regards this as a form of "psychic parochialism" (*ibid.*), a useful description for the kind of self-imposed isolationism of much of Jungian psychology (as well as psychoanalysis) that has been largely responsible for its decline in the wider world of academic and clinical discourse.

27. Sonu Shamdasani, "After Liber Novus," *Journal of Analytical Psychology* 57 (3, 2012): p. 365.

CHAPTER ONE

1. See Robert Hobson, "Critical Notice of *The Archetypes and the Collective Unconscious*, by C. G. Jung," *Journal of Analytical Psychology* 6 (2, 1961): 161–68, especially p. 166. Hobson draws attention to the looseness of Jung's language with regard to terms like *form* and *image* and questions the appropriateness of naming archetypes in terms of phenomenal images such as *snake, mother, child, trickster,* or even *rebirth* since these names imply a particular matter or content which is at odds with the notion of archetypes as abstract, contentless, *non*-phenomenal possibilities of ideas.

2. "Every man is born with a brain that is highly differentiated. This makes him capable of a wide range of mental functions, which are neither ontogenetically developed nor acquired." Jung, CW 7, § 455.

3. McGuire and Hull, *C. G. Jung Speaking*, p. 83.

4. Jung, "Instinct and the Unconscious," CW 8, § 270.

5. While suggesting that instinct and archetype determine one another (Jung, CW 8, § 271) he also states that intuition is a process analogous to instinct (Jung, CW 8, § 269) suggesting that while instinct is concerned with action, intuition is concerned with perception and apprehension.

6. Jung, "The Structure of the Psyche" (1927/1931), CW 8, § 339.

7. Jung, CW 8, § 342.

8. Jung, "The Nature of the Psyche" (1947), CW 8, § 406.

9. Jung, CW 8, § 375.

10. Jung, CW 8, § 420.

11. Jung, *Synchronicity: An Acausal Connecting Principle* (1952), CW 8, § 964.

12. Jung, CW 8, § 442.

13. Jung, CW 8, § 275.

14. Jung, CW 8, § 277.

15. Martin Parker, "Human Science as Conspiracy Theory," in J. Parish and M. Parker, eds., *The Age of Anxiety: Conspiracy Theory and the Human* Sciences (Oxford: Blackwell, 2001), p. 203.

16. Daniel Dennett, *Consciousness Explained* (London: Penguin Books, 2001).

17. Warren Colman, "Consciousness, the Self and the Isness Business," *British Journal of Psychotherapy* 21 (1, 2004): 83–102.

18. For a reformulation of psychoanalytic theory, showing the primacy of surface over depth, see the Boston Change Process Study Group, "The Foundational Level of Psychodynamic Meaning: Implicit Process in Relation to Conflict, Defense and the Dynamic Unconscious," *International Journal of Psychoanalysis* 88 (2007): 1–16, especially p. 1. They argue that, "traditionally, the intrapsychic entities were assumed to determine what happened at the interactive level. The interactive level was seen merely as the instantiation of deeper forces. We suggest instead that the interactive process itself is primary and generates the raw material from which we draw the generalized abstractions that we term *conflicts*, *defenses*, and *phantasy*."

19. Jung, *Synchronicity*, CW8, § 864.

20. Hobson, "Critical Notice," p. 163.

21. Jean Knox, *Archetype, Attachment, Analysis: Jungian Psychology and the Emergent Mind* (Hove: Brunner-Routledge, 2003), p. 28ff.

22. "We are forced to assume that the given structure of the brain does not owe its peculiar nature merely to the influence of surrounding conditions but also and just as much to the peculiar and autonomous quality of living matter—i.e., to a law inherent in life itself."; See C. G. Jung, *Psychological Types* (1921), in *The Collected Works of C. G. Jung*, vol. 6, ed. and trans. Gerhard Adler and R. F. C. Hull (London: Routledge and Kegan Paul, 1971), § 748.

23. Hobson, "Critical Notice"; and Michael Fordham, "The Self in Jung's Works," in *Explorations into the Self* (London: Academic Press, 1985), pp. 5–33.

24. Hobson, "Critical Notice," p. 162.

25. Stevens, *Two Million-Year-Old Self*, p. 4.

26. Knox, *Archetype, Attachment, Analysis*, pp. 31–2.

27. Hobson, "Critical Notice," p. 163.

28. C. G. Jung, *Memories, Dreams, Reflections* (London: Collins and Routledge and Kegan Paul, 1963), p. 153.

29. *Ibid.*

30. Sonu Shamdasani, *Jung and the Making of Modern Psychology: The Dream of a Science* (Cambridge: Cambridge University Press, 2003), p. 277.

31. Jung, "Instinct and the Unconscious," CW 8, § 278 and n. 11.

32. Raya Jones, "Vicissitudes of a Science-Complex," in Raya Jones, ed., *Jung and the Question of Science* (Hove and New York: Routledge, 2014), p. 54.

33. Robert Segal is an indefatigable critic of the malleability of archetypes that guarantees their applicability to any situation. See Robert Segal, "Explanation and Interpretation," in Jones, *Jung and the Question of Science*, p. 82.

34. Jones, *Jung and the Question of Science*, p. 2.

35. *Ibid.*

36. Personal e-mail communication, October 7, 2014.

37. The irreducibility of symbols would also follow from their being emergent phenomena which are not reducible to the sum of their parts by definition.

38. Jerry Fodor, "Précis of *The Modularity of Mind*," *The Behavioral and Brain Sciences* 8 (1985): 5; Fodor later clarified his view of modularity in *The Mind Doesn't Work That Way: The Scope and Limits of Computational Psychology* (Cambridge, MA: MIT Press, 2000) in which he argued for a much more limited form of modularity, partly in reaction against the "ebullient optimism" of Steven Pinker's *How the Mind Works*. He remains, however, "a committed—not to say fanatical— nativist" (*ibid.*, pp. 2–3). Presumably, his view of fiber-glass power boats hasn't changed much either.

39. C. G. Jung, "Marriage as a Psychological Relationship" (1925), in *The Collected Works of C. G. Jung*, vol. 17, trans. R. F. C. Hull (London: Routledge and Kegan Paul, 1954), § 338.

40. Anthony Stevens, *On Jung* (London: Penguin Books, 1991), p. 37; *Two Million-Year-Old Self*, p. 20; *Archetype Revisited: An Updated Natural History of the Self* (London: Brunner-Routledge, 2002), pp. 17–8; and "The Archetypes," in R. Papadopoulos, ed., *The Handbook of Jungian Psychology* (London & New York: Routledge, 2006), p. 77.

41. C. G. Jung, "Foreword to Harding: 'Woman's Mysteries'" (1949), in *The Symbolic Life*, vol. 18, *The Collected Works of C. G. Jung*, trans. R. F. C. Hull (London: Routledge and Kegan Paul, 1971), § 1228.

42. Robin Fox, *The Search for Society: Quest for a Biosocial Science and Morality* (New Brunswick and London: Rutgers University Press, 1989), p. 17.

43. *Ibid.*, p. 19.

44. Stevens, *Archetype Revisited*, p. xii.

45. *Ibid.*, p. 25. See also Fox, *Search for Society*, pp. 21–2.

46. *Ibid.*, p. 215.

47. *Ibid.*, p. 209.

48. George Hogenson, "Philosophy, the Thinking Function, and the Reading of Jung," in J. Kirsch & M. Stein, eds., *How and Why We Still Read Jung* (Hove and New York: Routledge, 2013), p. 171.

49. *Ibid.*, p. 172.

50. See Erik Goodwyn, "Approaching Archetypes: Reconsidering Innateness," *Journal of Analytical Psychology* 55 (4, 2010): 502–21 and Jean Knox's response (pp. 522–33). In his reply (*ibid.*, pp. 550–55), Goodwyn attempts to dodge Knox's criticism by dropping his references to the *tabula rasa* and shifting his ground to the more general notion of "innateness."

51. Stevens, *Archetype Revisited*, p. 259.

52. Ed West, "A Decade after Steven Pinker's *The Blank Slate, Why is Human Nature Still Taboo?*," *Daily Telegraph*, Aug. 17, 2012.

53. S. Rose, *Lifelines: Biology beyond Determinism* (New York: Oxford University Press, 1997), p. 70.

54. Steven Pinker, *The Blank Slate: The Modern Denial of Human Nature* (London and New York: Penguin Books, 2003); and *The Better Angels of Our Nature: Why Violence Has Declined* (New York: Viking, 2011).

55. Pinker, *Blank Slate*, p. 134.

56. David Buss, *The Evolution of Desire: Strategies of Human Mating* (New York: Basic Books, 1994); Martin Daly and Margo Wilson, "Discriminative Parental Solicitude: A Biological Perspective," *Journal of Marriage and Family* 42 (2, 1980): 277–88; and Randy Thornhill and Craig T. Palmer, *A Natural History of Rape: Biological Bases of Sexual Coercion* (Cambridge, MA: MIT Press, 2000).

57. Linda Gannon, "A Critique of Evolutionary Psychology," *Psychology, Evolution & Gender* 4 (2, 2002): 173–218.

58. Jung's social and cultural conservatism is well-known. See Jay Sherry, *Carl Gustav Jung: Avant Garde Conservative* (New York: Palgrave Macmillan, 2010).

59. George Lakoff and Mark Johnson, *Metaphors We Live By* (London and Chicago: Chicago University Press, 1980), p. 157.

60. David Sanderson, "Golliwog Remark Was Clear Racism, Judges Declare," *The Times*, Dec. 19, 2013.

61. Fox, *Search for Society*, pp. 221ff.

62. See, for example, the reports from White Horse Village by the BBC's China Editor Carrie Gracie. Over the past ten years, this remote rural village has become the site of a modern city with an expected population of 600,000 by 2020. "White Horse Village: Has Urbanising China Worked?" Accessed Jun. 28, 2015, at http://www.bbc.co.uk/news/world-asia-china-33255773.

63. Fox, *Search for Society*, p. 11, n. 44.

64. *Ibid.*, pp. 21–3.

65. Michael Tomasello, interviewed in "What Makes Us Human," presented by Alice Roberts, BBC Horizon, aired July 3, 2013.

66. Knox, *Archetype, Attachment, Analysis*, p. 46.

67. *Ibid.*, p. 47.

68. Jean Mandler, "How to Build a Baby: On the Development of an Accessible Representational System," *Cognitive Development* 3 (1988): 113–36; and Jean Mandler, "How to Build a Baby II: Conceptual Primitives," *Psychological Review* 99 (4, 1992): 587–604.

69. Knox, *Archetype, Attachment, Analysis*, p. 62.

70. See Jean Knox, *Self-Agency in Psychotherapy: Attachment, Autonomy, and Intimacy* (New York and London: W. W. Norton & Co., 2011), p. 98.

71. Vittorio Gallese and George Lakoff, "The Brain's Concepts: The Role of the Sensory-Motor System in Conceptual Knowledge," *Cognitive Neuropsychology* 22 (3/4, 2005): 455–79.

72. *Ibid.*, p. 467.

73. Knox, *Archetype, Attachment, Analysis*, pp. 67 and 96.

74. George Hogenson, "The Baldwin Effect: A Neglected Influence on C. G. Jung's Evolutionary Thinking," *Journal of Analytical Psychology* 46 (4, 2001): 591–611.

75. Jung, "Nature of Psyche," CW 8, § 398.

76. Hogenson, "Baldwin Effect," p. 600.

77. Esther Thelen and Linda B. Smith, *A Dynamic Systems Approach to the Development of Cognition and Action* (Cambridge, MA: MIT Press, 1998).

78. George Hogenson, "Reply to Maloney," *Journal of Analytical Psychology* 48 (2, 2003): 109.

79. K. Kaye and A. J. Wells, "Mothers' Jiggling and the Burst-Pause Pattern in Neonatal Feeding," *Infant Behavior and Development* 3 (1980): 29–46.

80. George Hogenson, "Responses to Erik Goodwyn's 'Approaching Archetypes: Reconsidering Innateness,'" *Journal of Analytical Psychology* 55 (4, 2010): 545.

81. E-mail to an online discussion seminar, International Association of Jungian Studies, January 26, 2011.

82. Hogenson, "Responses to Erik Goodwyn," p. 545.

83. Terrence Deacon, *The Symbolic Species: The Co-Evolution of Language and the Brain* (New York: W. W. Norton & Co., 1997).

84. Rodney Brooks, *Cambrian Intelligence: The Early History of the New AI* (Cambridge, MA: MIT Press, 1999).

85. George Hogenson and Anthony Stevens, "Debate: Psychology and Biology," in M. Mattoon & R. Hinshaw, eds., *Cambridge 2001:*

Proceedings of the Fifteenth International Congress for Analytical Psychology (Einsiedeln: Daimon Verlag, 2003), pp. 367–77.

86. Hogenson, "Baldwin Effect," p. 606.

87. See George Hogenson, "The Self, the Symbolic and Synchronicity: Virtual Realities and the Emergence of the Psyche," *Journal of Analytical Psychology* 50 (3, 2005): 271–84; and George Hogenson, "Archetypes as Action Patterns," *Journal of Analytical Psychology* 54 (3, 2009): 325–37.

88. *Shorter Oxford English Dictionary*, Sixth Edition, 2007.

89. Knox's redefinition of archetypes as image schemas might meet the definition of being a primitive model for the construction of metaphors but the extended meanings are themselves emergent and so do not constitute "typical examples." Grasping an object may be a primitive model for grasping a concept but the latter is not a typical example of the former.

90. Allan Schore, *Affect Regulation and the Origins of the Self: The Neurobiology of Emotional Development* (Hillsdale, NJ: Lawrence Erlbaum, 1994).

91. Knox, *Archetype, Attachment, Analysis*, pp. 31–2.

CHAPTER TWO

1. Warren Colman, "Synchronicity and the Meaning-Making Psyche," *Journal of Analytical Psychology* 56 (4, 2011): 471–91

2. Rene Descartes, Letter to Princess Elisabeth, May 21, 1643, in K. J. Warren, ed., *An Unconventional History of Western Philosophy: Conversations between Men and Women Philosophers* (Lanham, MD: Rowman and Littlefield, 2009), p. 163.

3. *Ibid.*

4. Antonio Damasio, *Descartes' Error: Emotion, Reason, and the Human Brain* (New York: G. P. Putnam, 1994).

5. Dennett, *Consciousness Explained.*

6. Wittgenstein said, "When I read Schopenhauer I seem to see to the bottom very easily. He is not deep in the sense that Kant and Berkeley are deep." Maurice Drury, "Some Notes on Conversations with Wittgenstein," in R. Rhees, ed., *Recollections of Wittgenstein* (Oxford: Oxford University Press, 1981), p. 158.

7. Julien Offray de La Mettrie, *Œuvres philosophiques de Monsieur de La Mettrie* (Amsterdam, 1764), I: xxviii.

8. Guy Toubiana, ed., 18th Century Online Encyclopedia: Enlightenment and Revolution. Accessed Nov. 5, 2014, at http://enlightenment-revolution.org/index.php/La_Mettrie,_Julien_Offray_de.

9. "Julian Offray de La Mettrie—Biography," *The European Graduate School Library*. Accessed Nov. 5, 2014, at http://www.egs.edu/library/julien-offray-de-la-mettrie/biography/.

10. Julien Offray de La Mettrie, *Machine Man and Other Writings*, ed. Anne Thompson (Cambridge University Press, 1996), p. 15.

11. The anti-vitalist pact was signed in 1842 by Helmholtz and three of his students, Emil du Bois-Reymond, Carl Ludwig, and Ernst Brücke, the four founders of the Berlin Physical Society. They declared that "no other forces than the common physical and chemical ones are active within the organism." Freud studied and trained as a neurologist under Brücke and declared, "[he] carried more weight with me than anyone else in my whole life." (Sigmund Freud, *The Question of Lay Analysis* (1926), in *The Standard Edition of the Complete Psychological Works of Sigmund Freud*, vol. 20, ed. and trans. J. Strachey (London: Hogarth Press, 1959), p. 253.

12. Sigmund Freud, "Project for a Scientific Psychology" (1895), in *The Standard Edition of the Complete Psychological Works of Sigmund Freud*, vol. 1, ed. and trans. J. Strachey (London: Hogarth Press, 1953), pp. 283–397.

13. Sigmund Freud, *The Three Essays on Sexuality* (1905), in *The Standard Edition of the Complete Psychological Works of Sigmund Freud*, vol. 7, ed. and trans. J. Strachey (London: Hogarth Press, 1953), p. 168. This passage was added in 1915.

14. Joe Cambray, "Romanticism and Revolution in Jung's Science," in Jones, *Jung and the Question of Science*, pp. 9–29.

15. *Ibid.*, pp. 16 and 21; and Mark Saban, "Science Friction: Jung, Goethe, and Scientific Objectivity," in Jones, *Jung and the Question of Science*, p. 43.

16. Jung, "The Real and the Surreal" (1933), CW 8, §§ 747–48.

17. Jung, "Basic Postulates of Analytical Psychology" (1931), CW 8, § 653.

18. Jung, CW 8, § 657.

19. Jung, "The Real and the Surreal," CW 8, § 747.

20. Jung, "Basic Postulates of Analytical Psychology," CW 8, § 657.

21. C. G. Jung, *Mysterium Coniunctionis*, vol. 14, *The Collected Works of C. G. Jung*, trans. R. F. C. Hull (Princeton, NJ: Princeton University Press, 1963), § 768.

22. C. G. Jung, "The Tavistock Lectures" (1935), in *The Collected Works of C. G. Jung*, vol. 18, trans. R. F. C. Hull (Princeton, NJ: Princeton University Press, 1963), § 69.

23 Jung, "The Real and the Surreal," § 745.

24 Jung, "Spirit and Life" (1926), CW 8, § 623.

25 Jung, "The Real and the Surreal," § 746.

26. Ann Addison, "Jung, Vitalism, and 'the Psychoid': An Historical Reconstruction," *Journal of Analytical Psychology* 54 (1, 2009): 138.

27. Jung, "On the Nature of Psyche," CW 8, § 418.

28. Jung, CW 8, § 417.

29. Jung, *Synchronicity*, CW 8, § 916.

30. The "hard problem" is a term introduced into the philosophy of consciousness by David Chalmers in 1995 to highlight the phenomenal nature of consciousness that is not susceptible to a reductionist explanation in purely material terms of mechanism and function. Chalmers distinguishes between the "easy problems" which consist of the functional, dynamical, and structural properties of the conscious mind (the *what* and *how* of consciousness) and the "hard problem" of *why* there should be conscious states at all. "How can we explain why there is something it is like to entertain a mental image, or to experience an emotion?" See David Chalmers, "Facing up to the Problem of Consciousness," *Journal of Consciousness Studies* 2 (3, 1995): 200–19.

31. Evan Thompson, *Mind in Life: Biology, Phenomenology, and the Sciences of Mind* (Cambridge and London: Harvard University Press, 2007), p. 225.

32. Semir Zeki, "Imagination," *In Our Time*, presented by Melvyn Bragg, aired November 28, 2002 (BBC Radio 4).

33. Lambros Malafouris, *How Things Shape the Mind* (Cambridge and London: MIT Press, 2013), p. 50; and similarly, Alva Noë says, "Brains don't have minds; people (and other animals) do" in Alva Noë, *Out of Our Heads* (New York: Hill and Wong, 2009), p. 10.

34. Alan Turing, "Computing Machinery and Intelligence," *Mind* 59 (1950): 433–60.

35. John Searle's original argument was in "Minds, Brains, and Programs," *Behavioral and Brain Sciences* 13 (3, 1980): 417–58; for a vigorous rebuttal see Dennett, *Consciousness Explained*, pp. 435–40; Searle addresses his many critics in *The Mystery of Consciousness* (London: Granta, 1997).

36. Rodney A. Brooks, "Computation as the Ultimate Metaphor," *Edge World Question Center*. Accessed Nov. 7, 2014, at http://edge.org/q2008/q08_5.html#brooks.

37. Christopher L. Passaglia, "In Memoriam Robert B. Barlow, Jr.," *Journal of Experimental Biology* (2010): 1397.

38. Horst Hendriks-Jansen, *Catching Ourselves in the Act* (Cambridge, MA and London: 1996), pp. 81–4.

39. *Ibid.*, p. 83.

40. *Ibid.*, p. 200.

41. Cf. the two examples cited in the previous chapter: proto-grasping and the "burst-pause" feeding pattern.

42. Hendriks-Jansen, *Catching Ourselves in the Act*, p. 283.

43. *Ibid.*, p. 285.

44. *Ibid.*, p. 273.

45. Thompson, *Mind in Life*, p. 128.

46. *Ibid.*, p. 98–9.

47. *Ibid.*, p. 13. Such species-specific modes of coupling with the environment might be considered archetypal albeit the term *archetype* would then be a misnomer, as previously argued.

48. *Ibid.*, p. 11.

49. *Ibid.*, p. 47.

50. Quoted in Maurice Merleau-Ponty, *The Structure of Behavior*, trans. A. Fisher (Pittsburgh, PA: Duquesne University Press, 1963), p. 63. The original quotation is from Kurt Goldstein, *The Organism* [1934] (New York: Zone Books, 1995), p. 85. Goldstein was an important influence on many of the founders of humanistic psychology, particularly Fritz Perls, the founder of gestalt therapy who worked as his assistant for a year in 1930.

51. Thompson, *Mind in Life*, p. 74.

52. *Ibid.*, p. 147.

53. *Ibid.*, p. 146.

54. Evan Thompson and Mog Stapleton, "Making Sense of Sense-Making: Reflections on Enactive and Extended Mind Theories," *Topoi* 28 (1, 2009): 27.

55. Thompson, *Mind in Life*, p. 78.

56. James Fisher, "The Evolution of the Analytic Process: Poetry and Psychoanalysis, Twin 'Sciences' of the Emotions," *Journal of the British Association of Psychotherapists* [reprinted in *Couple and Family Psychoanalysis* 4 (2014): 5–21].

57. Thompson, *Mind and Life*, p. 59.

58. *Ibid.*

59. Hans Jonas, *The Phenomenon of Life: Toward a Philosophical Biology* (Chicago, IL: Chicago University Press, 1966), p. 79; as quoted in Thompson, *Mind and Life*, p. 163.

60. Roger Brooke writes that The Enlightenment world that found its expression in Descartes "is a world in which reality is defined according to the vision of natural science. That reality defined as a system of mathematical and physical references was originally a vision, and still is, has long been forgotten." Roger Brooke, *Jung and Phenomenology* (London and New York: Routledge, 1991), p. 113.

61. Joe Hutto, *Illumination in the Flatwoods: A Season Living among the Wild Turkey* (Guildford, CT: The Lyons Press, 1995).

62. The significance of hunting for the development of symbolic imagination is discussed in Chapter 6.

63. Hutto, *Illumination*, p. 165.

64. *Ibid.*, p. 45.

65. *Ibid.*, p. 27.

66. *Ibid.*, p. 85.

67. *Ibid.,* p. 4.

68. *Ibid.*, p. 105.

69. Karl Popper, *Objective Knowledge: An Evolutionary Approach* (Oxford: Clarendon Press, 1972), pp. 238–39.

70. James Gleick, *Genius: The Life and Times of Richard Feynman* (New York: Vintage, 1993), p. 409 as quoted in Andy Clark, *Supersizing the Mind: Embodiment, Action, and Cognitive Extension* (Oxford University Press, 2011), p. xxv.

71. Andy Clark and David Chalmers, "The Extended Mind," *Analysis* 58 (1, 1998): pp. 7–19.

72. *Ibid.*

73. *Ibid.*

74. "Men make their own history, but they do not make it as they please; they do not make it under circumstances chosen by themselves, but under circumstances directly encountered, given and transmitted from the past." Karl Marx, "The 18th Brumaire of Louis Bonaparte" (1852), in Karl Marx and Frederick Engels, *Karl Marx and Frederick Engels: Selected Works in One Volume* (London: Lawrence and Wishart, 1968), p. 96.

75. Noë, *Out of Our Heads*, pp. 68–9.

76. Thompson and Stapleton, "Sense-Making," p. 27. I discuss the role of extended affectivity in relation to Lévy-Bruhl's concept of *participation mystique* in Chapter 8.

77. Shaun Gallagher, "The Over-Extended Mind," Versus 113 (2012): 67.

78. This is demonstrated by Wulf Hein in *Cave of Forgotten Dreams, A Film by Werner Herzog* (2010), DVD available at Amazon, at 53:00–55:00.

79. Lambros Malafouris and Colin Renfrew, eds., *The Cognitive Life of Things: Recasting the Boundaries of the Mind* (Cambridge: McDonald Institute for Archaeological Research, 2010); and see Chapter 4 for a discussion of Renfrew and Malafouris' theory of material engagement.

80. Andy Clark, "Natural Born Cyborgs?," *Edge Conversations* (2000). Accessed Nov. 9, 2014, at http://www.edge.org/3rd_culture/clark/clark_p6.html.

81. Andy Clark, *Natural-Born Cyborgs: Minds, Technologies, and the Future of Human Intelligence* (Oxford: Oxford University Press, 2003), p. 197.

82. Dana L. Strait et al., "Musical Experience and Neural Efficiency—Effects of Training on Subcortical Processing of Vocal Expressions of Emotion," *European Journal of Neuroscience* 29 (3, 2009): 661–68.

83. Susan R. Barry, "Do Musicians Have Different Brains?," *Psychology Today*, Jun. 11, 2010. Accessed Jan. 31, 2015, at http://www.psychologytoday.com/blog/eyes-the-brain/201006/do-musicians-have-different-brains.

84. Oliver Sacks, *Musicophilia: Tales of Music and the Brain* (New York: Knopf, 2008).

85. Thompson, *Mind in Life*, p. 71.

86. Gallagher, "Over-Extended Mind," p. 63.

87. Edwin Hutchins, *Cognition in the Wild* (Cambridge, MA: MIT Press, 1995). Introduction available at http://hci.ucsd.edu/hutchins/citw.html.

88. Edwin Hutchins, "Imagining the Cognitive Life of Things," in Malafouris and Renfrew, *Cognitive Life of Things*, pp. 91–102 (also available at https://www.ida.liu.se/~729G12/mtrl/ImaginingCogLifeThings.pdf).

89. Andy Clark, "Material Surrogacy and the Supernatural: Reflections on the Role of Artefacts in 'Off-line' Cognition,'" in Malafouris and Renfrew, *Cognitive Life of Things*, p. 23–8.

90. Hutchins, "Imagining the Cognitive Life of Things."

91. Edwin Hutchins, "The Distributed Cognition Perspective on Human Interaction," in N. J. Enfield and Stephen C. Levinson, eds., *Roots of Human Sociality: Culture, Cognition, and Interaction* (Oxford and New York: Berg, 2006), pp. 393–94.

92. Michael Cole and James V. Wertsch, "Beyond the Individual-Social Antimony in Discussions of Piaget and Vygotsky," *Human Development* 39 (1996): 250–56.

93. For further information and a series of fascinating videos of research experiments testing the New Caledonian crows' problem-solving abilities, see the website of the Auckland University psychology research team led by Gavin Hunt and Alex Taylor: "Cognition and Culture in New Caledonian Crows." Accessed at http://www.psych.auckland.ac.nz/en/about/our-research/research-groups/new-caledonian-crow-cognition-and-culture-research.html.

94. Rom Harré, *Personal Being* (Oxford: Blackwell, 1983).

95. Louis Zinkin, "Your Self: Did You Find It or Did You Make It?" [1991], *Journal of Analytical Psychology* 53 (3, 2008): 389–406.

96. Edwin Hutchins, "Distributed Cognition," *International Encyclopedia of the Social and Behavioral Sciences*. Accessed Nov. 9, 2014, at http://eclectic.ss.uci.edu/~drwhite/Anthro179a/DistributedCognition.pdf.

97. Edwin Hutchins and Brian Hazlehurst, "Learning in the Cultural Process" in C. G. Langton, C. Taylor, J. D. Farmer, and S. Rasmussen, eds., *Artificial Life II* (Redwood City, CA: Addison-Wesley, 1990), pp. 689–706.

98. Norbert Elias, "The Symbol Theory," vol. 13, *The Collected Works of Norbert Elias*, ed. Richard Kilminster (Dublin: UCD Press, 2011), p. 48.

99. *Ibid.*, p. 39.

100. *Ibid.*, p. 47.

101. *Ibid.*, p. 52.

102. See Chapter 1, p. 41 and n. 65

CHAPTER THREE

1. Deacon, *Symbolic Species*.

2. *Ibid.*, p. 71.

3. Susanne Langer, *Philosophy in a New Key* (Cambridge, MA: Harvard University Press, 1942).

4. Charles Rycroft, *The Innocence of Dreams* (London: Hogarth Press, 1979), p. 162.

5. For this view, I am indebted to an anonymous internet commentator with the online name *rationalrevolution*, in John Horgan, "Crows like My Pal George Aren't Just Smart, They're Also Jokers." Accessed Jan. 10, 2015, at http://blogs.scientificamerican.com/cross-check/2014/04/16/crows-like-my-pal-george-arent-just-smart-theyre-also-jokers/.

6. Cole and Wertsch, "Beyond the Individual-Social Antimony," pp. 250–56.

7. Antonio Damasio, *The Feeling of What Happens: Body, Emotion, and the Making of Consciousness* (London: Vintage, 1999), p. 5. Note, too, the centrality of affect in this vignette; Damasio is laying the ground for his argument that "elaborated consciousness" is dependent on a higher-level monitoring of affective states generated by external events. In later chapters, I argue that symbolization facilitates the representation of states of "extended affectivity," thus strengthening the linkage between symbols, consciousness, imagination, and affect.

8. Michael Tomasello, *A Natural History of Human Thinking* (Cambridge, MA: Harvard University Press, 2014), p. 16.

9. Terry Pratchett says, "Imagination, not intelligence, made us human," but I first heard the idea from a poet who was fed up with his wife telling him to be reasonable. [See Foreword to David Pringle, *The Definitive Illustrated Guide to Fantasy* (London: Carlton Books, 2003).]

10. Deacon, *Symbolic Species*, p. 22.

11. *Ibid.*, p. 31.

12. Elizabeth Hess, *Project Nim*, directed by James Marsh (Red Box Films with Passion Pictures and BBC Films, 2011), DVD.

13. Herbert Terrace, reply by Pete Singer, "Can Chimps Converse?: An Exchange," *New York Review of Books*, Nov. 24, 2011. Also accessed at http://www.nybooks.com/articles/archives/2011/nov/24/can-chimps-converse-exchange/.

14. Deacon, *Symbolic Species*, p. 96.

15. Paul Raphaele, "Speaking Bonobo," *Smithsonian Magazine*, Nov. 2006. Accessed Nov. 20, 2014, at http://www.smithsonianmag.com/science-nature/speaking-bonobo-134931541/?no-ist.

16. Deacon, *Symbolic Species*, pp. 122–27.

17. *Ibid.*, p. 109.

18. British audiences will recognize the reference to Eric Morecambe's well-known riposte to Andre Previn's complaints about his rendition of the Grieg piano concerto. Others are recommended to watch the classic comedy sketch on YouTube.

19. Sarah Hrdy, "Mothers and Others," *Natural History*, May 2001. Accessed Feb. 2, 2015, at http://www.naturalhistorymag.com/features/11440/mothers-and-others.

20. Sarah Hrdy, "How Humans Became Such Other-Regarding Apes," Salk Center for Academic Research and Training in Anthropogeny, UCSD-TV. Accessed Nov. 20, 2014, at http://www.youtube.com/watch?v=mDlPhExR664.

21. Hrdy, "Mothers and Others."

22. Levinson, "Interactional Biases in Human Thinking," p. 232.

23. *Ibid.*, p. 237.

24. This is probably also the reason why psychotherapy patients find silent analysts who do not join in ordinary conversation so bewildering, especially as many analysts fail to explain the "fundamental rule" of free association beforehand and then interpret the patient's confusion or anger in terms of their own special rules of understanding.

25. Stephen Levinson, "On the 'Human Interaction Engine,'" in Enfield and Levinson, *Roots of Human Sociality*, p. 42.

26. Tomasello, *Natural History of Human Thinking*, p. 15.

27. Demonstrated by Franz de Waal in Chris Packham, "Secrets of the Social World," *Inside the Animal Mind*, episode 3, aired February 11, 2014 (BBC2). There is a large literature on the topic of intentional deception in animals, especially chimpanzees. For a fairly recent summary and further evidence, see Brian Hare, Josep Call, and Michael Tomasello, "Chimpanzees Deceive a Human Competitor by Hiding," *Cognition* 101 (2006): 495–514. Available online at http://www.sciencedirect.com/science/article/pii/S0010027705002179.

28. Josep Call and Michael Tomasello, "Does the Chimpanzee Have a Theory of Mind?: 30 Years Later," *Trends in Cognitive Sciences* 12 (5, 2008): 187–92.

29. Paul Bloom and Tim P. German, "Two Reasons to Abandon the False Belief Task as a Test of Theory of Mind," *Cognition* 77 (2000): B2–B31; and Marco Fenici, "What Does the False Belief Test Test?" *Phenomenology and Mind* 1, (2011): 197–207.

30. Call and Tomasello, "Does the Chimpanzee Have a Theory of Mind?."

31. *Ibid.*

32. Juan-Carlos Gómez and Beatrice Martín-Andrade, "Fantasy Play in Apes," in A. D. Pellegrini and P. K. Smith, eds., *The Nature of Play: Great Apes and Humans* (New York: Guildford Press, 2005), p. 141.

33. Judith Kerr, *The Tiger Who Came to Tea* [1968] (London: HarperCollins, 2006).

34. Knox, *Self-Agency in Psychotherapy*, p. 109ff.

35. Gómez and Martín-Andrade, "Fantasy Play in Apes," p. 145.

36. Heidi Lyn, Patricia Greenfield, and Sue Savage-Rumbaugh, "The Development of Representational Play in Chimpanzees and Bonobos: Evolutionary Implications, Pretense, and the Role of Interspecies Communication," *Cognitive Development* 21 (3, 2006): 199–213.

37. Hanna Segal, "Notes on Symbol Formation," *International Journal of Psychoanalysis* 38 (1957): 391–97.

38. Gómez and Martín-Andrade, "Fantasy Play in Apes," p. 167.

39. Felix Warneken and Michael Tomasello, "Altruistic Helping in Human Infants and Young Chimpanzees," *Science* 311 (2006): 1301–304.

40. Tomasello, *Origins of Human Communication*, p. 41.

41. Ulf Liszkowski, Malinda Carpenter, Anne Henning, Tricia Striano and Michael Tomasello, "Twelve-Month-Olds Point to Share Attention and Interest," *Developmental Science* 7 (3, 2004): 297–307.

42. Sandeep Ravindran, "African Elephants Understand Human Gestures," *National Geographic*, Oct. 10, 2013.

43. Anna F. Smet and Richard W. Byrne, "African Elephants Can Use Human Pointing Cues to Find Hidden Food," *Current Biology* 23 (20, 2013): 2033–037.

44. Jingzhi Tan and Brian Hare, "Bonobos Share with Strangers," *PLOS ONE* 8 (1, 2013): e51922. doi: 10.1371/journal.pone.0051922.

45. Zanna Clay and Frans B. M. de Waal, "Bonobos Respond to Distress in Others: Consolation across the Age Spectrum," *PLOS ONE* 8 (1, 2013): e55206. doi:10.1371/journal.pone.0055206.

46. Katharina Hamann, Felix Warneken, Julia R. Greenberg and Michael Tomasello, "Collaboration Encourages Equal Sharing in Children but Not Chimpanzees," *Nature 476* (2011): 328–31.

47. Tomasello, *Origins of Human Communication*, p. 174. Tomasello's view is contested by Frans de Waal and his team at Emory University who argue there is evidence of chimpanzees helping each other in the wild and claim to have demonstrated this in the laboratory; however, Tomasello considers their study poorly designed. See Carl Zimmer, "Chimpanzees Clear Some Doubt after Generosity Is Questioned," *New York Times*, Aug. 8, 2011, D3.

48. Richard W. Byrne and Andrew Whiten, *Machiavellian Intelligence: Social Expertise and the Evolution of Intelligence in Monkeys, Apes, and Humans* (New York: Oxford University Press, 1988).

49. Nicholas Humphrey, "The Social Function of Intellect," in P. P. G. Bateson and R. A. Hinde, eds., *Growing Points in Ethology* (Cambridge: Cambridge University Press, 1976), pp. 303–17.

50. Tomasello, *Origins of Human Communication*, p. 190.

51. Tomasello, *Natural History of Human Thinking*, p. 36.

52. Paul L. Harris, *The Work of the Imagination* (Oxford: Blackwell, 2000), p. 10.

53. For a discussion of the importance of shared play in the development of a "third perspective," see Peter Hobson, *The Cradle of Thought* (London: Macmillan, 2002) and Elizabeth Urban, "The 'Self' in Analytical Psychology: The Function of the 'Central Archetype' Within Fordham's Model," *Journal of Analytical Psychology* 53 (3, 2008): 329–50. Hobson argues that developmental failures in this regard are associated with certain kinds of autism and borderline states of mind.

54. Tomasello, *Origins of Human Communication*, p. 5.

55. Cortina and Liotti, "Attachment Is about Safety and Protection," pp. 410–41. Original reference: D. L. Cheney and R. M. Seyfarth, *Baboon Metaphysics: The Evolution of a Social Mind* (Chicago, IL: University of Chicago, 2007), pp. 163–64.

56. John Searle, *The Construction of Social Reality* (London and New York: Penguin Books, 1995).

57. *Ibid.*, p. 25.

58. *Ibid.*

59. Giles Clark, "A Spinozan Lens onto the Confusions of Borderline Relations," *Journal of Analytical Psychology* 51 (1, 2006): 67–86.

60. *Ibid.*, p. 73.

61. Knox, *Self-Agency in Psychotherapy*, p. 99.

62. Deacon, *Symbolic Species*, p. 70.

63. Tomasello, *Natural History of Human Thinking*, p. 102.

64. Hobson, *Cradle of Thought.*

65. Tomasello, *Natural History of Human Thinking*, p. 76.

CHAPTER FOUR

1. Glynn Isaac, "The Food-Sharing Behavior of Protohuman Hominids," in G. Isaac and R. Leakey, eds., *Human Ancestors: Readings from Scientific American* (San Francisco: W. H. Freeman, 1979), pp. 110–23.

2. Steven Mithen, *The Prehistory of the Mind: A Search for the Origins of Art, Religion, and Science* (London: Thames and Hudson, 1996), p. 116.

3. Richard Byrne, Crickette M. Sanz, and David B. Morgan, "Chimpanzees Plan Their Tool Use," in C. M. Sanz, J. Call, and C. Boesch, eds., *Tool Use in Animals: Cognition and Ecology* (Cambridge: Cambridge University Press, 2013), pp. 48–63.

4. Isaac, "Food-Sharing Behavior," p. 122.

5. David J. Meltzer, *Lewis Roberts Binford 1934–2011: A Biographical Memoir* (Washington, DC: National Academy of Sciences, 2011), p. 3.

6. Mithen, *Prehistory of the Mind*, p. 112.

7. Richard Potts, *Early Hominid Activities at Olduvai* (New York: Aldine de Gruyter, 1988); also see Mithen, *Prehistory of the Mind*, p. 116.

8. As demonstrated in *Monkey Planet*, presented by George McGavin, aired April 16, 2014 (BBC One).

9. Nicholas Toth et al., "Pan the Tool-Maker: Investigations into the Stone Tool-Making and Tool-Using Capabilities of a Bonobo (*Pan Paniscus*)," *Journal of Archaeological Science* 20 (1, 1993): 81–91.

10. Mithen, *Prehistory of the Mind*, p. 108.

11. Lewis-Williams, *Mind in the Cave*, p. 111.

12. Richard Young, "Evolution of the Human Hand: The Role of Throwing and Clubbing," *Journal of Anatomy* 202 (1, 2003): 165–74.

13. Tomasello, *Origins of Human Communication*, p. 258.

14. Geoffrey Pullman, quoted in Raffaele, "Speaking Bonobo."

15. See Malafouris and Renfrew, *Cognitive Life of Things*; and Malafouris, *How Things Shape the Mind*.

16. Lewis Binford, "Archaeology as Anthropology," *American Antiquity* 28 (1962): 217–25. Quoted in Meltzer, *Lewis Roberts Binford*, p. 7.

17. Colin Renfrew, *Prehistory: The Making of the Human Mind* (London: Weidenfeld & Nicolson, 2007), p. 107.

18. Malafouris, *How Things Shape the Mind*, p. 40.

19. Malafouris and Renfrew, *Cognitive Life of Things*, p. 7.

20. Klein and Edgar, *Dawn of Human Culture*, p. 72.

21. Malafouris, *How Things Shape the Mind*, p. 154.

22. Atsushi Iriki and Osamu Sakura, "The Neuroscience of Primate Intellectual Evolution: Natural Selection and Passive and Intentional Niche Construction," *Philosophical Transactions of the Royal Society B: Biological Sciences* 363 (1500, 2008): 2229–241. Published online Apr. 15, 2008, doi: 10.1098/rstb.2008.2274.

23. Quoted in Mithen, *Prehistory of the Mind*, p. 19.

24. Malafouris, *How Things Shape the Mind*, p. 154. Referring to Henri Bergson, *Creative Evolution* [1911] (Dover, 1998), p. 139.

25. These discoveries provided the inspiration for an exhibition at the Natural History Museum in London in 2014. They are reported in Rob Dinnis and Chris Stringer, *Britain: One Million Years of the Human Story* (London: Natural History Museum, 2013).

26. Hutchins, "Imagining the Cognitive Life of Things," p. 99.

27. Michael Tomasello, Ann Kruger, and Hilary Ratner, "Cultural Learning," *Behavioral and Brain Sciences* 16 (1993): 495–552.

28. Malafouris, *How Things Shape the Mind*.

29. *Ibid.*, p. 174.

30. *Ibid.*, p. 176.

31. *Ibid.*, p. 168.

32. David W. Cameron and Colin P. Groves, *Bones, Stones, and Molecules* (California and London: Elsevier, 2004), p. 158. My discussion is drawn from Penny Spikins, Holly Rutherford, and Andy Needham, "From Homininity to Humanity: Compassion from the Earliest Archaic to Modern Humans," *Time and Mind* 3 (3, 2010).

33. Interviewed in *"Homo erectus,"* Episode 2 of *Prehistoric Autopsy*, presented by Alice Roberts and George McGavin, aired Oct. 23, 2012 (BBC2). Clip available at http://www.bbc.co.uk/programmes/p00zy4d3.

34. Teresa Romero, Miguel A. Castellanos, and Frans B. M. de Waal, "Consolation as Possible Expression of Sympathetic Concern among Chimpanzees," *Proceedings of the National Academy of Sciences* 107 (27, 2010): 12110–1115.

35. Zanna Clay and Frans B.M. de Waal, "Development of Socio-emotional Competence in Bonobos," *Proceedings of the National Academy of Sciences* 110 (45, 2013): 18121-8126.

36. David Lordkipanidze et al., "A Complete Skull from Dmanisi, Georgia, and the Evolutionary Biology of Early *Homo*," *Science* 342 (6156, 2013): 326–31.

37. Francesco Berna et al., "Microstratigraphic Evidence of In Situ Fire in the Acheulean Strata of Wonderwerk Cave, Northern Cape Province, South Africa," *Proceedings of the National Academy of Sciences* 109 (20, 2012): E1215–E1220.

38. Since the time of writing, discoveries in China of modern human teeth at least 80,000 years old have thrown this time-scale into question. "Fossil Teeth Place Humans in Asia 20,000 years Early." Accessed Mar. 31 2016 at http://www.bbc.co.uk/news/science-environment-34531861.

39. Stringer, *Origins of Our Species*, pp. 138–39.

40. Dinnis and Stringer, *Britain*, p. 44.

41. Abram, *Spell of the Sensuous*.

42. Ruggero D'Anastasio et. al., "Micro-Biomechanics of the Kebara 2 Hyoid and Its Implications for Speech in Neanderthals," *PLOS ONE* 8 (12, 2013): e82261.

43. Johannes Krause et al., "The Derived FOXP2 Variant of Modern Humans Was Shared with Neanderthals," *Current Biology* 17 (2007): 1908–912.

44. This is not necessarily the same as "belief": there may be beliefs involved, but these may be derived from experiences in the sensible world that do not meet the criteria of scientific materialism for what counts as physical manifestations. Modern indigenous cultures do not necessarily regard all these as "spiritual" so it is even less likely that early humans would have done so. Even so, I would contend that they do constitute an imaginal engagement with the world that experiences the symbolic in concrete form. These questions are considered in more detail later in the book, mainly in Chapters 6 and 8.

45. Stringer, *Origin of Our Species*, p. 126.

46. The evidence is reviewed in Philip Lieberman, *Uniquely Human: The Evolution of Speech, Thought, and Selfless Behavior* (Cambridge, MA: Harvard University Press, 1993), p. 163.

47. William Rendu et al., "Evidence Supporting an Intentional Neandertal Burial at La Chapelle-aux-Saints," *Proceedings of the National Academy of Sciences* 111 (1, 2014): 81–6.

48. Paul Pettit, "When Burial Begins," *British Archaeology* 66 (2002). Pettit points out that symbolic burials with spiritual significance may have been the exception rather than the rule amongst early modern humans, too—there are, for example, no examples of burials amongst the Aurignacians who produced the Lion Man and the Chauvet cave-paintings.

49. Francesco d'Errico and Chris Stringer, "Evolution, Revolution, or Saltation Scenario for the Emergence of Modern Cultures?," *Philosophical Transactions of the Royal Society* 366 (2011): 1064.

50. Klein and Edgar, *Dawn of Human Culture*, p.14.

51. Joaõ Zilhaõ, "The Emergence of Language, Art, and Symbolic Thinking: A Neanderthal Test of Competing Hypotheses," in Christopher S. Henshilwood and Francesco d'Errico, eds., *Homo Symbolicus: The Dawn of Language, Imagination, and Spirituality* (Amsterdam: John Benjamins, 2011), pp. 111–32.

52. Marian Vanhaeren et. al., "Middle Paleolithic Shell Beads in Israel and Algeria," *Science* 312 (5781, 2006): 1788.

53. Stringer, *Origin of Our Species*, p. 128.

54. *Ibid.*, p. 126.

55. Quoted in Elizabeth J. Himelfarb, "Prehistoric Body Painting," *Archaeology* 53 (4, 2000).

56. In relation to Aurignacian use of red ochre, Leroi-Gourhan comments, "it is not unusual to find a layer of the cave floor impregnated with a purplish red to a depth of eight inches. ... The colouring is so intense that practically all the loose ground seems to consist of ochre. One can imagine that the Aurignacians regularly painted their bodies red, dyed their animal skins, coated their weapons, and sprinkled the ground of their dwellings, and that a paste of ochre was used for decorative purposes in every phase of their domestic life." André Leroi-Gourhan, *The Art of Prehistoric Man in Western Europe* (London: Thames & Hudson, 1968), p. 40.

57. Red, black, and white body paint plays an important role in the symbolic ritual of the Ndembu, reported by Victor Turner in *The*

Forest of Symbols: Aspects of Ndeumbu Ritual (Ithaca and London: Cornell University Press, 1967).

58. Wil Roebroeks et al., "Use of Red Ochre by Early Neanderthals," *Proceedings of the National Academy of Science* 109 (6, 2012): 1889–894.

59. Joaõ Zilhaõ, "Personal Adornments and Symbolism among the Neanderthals," in S. Elias, ed., *Origins of Human Creativity and Innovation* (Amsterdam: Elsevier, 2012), pp. 35–49.

60. Clive Finlayson et al., "Birds of a Feather: Neanderthal Exploitation of Raptors and Corvids," *PLOS ONE* 7 (9, 2012): e45927.

61. Renfrew, *Prehistory*, pp. 93ff.

62. Deacon, *Symbolic Species*, p. 366.

63. *Ibid.*, p. 367.

64. Turner, *Forest of Symbols*.

65. "And like this insubstantial pageant faded, / Leave not a rack behind." William Shakespeare, *The Tempest*, ed. Virginia Mason Vaughan and Alden T. Vaughan, *The Arden Shakespeare* (London: Thomas Nelson and Sons, 1999), 4.1.155–56. References are to act, scene, and line.

66. Adam R. Brumm and Mark W. Moore, "Symbolic Revolutions and the Australian Archaeological Record," *Cambridge Archaeological Journal* 15 (2, 2005): 157–75.

67. *Ibid.*, p. 167.

68. Klein and Edgar, *Dawn of Human Culture*; and Frederick L. Coolidge and Thomas Wynn, "Working Memory, Its Executive Functions, and the Emergence of Modern Thinking," *Cambridge Archaeological Journal* 15 (1, 2005): 5–26.

69. Mithen, *Prehistory of the Mind*, pp. 211ff.

70. Zilhaõ, "Personal Adornments and Symbolism," p. 46.

71. Renfrew, *Prehistory*, pp. 84–5.

72. Joseph Henrich, "Demography and Cultural Evolution: How Adaptive Cultural Processes Can Produce Maladaptive Losses," *American Antiquity* 69 (2, 2004): 197–214.

73. Adam Powell, Stephen Shennan, and Mark G. Thomas, "Late Pleistocene Demography and the Appearance of Modern Human Behavior," *Science* 324 (2009): 1298–301.

74. Erella Hovers and Anna Belfer-Cohen, "'Now You See It, Now You Don't': Modern Human Behavior in the Middle Paleolithic," in E. Hovers and S. L. Kuhn, eds., *Transitions Before the Transition:*

Evolution and Stability in the Middle Paleolithic and Middle Stone Age (New York: Springer, 2006), pp. 295–304.

75. Karl Marx. See Chapter 2, note 74.

76. Recent research suggests that Neanderthals had already suffered a severe population loss around 50,000 years ago (well before the arrival of *Homo sapiens*) after which their genetic diversity was sharply reduced. They recovered from near-extinction to recolonize parts of Central and Western Europe where they survived for another 10,000 years. See Paul Rincon, "DNA Reveals Neanderthal Extinction Clues," *BBC Science and Environment News*, Feb. 27, 2012. Accessed Dec. 7, 2014, at http://www.bbc.co.uk/news/science-environment-17179608; and Uppsala Universitet, "European Neanderthals Were on the Verge of Extinction Even before the Arrival of Modern Humans," *Science Daily*. Accessed Dec. 7, 2014, at http://www.sciencedaily.com/releases/2012/02/120225110942.htm.

77. d'Errico and Stringer, "Evolution, Revolution, or Saltation," p. 1064.

78. *Ibid.*, p. 1067.

79. Stringer, *Origin of Our Species*, p. 207.

80. *Ibid.*, pp. 71–2.

CHAPTER FIVE

1. Abram, *Spell of the Sensuous.*

2. I am using *intentional* here in its philosophical sense of being *about* something rather than in the sense of being *deliberate.* That is, by intentional activity I mean the sense-making purposive activity through which humans enact their world.

3. For the "more-than-human world" see Abram, *Spell of the Sensuous.*

4. Renfrew, *Prehistory*, p. 117.

5. Searle, *Construction of Social Reality.*

6. *Ibid.*, p. 76.

7. *Ibid.*, pp. 28 and 37ff.

8. See Chapter 3, pp. 104–05.

9. Stephen L. Kuhn and Mary C. Stiner, "Body Ornamentation as Information Technology: Towards an Understanding of the Significance of Early Beads," in P. Mellars, K. Boyle, O. Bar-Yosef, and C. Stringer, eds., *Rethinking the Human Revolution: New*

Behavioural and Biological Perspectives on the Origin and Dispersal of Modern Humans (Cambridge: McDonald Institute Monographs, 2007), p. 47.

10. *Ibid.*, p. 51.

11. Clark, "Material Surrogacy and the Supernatural," p. 24.

12. *Ibid.* Referring to Matthew Day, "Religion, Off-Line Cognition and the Extended Mind," *Journal of Cognition and Culture* 4 (1, 2007): 101–21.

13. Enkapune Ya Muto (Twilight Cave) in Kenya was excavated by Stanley Ambrose in the 1980s. The oldest ostrich shell beads found there have been dated to more than 46,000 years old [Stringer, *Origin of Our Species*, p. 227]. The Üçagizli ("three mouths") cave in Turkey, near the Syrian border, dates from 36,000 years ago. An international team including Steven Kuhn and Mary Stiner has been excavating the cave since 1997 (*ibid.*, p. 94).

14. Kim Sterelny, *The Evolved Apprentice: How Evolution Made Humans Unique* (Boston: MIT Press, 2012), p. 51.

15. *Ibid.*

16. See Chapter 1, note 18.

17. Malafouris, *How Things Shape the Mind*, p. 91; quoting Gregory Bateson, *Steps to an Ecology of Mind: Collected Essays in Anthropology, Psychiatry, Evolution, and Epistemology* (Northvale, NJ and London: Jason Aronson Inc., 1972), p. 139.

18. *Ibid.*, p. 118.

19. Lambros Malafouris, "The Sacred Engagement: Outline of a Hypothesis about the Origin of Human 'Religious Intelligence,'" in D. A. Barrowclough and C. Malone, eds., *Cult in Context: Reconsidering Ritual in Archaeology* (Oxford: Oxbow Books, 2007), p. 202.

20. Malafouris, *How Things Shape the Mind*, p. 95.

21. Vygotsky uses the example of a child using a stick as a horse to illustrate the separation of thought from objects and action. The stick becomes a pivot by which the child can sever the meaning of a horse from a real horse, albeit I would prefer to say that the meaning is elaborated or given an additional dimension rather than "severed" which has too much of a Cartesian implication. Similarly, I have avoided the use of the term *internalized* in this discussion which literalizes the metaphor of mind as internal to the body. (See Lev Vygotsky, *Mind in Society*, trans. Michael Cole (Cambridge, MA: Harvard University Press, 1978), pp. 97–8.

22. Paul Pettit, "The Living as Symbols, the Dead as Symbols: Problematising the Scale and Pace of Hominin Symbolic Evolution," in Henshilwood and d'Errico, *Homo Symbolicus*, pp. 141–61.

23. Stringer, *Origin of Our Species*, p. 211.

24. *Hamlet*, ed. Philip Edwards (Cambridge: Cambridge University Press, 2003), 1.2.133 and 2.2.317. References are to act, scene, and line.

25. Colin Renfrew, "Neuroscience, Evolution, and the Sapient Paradox: The Factuality of Value and the Sacred," *Philosophical Transactions of the Royal Society B: Biological Sciences* 363 (1499, 2008): 2044.

26. *Ibid.*

27. *Hamlet*, ed. Philip Edwards, 1.2.133; *Macbeth, The Arden Shakespeare,* Ninth Edition ed. Kenneth Muir (Methuen, 1964) 5.5.26–28. References are to act, scene, and line.

28. James Fisher, "The Evolution of the Analytic Process: Poetry and Psychoanalysis, Twin 'Sciences' of the Emotions," *Couple and Family Psychoanalysis* 4 (2014): 5–21. First published in *Journal of the British Association of Psychotherapists*.

29. Renfrew, "Neuroscience, Evolution, and the Sapient Paradox," p. 2045.

30. In 1984, Serge Gainsbourg created a cause célèbre by burning a 500 franc note on live French TV, in protest against heavy taxation. His action, illegal in France, provoked outrage and 'to this day, remembering this remains troubling' (Claire Bruas-Jacquess, personal communication, March 25, 2015).

31. What then of those religious traditions that exclude material representations, notably the Jewish commandment that "thou shalt have no graven images?" Here, it is interesting to note that it is the *Word* of God itself that has become the sacred object, made manifest in the holy scrolls of the Torah which are the focal point of worship in every synagogue. This would seem to support David Abram's argument that written language introduced a major change of focus from that of oral cultures in which it is the sensory environment that provides the location and symbology for spiritual meaning. In Judaism, the Word has become the sacred object *per se.* Christians go even further—for them, the historical Jesus is "the word made flesh" thus subsuming even bodily existence to the supremacy of the Word. Even in Eastern mystical traditions that foster states of mind beyond thought there are representations of the Buddha and mandalas.

Clearly, it is very difficult to experience the spiritual without some material aid, even where a distinction is made between the image and the spiritual reality it signifies.

32. Roger Brooke, "The Self, the Psyche, and the World: A Phenomenological Interpretation," *Journal of Analytical Psychology* 54 (5, 2009): 609.

33. *Ibid.*

34. *Ibid.*

CHAPTER SIX

1. Archaeologists divide the peoples of the Upper Paleolithic into a series of prehistorical cultures on the basis of their characteristic tool industries. The earliest culture was the Aurignacians who produced the Lion Man and the Chauvet caves. The Sunghir burial with thousands of beads was part of the Gravettian culture, and the caves at Lascaux (17,000 years ago) were the work of the Magdalenian peoples.

2. Tim D. White et al., "Pleistocene *Homo sapiens* from Middle Awash, Ethiopia," *Nature* 423 (Jun. 12, 2003): 742–47. See Robert Sanders, "160,000-year-old fossilized skulls uncovered in Ethiopia are oldest anatomically modern humans," *UCBerkeley News*, Jun. 11, 2003. Accessed Feb. 25, 2015, at http://berkeley.edu/news/media/releases/2003/06/11_idaltu.shtml.

3. Stringer, *Origin of Our Species*, p. 103.

4. Marx, "18th Brumaire," p. 96.

5. Jean Morris and Eleanor Preston-Whyte, *Speaking with Beads: Zulu Arts from Southern Africa* (New York : Thames and Hudson, 1994), p. 55. Quoted in Spikins et al., "From Homininity to Humanity," p. 11.

6. Daniella Bar-Yosef Mayer and Naomi Porat, "Green Stone Beads at the Dawn of Agriculture," *Proceedings of the National Academy of Sciences* 105 (25, 2008): 8549.

7. Joy Schaverien, "Gifts, Talismans, and Tokens in Analysis: Symbolic Enactments or Sinister Acts," *Journal of Analytical Psychology* 56 (2, 2011): 160–83.

8. Lewis-Williams, *Mind in the Cave.*

9. *Ibid.*, p. 93.

10. Paul Bahn, "Religion and Ritual in the Upper Paleolithic," in T. Insoll, ed., *Handbook of Archaeology of Ritual and Religion* (Oxford and New York: Oxford University Press, 2011), p. 350.

11. *Ibid.*

12. *Ibid.*, p. 352.

13. Lewis-Williams, *Mind in the Cave*, p. 131.

14. Anne Solomon, "The Myth of Ritual Origins? Ethnography, Mythology and Interpretation of San Rock Art," *South African Archaeological Bulletin* 52 (1997): 3–13.

15. *Ibid.*, p. 6.

16. Alan P. Garfinkel, "Paradigm Shifts, Rock Art Studies, and the 'Coso Sheep Cult' of Eastern California," *North American Archaeologist* 27 (3, 2006): 203–44.

17. *Ibid.*, p. 215.

18. Thomas A. Dowson, "Debating Shamanism in Southern African Rock Art: Time to Move On," *South African Archaeological Bulletin* 62 (185, 2007): 49.

19. Tim Ingold, *The Perception of the Environment: Essays on Livelihood, Dwelling and Skill* (London and New York: Routledge, 2000), p. 130.

20. Dowson, "Debating Shamanism," p. 55.

21. Warren Colman, "Dream Interpretation and the Creation of Symbolic Meaning," in M. Stein, ed., *Jungian Psychoanalysis* (Chicago and La Salle, IL: Open Court, 2010), pp. 94–108.

22. Lewis-Williams, *Mind in the Cave*, p. 170.

23. *Ibid.*, p. 172.

24. *Ibid.*, p. 51.

25. Jung, *Memories, Dreams, Reflections*, p. 216.

26. C. G. Jung, "Psychological Commentary on 'The Tibetan Book of the Great Liberation'" (1939/1954), in *The Collected Works of C. G. Jung*, vol. 11, trans. R. F. C. Hull, 2nd ed. (London: Routledge and Kegan Paul, 1969), § 782.

27. For an account of just such a dialogue between a psychoanalyst and a sangoma, see Suzanne Maiello, "Encounter with a Traditional Healer: Western and African Therapeutic Approaches in Dialogue," *Journal of Analytical Psychology* 53 (2, 2008): 241–60.

28. Ingold, *Perception of the Environment*, p. 121.

29. Abram, *Spell of the Sensuous*, p. 168ff.

30. Bruce Chatwin, *The Songlines* (London: Penguin Books, 1987), p. 52. Quoted in Abram, *Spell of the Sensuous*, p. 171.

31. Ingold, *Perception of the Environment*, p. 123.

32. Turner, *Forest of Symbols*, p. 48.

33. *Ibid.*, p. 49.

34. Colman, "Dream Interpretation," p. 99.

35. Thompson, *Mind in Life*, p. 12.

36. Mettrie, *Machine Man*, p. 15.

37. Brooke, *Jung and Phenomenology*, p. 89.

38. Lewis-Williams, *Mind in the Cave*, p. 210.

39. Jerome Bernstein, "Healing Our Split: *Participation Mystique* and C. G. Jung," in Mark Winborn, ed., *Shared Realities: Participation Mystique and Beyond* (Skiatook, OK: Fisher King Press, 2014), p. 171, fn. 428.

40. See Chapter 5, pp. 158–59.

41. I am using the term *collective* here in its original Durkheimian sense as *socially* collective rather than Jung's sense of an unconscious that is *psychologically* collective. See Chapter 8 for further discussion.

42. Cortina and Liotti, "Attachment Is about Safety and Protection."

43. The video turned up on my Facebook page via one of my animal-loving friends. It can be found on Jane Goodall's website. Posted on Dec. 31, 2013. Accessed on Jan. 4, 2015, at http://www.janegoodall.be/index.php/the-incredible-gesture-of-gratitude-of-wounda-to-jane-goodall/.

44. See Chapter 4, p. 127.

45. The evidence for compassion and empathy amongst elephants is also likely to be due to their pattern of group living, although it does not seem to have led to the same level of cooperation and collaboration in shared tasks.

46. Penny Spikins, "The Evolution of Emotion," talk given at Natural History Museum, London, May 30, 2014.

47. *Ibid.* See also Spikins et al., "From Homininity to Humanity."

48. This is an example of *participation mystique*, Lévy-Bruhl's important and widely misunderstood concept, discussed in Chapter 8.

49. Warren Colman, "Mourning as a Symbolic Process," *Journal of Analytical Psychology* 55 (2, 2010): 275–97.

50. In *Memories, Dreams, Reflections*, Jung recounts the making of an important symbolic object of this kind—the carved manikin that he hid in the attic together with a little stone that he had painted.

When, as an adult, he read about Australian *churingas* (sacred stones kept hidden and secret), he connected these with his own secret stone and this produced his first conviction "that there are archaic psychic components which have entered the individual psyche without any direct line of tradition." Shamdasani has shown that Jung's source was Lévy-Bruhl, who regarded the practices around churingas as examples of *participation mystique*. But for Jung, it was not only the participatory state of mind that was common between him and the Aranda peoples of central Australia, it was also the content of the act that he took as an indication of an "atemporal component of the soul." Typically, Jung takes similarity as identity and accommodates the experiences of others to his own. (See Jung, *Memories, Dreams, Reflections*, pp. 36–8; Shamdasani, *Making of Modern Psychology*, pp. 296–97).

51. Malcolm Hamilton, *The Sociology of Religion*, 2nd ed. (New York: Routledge, 2011), p. 56.

52. Wikipedia entries for "*mana*" and "Robert Codrington."

53. R. R. Marett, *The Threshold of Religion*, 2nd ed. (London: Methuen, 1914).

54. E. O. James, *The Beginnings of Religion* (London: Hutchinson's University Library, 1937), p. 17.

55. Marett, *Threshold of Religion*, p. xxxi.

56. *International Encyclopedia of the Social Sciences*, 1968. Accessed Jan. 4, 2014, at http://www.encyclopedia.com/doc/1G2-3045000765.html.

57. William Wordsworth, *Preface to Lyrical Ballads* (1802).

58. Hamilton, *Sociology of Religion*, p. 57.

59. *Ibid.*, p. 59.

60. In the Chamber of the Lions at the furthest end of the caves; see Werner Herzog, *Cave of Forgotten Dreams* (Creative Differences et al., 2010), DVD and available at Amazon.com. The scene featuring the rock pendant occurs at 42:30.

61. It is a different matter for agricultural communities, of course, which give rise to many myths concerning gods and goddesses of the harvest, the main subject matter of Frazer's *Golden Bough*.

62. Mithen, *Prehistory of the Mind*.

63. Pamela B. Vandiver, Olga Soffer, Bohuslav Klima, and Jiři Svoboda, "The Origins of Ceramic Technology at Dolni Věstonice, Czechoslovakia," *Science* 246 (4933, 1989): 1002–008.

64. Interviewed in *Sacred Wonders of Britain*, episode 1, presented by Neil Oliver, aired December 30, 2013 (BBC Two, 2013–2014).

65. Mathias Guenther, "Animals in Bushman Thought, Myth, and Art," in Tim Ingold, David Riches, and James Woodburn, eds., *Hunters and Gatherers 2: Property, Power, and Ideology* (Oxford: Berg, 1988), p. 199.

66. Brian Morris, *Animals and Ancestors: An Ethnography* (Oxford: Berg, 2000), p. 39.

67. "Is the world composed of just so many 'natural resources' or is the world, in fact, a sacred entity? And as humans, do we have the integrity and intelligence to know the difference?" Joe Hutto, *The Light in High Places: A Naturalist Looks at Wyoming Wilderness, Rocky Mountain Bighorn Sheep, Cowboys, and Other Rare Species* (New York: Skyhorse Publishing, 2009), p. v.

68. Tim Ingold, *Being Alive: Essays on Movement, Knowledge and Description* (Abingdon and New York: Routledge, 2011), p. 68.

69. Ingold, *Perception of the Environment*, p. 72.

70. Robert J. Losey et al., "The Bear-able Likeness of Being: Ursine Remains at the Shamanka II Cemetery, Lake Baikal, Siberia," in Christopher Watts, ed., *Relational Archaeologies: Humans, Animals, Things* (London and New York: Routledge, 2013), p. 67.

71. *Ibid.*, p. 94.

72. Chantal Conneller, "Becoming Deer: Corporeal Transformations at Star Carr," *Archaeological Dialogues* 11 (2004): 37–56; and Viveiros de Castro, "Cosmological Deixis and Amerindian Perspectivism," *The Journal of the Royal Anthropological Institute* 4 (3, 1998): 469–88.

73. Hanna Cobb, "Materials, Biographies, Identities, Experience," in V. Cummings, P. Jordan, and M. Zvelebil, eds., *Handbook of Archaeology and Anthropology of Hunter-Gatherers* (Oxford: Oxford University Press, 2014), p. 1212.

74. Abram, *Spell of the Sensuous*, pp. 12–3.

75. The unpublished manuscript entitled "African Journey" can be found in the Jung Papers at the ETH [*Eidgenössische Technische Hochschule*] in Zürich. My reference to it is taken from Shamdasani, *Making of Modern Psychology*, p. 324.

76. Losey et al., *Bear-able Likeness*, p. 87; referencing Mietje Germonpré and Riku Hämäläinen "Fossil Bear Bones in the Eurasian

Upper Paleolithic: The Possibility of a Proto Bear-Ceremonialism,"
Arctic Anthropology 44 (2, 2007): 1–30.

77. *Ibid.*, p. 67.

78. R. K. Nelson, *Make Prayers to the Raven: The Life in the Bear*,
produced by M. O. Badger and R. K. Nelson (KUAC-TV; University
of Alaska Fairbanks, 1987), VHS.

79. The symbolic "as if" view might then be contrasted with
the state of *participation mystique* in which there is a "symbolic
equation" between symbol and symbolized. Cf. Segal, "Notes on
Symbol Formation."

80. This pithy comment is reported by Richard Mizen who can
no longer remember his source, so it may well be apocryphal. See
Richard Mizen, "On the Capacity to Suffer One's Self," *Journal of
Analytical Psychology* 59 (3, 2014): 316.

81. Hamilton, *Sociology of Religion*, p. 27–8.

82. *Ibid.*

83. E. E. Evans-Pritchard, *Theories of Primitive Religion* (Oxford:
Clarenden Press), p. 24.

84. Max Gluckman, *Politics, Law and Ritual in Tribal Society*
(Oxford: Basil Blackwell, 1965), p. 2; see also J. M. Coetzee, *The
Lives of Animals* (Princeton, NJ: Princeton University Press, 1999),
p. 101 with reference to R. Angus Downie, *Frazer and the Golden
Bough* (London: Gollancz 1970), p. 42.

85. The phrase "the more than human world" was coined by David
Abram (see *Spell of the Sensuous*) and has become a key phrase within
the lingua franca of the cultural ecology movement (Wikipedia entry
for David Abram).

86. Godfrey Lienhardt, *Divinity and Experience: The Religion of
the Dinka* (Oxford University Press, 1961), p. 117.

87. Jonathan Z. Smith, "I am a Parrot (Red)," in J. Z. Smith, *Map
is not Territory: Studies in the History of Religions* (University of
Chicago Press, 1978), p. 281.

CHAPTER SEVEN

1. One exception is Bradd Shore for whom Lévy-Bruhl "conceives
of the mind as an emergent phenomenon at the nexus of the nervous
system and a variable field of social values." See *Culture in Mind:
Cognition, Culture and the Problem of Meaning* (Oxford and New York:

Oxford University Press, 1996), p. 28. Boas contrasts "an essential similarity of mental endowment in difference races, with the probability of variations in the type of mental characteristics" in "Psychological Problems in Anthropology" (1910) in George W. Stocking, ed., *A Franz Boas Reader: The Shaping of American Anthropology, 1883–1911* (University of Chicago Press, 1974), p. 244.

2. *Ibid.*, p. 247. Shamdasani is somewhat misleading here, implying that Freud and Jung simply failed to take notice of Boas (*Making of Modern Psychology*, p. 277). Boas certainly critiqued the comparative method used by Jung (as mentioned in Chapter 1), but even if outward similarities might have very different historical origins in context-specific ways of life, psychoanalysis could claim to have identified the psychological processes underlying those historically variant similarities. The dislocation between anthropology and psychoanalysis has more to do with the split between culture and mind. In other words, anthropology has as much responsibility as psychoanalysis for the disconnection between the two—both have been caught up in the Cartesian problematic.

3. I heard this from a guide at Uluru in August 2009.

4. Translated as "The Psychology of the Unconscious" by Beatrice Hinkle in 1916 (New York: Moffat, Yard and Company, 1916) and later published as Volume 5 in *the Collected Works of C. G. Jung* as "Symbols of Transformation," retranslated by R. F. C. Hull (London: Routledge and Kegan Paul, 1956).

5. Jung, trans. Hinkle, *Psychology of Unconscious*, p. 14 (cf. CW 5, § 11).

6. Jung, CW 5, § 14 (cf. 1916 version, p. 15).

7. Jung, CW 5, § 20.

8. Jung, CW 5, § 23; Boas, "Psychological Problems," p. 244.

9. Jung, CW 5, § 24.

10. Jung, CW 5, p. xxiii.

11. Jung, CW 5, § 29. Jung is quoting from Karl Abraham, *Dreams and Myths: A Study in Folk Psychology*," in Hilda C. Abraham, ed., *Clinical Papers and Essays on Psychoanalysis* (London: Hogarth Press, 1955), p. 36 [Originally published in 1909].

12. *Ibid.*

13. Jung, CW 5, § 37.

14. Jung, CW 5, § 38 and n. 38.

15. D.W. Winnicott, "Transitional Objects and Transitional Phenomena" (1953), in *Playing and Reality* (London: Tavistock, 1971), p. 14.

Winnicott distinguishes this from the "intermediate area" which is partly shared and partly private, thus tentatively acknowledging the social aspect of the mind.

16. Jung, CW 5, § 17.

17. The notion of "inanimate matter" is considerably more recent, of course, as discussed in the previous chapter.

18. Stringer, *Origin of Our Species*, p. 138.

19. Lyn Wadley, "Complex Cognition Required for Compound Adhesive Manufacture," in Henshilwood and d'Errico, *Homo Symbolicus*, pp. 100 and 104.

20. Shamdasani, *Making of Modern Psychology*, p. 105. In this and the following section I am indebted to Sonu Shamdasani's extensive research.

21. Frank Seafield in an 1865 dream encyclopaedia quoted by Natalya Lusty and Helen Groth, *Dreams and Modernity: A Cultural History* (Hove and New York: Routledge, 2013), p. 24.

22. Gotthilf Heinrich von Schubert quoted in Shamdasani, *Making of Modern Psychology*, p. 109.

23. See Neville Symington, *The Analytic Experience* (London: Free Association Books, 1986), p. 80.

24. D. M. Thomas, *The White Hotel* (London: Gollancz, 1981).

25. Frank J. Sulloway, *Freud, Biologist of the Mind: Beyond the Psychoanalytic Legend* (Cambridge, MA: Harvard University Press, 1992), p. 270.

26. Quoted in Shamdasani, *Making of Modern Psychology*, p. 117.

27. Nietzsche, *Human, All Too Human* (1880), pp. 24–7. The translation is taken from Jung, CW 5, § 27. For a slightly different translation, see Shamdasani, *Making of Modern Psychology*, p. 117.

28. Lucien Lévy-Bruhl, *How Natives Think* (1910), trans. Lilian A. Clare (London: Allen & Unwin, 1926), p. 382.

29. Sigmund Freud, "The Unconscious," (1915), in *The Standard Edition of the Complete Psychological Works of Sigmund Freud*, vol. 14 (London: Hogarth Press, 1957), p. 186.

30. James Strachey, "Sigmund Freud: His Life and Ideas," in *The Pelican Freud Library*, vol. 11 (London: Penguin Books, 1984), p. 22.

31. C. G. Jung, "Archaic Man" (1930), in *The Collected Works of C. G. Jung*, vol. 10, trans. R. F. C. Hull, 2nd ed. (London: Routledge and Kegan Paul, 1970), § 106

32. According to Jonathan Z. Smith, Lévy-Bruhl's interpretation was a misreading of the original anthropological data: the Bororo

did not claim any such thing. Rather they were expressing a special relationship of identity with parrots that included becoming parrots after death, but not that they were here and now identical with parrots in the sense that an insane person might claim to be Napoleon. See Smith, "I am a Parrot (Red)," p. 267.

33. In Jones' view, "Symbolism thus appears as the unconscious precipitate of primitive means of adaption to reality that have become superfluous and useless." See Ernest Jones, "The Theory of Symbolism," in *Papers on Psychoanalysis* (London: Balliere, Tindall & Cox, 1938), p. 152.

34. Abram Kardiner, *My Analysis with Freud: Reminiscences* (New York: W. W. Norton & Co., 1977), p. 75.

35. Sigmund Freud, *The Interpretation of Dreams* (1900), in *The Standard Edition of the Complete Psychological Works of Sigmund Freud*, vol. 4 (London: Hogarth Press, 1953), p. 352.

36. Sigmund Freud, *Introductory Lectures on Psycho-Analysis* (1915–1916), in *The Standard Edition of the Complete Psychological Works of Sigmund Freud*, vol. 15 (London: Hogarth Press, 1961), p. 181.

37. *Ibid.*, p. 199.

38. *Ibid.*

39. Clifford Geertz, *The Interpretation of Cultures: Selected Essays* (New York: Basic Books, 1973), p. 119.

40. Iain McGilchrist, *The Master and His Emissary: The Divided Brain and the Making of the Western Mind* (New Haven and London: Yale University Press, 2009).

41. *Ibid.*, pp. 39–40.

42. *Ibid.*, pp. 46–51.

43. *Ibid.*, p. 51.

44. *Ibid.*, p. 70.

45. *Ibid.*, pp. 46 and 50.

46. *Ibid.*, p. 93.

47. Murray Stein, *Minding the Self: Jungian Meditations on Contemporary Spirituality* (Hove and New York: Routledge, 2014), p. 33. Stein includes the neurology of right and left brain functioning in his reformulation but does not reference McGilchrist specifically.

48. See Peter Amman, *The Spirit of the Rocks* (Zürich: Triluma Film, 2002), 01:01–03.

49. Michael Robbins, *The Primordial Mind in Health and Illness: A Cross-Cultural Perspective* (Hove & New York: Routledge, 2011).

50. *Ibid.*, p. 6.

51. *Ibid.*, p. 129.

52. For examples, see Maiello, "Encounter with a Traditional Healer" and an interview with West African writer and healer, Malidoma Patrice Somé, in Stephanie Marohn, *The Natural Medicine Guide to Schizophrenia* (Charlottesville, VA: Hampton Roads, 2003), p. 178.

53. D. W. Winnicott, "The Use of an Object and Relating through Identifications," in *Playing and Reality*, p. 89.

54. *Ibid.*

55. Wilfred R. Bion, "A Theory of Thinking (1962)," in *Second Thoughts* (London: Karnac Books, 1984).

56. Geertz, *Interpretation of Cultures*, p. 99.

57. Erik Erikson, *Childhood and Society* (New York: W. W. Norton & Co., 1950).

58. Boston Change Process Study Group, "Foundational Level of Psychodynamic Meaning."

59. See Donnell Stern, *Unformulated Experience: From Dissociation to Imagination* (Hillsdale, NJ: Analytic Press, 2003) and Christopher Bollas, *The Shadow of the Object: Psychoanalysis of the Unthought Known* (London: Karnac Books, 1987).

60. Richard Carvalho, "A Vindication of Jung's Unconscious and Its Archetypal Expression: Jung, Bion, and Matte Blanco," in A. Cavalli, L. Hawkins, and M. Stevens, eds., *Transformation: Jung's Legacy and Clinical Work Today* (London: Karnac Books, 2013), p. 53.

61. Eric Rayner and David Tuckett, "An Introduction to Matte-Blanco's Reformulation of the Freudian Unconscious and his Conceptualization of the Internal World," in Ignacio Matte Blanco, *Thinking, Feeling, and Being: Clinical Reflections on the Fundamental Antinomy of Human Beings and World* (London and New York: Tavistock/Routledge, 1998), p. 16.

62. Rodney Bomford, "The Question of God and the Doctrine of the Trinity," *British Journal of Psychotherapy* 26 (3, 2010): 361.

63. Richard Carvalho, "Matte Blanco and the Multidimensional Realm of the Unconscious," *British Journal of Psychotherapy* 26 (3, 2010): 326.

64. Carvalho acknowledges this: "As a rule, the higher the ratio of symmetry to asymmetry, the greater the likelihood of unconsciousness. But not necessarily: poets after all make explicit conscious use of symmetry to produce their effects" (personal communication, January 12, 2015).

65. *Ibid.*

66. Lévy-Bruhl, *How Natives Think*, pp. 58–9.

67. I made a similar point in the last chapter in relation to the distinction between the ants and the household spirits in Bali. Symmetrically, they are the same but, at the same time they are distinct—a clear example of bi-logic.

68. Geertz, *Interpretation of Cultures*, p. 81.

69. Abridged and adapted from Richard Carvalho, "Synchronicity, the Infinite Unrepressed, Dissociation, and the Interpersonal," *Journal of Analytical Psychology* 59 (3, 2014): 374–75.

70. See my paper on "Sexual Metaphor and the Language of Unconscious Phantasy" for a similar example in relation to an interpretation of the "faecal penis." I argue that rather than referring to a pre-existent unconscious phantasy (cf. "archetype"), the interpretation was "dreamed up" out of the *coniunctio* between the patient's material and my own immersion in the metaphorical language of Freud, Klein, and Meltzer. Warren Colman, "Sexual Metaphor and the Language of Unconscious Phantasy," *Journal of Analytical Psychology* 50 (5, 2005): 641–60.

CHAPTER EIGHT

1. Jung, *Memories, Dreams, Reflections*, pp. 182–83.

2. Miriam Webster on-line dictionary. Accessed on Feb. 16, 2015, at www.merriam-webster.com/dictionary/collective%20representation.

3. Emil Durkheim, *The Elementary Forms of Religious Life*, trans. Joseph Ward Swain (London: George Allen and Unwin, 1915), p. 15.

4. Lévy-Bruhl, *How Natives Think*, p. 382.

5. *Ibid.*, p. 36.

6. *Ibid.*, p. 38.

7. Susanne Langer, *Feeling and Form: A Theory of Art* (New York: Charles Scribner's Sons, 1953), p. 44.

8. Susanne Langer, *Mind: An Essay on Human Feeling*, vol. 1 (Baltimore, MD: The Johns Hopkins Press, 1967), p. 76.

9. *Ibid.*, p. 152.

10. Lucien Lévy-Bruhl, *The Notebooks on Primitive Mentality*, trans. Peter Riviere (Oxford: Basil Blackwell, 1975), p. 102.

11. S. A. Mousalamis, "The Concept of Participation in Lévy-Bruhl's 'Primitive Mentality,'" *Journal of the Anthropological Society of Oxford* 21 (1, 1990): 43.

12. Kenneth Grahame, *The Wind in the Willows* (Project Gutenberg e-books, 2008). Accessed Aug. 8 2014, at http://www.gutenberg.org/files/289/289-h/289-h.htm#link2H_4_0007. Originally published (London: Methuen, 1908).

13. Dowson, "Debating Shamanism," p. 58.

14. Colman, "Synchronicity," p. 475.

15. Bruno Latour, *We Have Never Been Modern* (Cambridge, MA: Harvard University Press, 1993).

16. Alf Hornborg, "Animism, Fetishism, and Objectivism as Strategies for Knowing (or Not Knowing) the World," *Ethnos: Journal of Anthropology* 71 (1, 2006): 21–32.

17. Maurice Merleau-Ponty, *The Phenomenology of Perception*, trans. C. Smith (London and New York: Routledge, 1965), p. 143.

8. Abram, *Spell of the Sensuous*, p. 59.

19. Lévy-Bruhl, *How Natives Think*, p. 77.

20. *Ibid.*, p. 123.

21. *Ibid.*, p. 125.

22. Carvalho, "Multidimensional Realm of Unconscious," p. 326.

23. William Hazlitt was an early nineteenth-century artist and critic associated with the English Romantics. The full quotation shows Hazlitt's awareness of the reality of the imagination and indicates the participatory distribution of cognition between audience, actor, and author: "Hamlet is a name; his speeches and sayings but the idle coinage of the poet's brain. What then, are they not real? They are as real as our own thoughts. Their reality is in the reader's mind. It is we who are Hamlet." From *Characters of Shakespeare's Plays* (1817).

24. Evans-Pritchard, *Nuer Religion*, p. 131. Quoted in Smith, "I am a Parrot (Red)," p. 281.

25. As Haruki Murakami expresses it, "Fact may not be truth and truth may not be factual." *The Wind-Up Bird Chronicle* (London: Vintage Books, 2003), p. 525.

26 Day, "Religion"; see Chapter 5, p. 154–55.

27. Jung, CW 6, § 781.

28. Lévy-Bruhl, *How Natives Think*, p. 382.

29. C. G. Jung, "The Relations between the Ego and the Unconscious" (1928), in *The Collected Works of C. G. Jung*, vol. 7, ed. and trans. Gerhard Adler and R. F. C. Hull (Princeton, NJ: Princeton University Press, 1966), § 269.

30. Mark Winborn, "Introduction: An Overview of *Participation Mystique*," in *Shared Realities*, p. 1.

31. *Ibid.*, pp. 16–8.

32. Erich Neumann, *The Place of Creation* (Princeton, NJ: Princeton University Press, 1989).

33. Ingold, *Being Alive*, p. 68.

34. Deborah Bryon, "*Participation Mystique* in Peruvian Shamanism," in Winborn, *Shared Realities*, pp. 144–61.

35. *Ibid.*, p. 158.

36. *Ibid.*, pp. 157 and 152.

37. *Ibid.*, p. 150; Cf. the wily fox in Saint-Exupéry's *The Little Prince* who says, "It is only with the heart that one can see rightly; what is essential is invisible to the eye."

38. *Ibid.*, p. 152.

39. Robert Segal, "Jung and Lévy-Bruhl," *Journal of Analytical Psychology* 52 (5, 2007): 636.

40. Jung, CW 6, § 692.

41. Jung, "The Archaic" (1931), in Jung, CW 10, § 128. See also Segal, "Jung and Lévy-Bruhl," p. 644.

42. C. G. Jung, "The Concept of the Collective Unconscious" (1936), in *The Collected Works of C. G. Jung*, vol. 9i, ed. and trans. Gerhard Adler and R. F. C. Hull, 2nd ed. (London: Routledge and Kegan Paul, 1968), § 89.

43. D. W. Winnicott, "The Location of Cultural Experience" (1967), in *Playing and Reality*, p. 99.

44. Geertz, *Interpretation of Cultures*, p. 12.

45. Frances Densmore, *Teton Sioux Music*, Bureau of American Ethnology Bulletin 61 (Washington, DC: Government Printing Office 1918; Lincoln, NB: University of Nebraska Press, reprint 1992), pp. 184–88. Quoted in Vine Deloria, Jr., *C. G. Jung and the Sioux Traditions: Dreams, Visions, Nature, and the Primitive* (New Orleans, LA: Spring Journal Books), p. 156.

46. Warren Colman, "The Analyst in Action: An Individual Account of What Jungians Do and Why They Do It," *International Journal of Psychoanalysis* 91 (2010): 301.

47. Geertz, *Interpretation of Cultures*, pp. 87–125.

48. *Ibid.*, p. 112.

49. *Ibid.*, p. 114–18.

50. The death temple is concerned with honouring the dead and appeasing the divinities of evil and destruction. See Clifford Geertz, "Tihungan" in Koentjaraningrat, ed., *Villages in Indonesia* (Ithaca, NY: Cornell University Press, 1967), p. 240.

51. Geertz, *Interpretation of Cultures*, pp. 6ff. The term *thick description* and the winking example are taken from Gilbert Ryle.

52. *Ibid.*, p. 114.

53. *Ibid.*, p. 116.

54. *Ibid.*, p. 117.

55. *Ibid.*, p. 115.

56. *Ibid.*, p. 114.

57. *Ibid.*, p. 116.

58. *Ibid.*, p. 118.

59. Jung, CW 16, §§ 399 and 163.

60. Victor Turner, *The Ritual Process: Structure and Anti-Structure* (Chicago, IL: Aldine, 1969), pp. 42–3.

61. Geertz, *Interpretation of Cultures*, p. 104.

62. Roger Brooke, "Notes on the Phenomenology of Interiority and the Foundations of Psychology," *International Journal of Jungian Studies* 5 (1, 2013): 10–1.

63. "To understand the dream's meaning I must stick as close as possible to the dream images." Jung, CW 16, § 320.

SELECTED BIBLIOGRAPHY

Abram, David. *The Spell of the Sensuous: Perception and Language in a More-Than-Human World*. New York: Vintage Books, 1997.

Boas, Franz. "Psychological Problems in Anthropology" (1910), in George W. Stocking, ed., *A Franz Boas Rader: The Shaping of American Anthropology, 1883–1911*. Chicago, IL: University of Chicago Press, 1974.

Boston Change Process Study Group (BCPSG). "The Foundational Level of Psychodynamic Meaning: Implicit Process in Relation to Conflict, Defense, and the Dynamic Unconscious." *International Journal of Psychoanalysis* 88 (2007): 1–16.

Brooke, Roger. *Jung and Phenomenology*. London and New York: Routledge, 1991.

Carvalho, Richard. "Matte Blanco and the Multidimensional Realm of the Unconscious." *British Journal of Psychotherapy* 26 (3, 2010): 324–34.

Clark, Andy. "Material Surrogacy and the Supernatural: Reflections on the Role of Artefacts in 'Off-line' Cognition," in Lambros Malafouris and Colin Renfrew, eds., *The Cognitive Life of Things: Recasting the Boundaries of the Mind*. Cambridge: McDonald Institute for Archaeological Research, 2010.

Clark, Andy and David Chalmers. "The Extended Mind." *Analysis* 58 (1, 1998): 7–19.

Cole, Michael and James V. Wertsch. "Beyond the Individual-Social Antimony in Discussions of Piaget and Vygotsky." *Human Development* 39 (1996): 230–36.

Colman, Warren. "Sexual Metaphor and the Language of Unconscious Phantasy." *Journal of Analytical Psychology* 50 (5, 2005): 641–60.

Colman, Warren. "Theory as Metaphor: Clinical Knowledge and Its Communication." *Journal of Analytical Psychology* 54 (2, 2009): 199–215.

Colman, Warren. "Dream Interpretation and the Creation of Symbolic Meaning," in M. Stein, ed., *Jungian Psychoanalysis*. Chicago and La Salle, IL: Open Court, 2010, pp. 94–108.

Colman, Warren. "Synchronicity and the Meaning-Making Psyche." *Journal of Analytical Psychology* 56 (4, 2011): 471–91.

Cook, Jill. *Ice-Age Art: The Arrival of the Modern Mind.* London: British Museum Press, 2013.

Cortina, Mauricio and Giovanni Liotti. "Attachment Is about Safety and Protection, Intersubjectivity Is about Sharing and Social Understanding: The Relationships between Attachment and Intersubjectivity." *Psychoanalytic Psychology* 27 (2010): 410–41.

Day, Matthew. "Religion, Off-Line Cognition, and the Extended Mind." *Journal of Cognition and Culture* 4 (1, 2007): 101–21.

Deacon, Terrence. *The Symbolic Species: The Co-Evolution of Language and the Brain.* New York: W. W. Norton & Co., 1997.

Dowson, Thomas A. "Debating Shamanism in Southern African Rock Art: Time to Move On." *South African Archaeological Bulletin* 62 (185, 2007): 49–61.

Durkheim, Emil. *The Elementary Forms of Religious Life,* trans. Joseph Ward Swain. London: George Allen and Unwin, 1915.

d'Errico, Francesco and Chris Stringer. "Evolution, Revolution or Saltation Scenario for the Emergence of Modern Cultures?" *Philosophical Transactions of the Royal Society* 366 (2011): 1060–069.

Dinnis, Rob and Chris Stringer. *Britain: One Million Years of the Human Story.* London: Natural History Museum, 2013.

Elias, Norbert, *The Symbol Theory,* vol. 13, *The Collected Works of Norbert Elias,* ed. Richard Kilminster. Dublin: University College Dublin Press, 2011.

Elias, Scott, ed. *Origins of Human Creativity and Innovation.* Amsterdam: Elsevier, 2012.

Enfield, N. J. and Stephen C. Levinson, eds. *Roots of Human Sociality: Culture, Cognition, and Interaction.* Oxford and New York: Berg, 2006.

Fisher, James. "The Evolution of the Analytic Process: Poetry and Psychoanalysis, Twin 'Sciences' of the Emotions," *Couple and Family Psychoanalysis* 4 (2014): 5–21. First published in *Journal of the British Association of Psychotherapists.*

Fox, Robin. *The Search for Society: Quest for a Biosocial Science and Morality.* New Brunswick and London: Rutgers University Press, 1989.

Gallagher, Shaun. "The Over-Extended Mind," *Versus* 113 (2012): 57–68.

Geertz, Clifford. *The Interpretation of Cultures: Selected Essays*. New York: Basic Books, 1973.

Hamilton, Malcolm. *The Sociology of Religion*, 2nd ed. New York: Routledge, 2011.

Hendriks-Jansen, Horst. *Catching Ourselves in the Act: Situated Activity, Interactive Emergence, Evolution, and Human Thought*. Cambridge, MA and London: MIT Press, 1996.

Hobson, Peter. *The Cradle of Thought*. London: Macmillan, 2002.

Hogenson, George. "The Baldwin Effect: A Neglected Influence on C. G. Jung's Evolutionary Thinking." *Journal of Analytical Psychology* 46 (4, 2001): 591–611.

Hutchins, Edwin. *Cognition in the Wild*. Cambridge, MA: MIT Press, 1995.

Hutto, Joe. *Illumination in the Flatwoods: A Season Living Among the Wild Turkey*. Guildford, CT: The Lyons Press, 1995.

Ingold, Tim. *The Perception of the Environment: Essays on Livelihood, Dwelling, and Skill*. London and New York: Routledge, 2000.

Jones, Raya, ed. *Jung and the Question of Science*. London & New York: Routledge, 2014.

Jung, C. G. *Memories, Dreams, Reflections*. London: Collins and Routledge & Kegan Paul, 1963, p. 153. Reprinted by New York: Vintage Books, 1989.

Klein, Richard and Blake Edgar. *The Dawn of Human Culture*. New York: John Wiley & Sons, 2002.

Knox, Jean. *Archetype, Attachment, Analysis: Jungian Psychology and the Emergent Mind*. Hove: Brunner-Routledge, 2003.

Knox, Jean. *Self-Agency in Psychotherapy: Attachment, Autonomy and Intimacy*. London and New York: W. W. Norton & Co., 2011.

Lakoff, George and Mark Johnson. *Metaphors We Live By*. London and Chicago: Chicago University Press, 1980.

Langer, Susanne. *Philosophy in a New Key: A Study in the Symbolism of Reason, Rite and Art*. Cambridge, MA: Harvard University Press, 1942. (2nd Edition: 1951).

Levinson, Stephen. "Interactional Biases in Human Thinking," in Esther Goody, ed., *Social Intelligence and Interaction: Expressions and Implications of the Social Bias in Human Intelligence*. Cambridge University Press, 1995, pp. 221–60.

Lévy-Bruhl, Lucien. *How Natives Think* [1910], trans. Lilian A. Clare. London: Allen & Unwin, 1926.

Lewis-Williams, David. *The Mind in the Cave*. London: Thames & Hudson, 2002.

Maiello, Suzanne. "Encounter with a Traditional Healer: Western and African Therapeutic Approaches in Dialogue," *Journal of Analytical Psychology* 53 (2, 2008): 241–60.

Malafouris, Lambros. *How Things Shape the Mind*. Cambridge, MA & London: MIT Press, 2013.

Malafouris, Lambros and Colin Renfrew ed., *The Cognitive Life of Things: Recasting the Boundaries of the Mind*. Cambridge: McDonald Institute for Archaeological Research, 2010.

Marx, Karl. "The 18th Brumaire of Louis Bonaparte" (1852). In *Karl Marx and Frederick Engels. Selected Works*. London: Lawrence and Wishart: 1968.

Mettrie, Julien Offray de la. *Machine Man and Other Writings*, ed. Anne Thompson. Cambridge University Press, 1996.

McGilchrist, Iain. *The Master and His Emissary: The Divided Brain and the Making of the Western Mind*. New Haven and London: Yale University Press, 2009.

Mithen, Steven. *The Prehsitory of the Mind: A Search for the Origins of Art, Religion and Science*. London: Thames and Hudson, 1996.

Noë, Alva. *Out of Our Heads. Why You Are Not Your Brain, and Other Lessons from the Biology of Consciousness*. New York: Hill and Wang, 2009.

Pinker, Steven. *The Blank Slate: The Modern Denial of Human Nature*. London and New York: Penguin Books, 2003.

Robbins, Michael. *The Primordial Mind in Health and Illness: A Cross-Cultural Perspective*. Hove & New York: Routledge, 2011.

Searle, John. *The Construction of Social Reality*. London and New York: Penguin Books, 1995.

Segal, Hanna. "Notes on Symbol Formation," *International Journal of Psychoanalysis* 38, (1957): 391–97.

Segal, Robert. "Jung and Lévy-Bruhl," *Journal of Analytical Psychology* 52 (5, 2007): 635–58.

Shamdasani, Sonu. *Jung and the Making of Modern Psychology: The Dream of a Science*. Cambridge University Press, 2003.

Shore, Bradd. *Culture in Mind: Cognition, Culture and the Problem of Meaning*. Oxford and New York: Oxford University Press, 1996.

Smith, Jonathan Z. "I am a Parrot (Red)," in *The Map is Not the Territory: Studies in the Histories of Religions.* Chicago, IL: University of Chicago Press: 1978, p. 281.

Spikins, Penny, Holly Rutherford and Andy Needham. "From Hominity to Humanity: Compassion From the Earliest Archaic to Modern Humans," *Time and Mind* 3:3, 2010.

Stein, Murray. *Minding the Self: Jungian Meditations on Contemporary Spirituality.* Hove and New York: Routledge, 2014.

Stevens, Anthony. *Archetype: A Natural History of the Self.* London: Routledge & Kegan Paul, 1982.

Stevens, Anthony. *The Two Million-Year-Old Self.* (No. 3, Carolyn and Ernest Fay Series in Analytical Psychology). College Station, TX: Texas A&M Press, 1993.

Stringer, Chris. *The Origin of Our Species.* London: Allen Lane, 2011.

Thompson, Evan. *Mind in Life: Biology, Phenomenology and the Sciences of Mind.* Cambridge, MA & London: Harvard University Press, 2007.

Thompson, Evan and Mog Stapleton. "Making Sense of Sense-Making: Reflections on Enactive and Extended Mind Theories." *Topoi* 28:1 (2009): 23–30.

Tomasello, Michael. *Origins of Human Communication.* Cambridge, MA: MIT Press, 2008.

Tomasello, Michael. *A Natural History of Human Thinking.* Cambridge, MA: Harvard University Press, 2014.

Turner, Victor. *The Forest of Symbols: Aspects of Ndeumbu Ritual.* Ithaca and London: Cornell University Press, 1967.

Winborn, Mark, ed., *Shared Realities: Participation Mystique and Beyond.* Skiatook, OK: Fisher King Press, 2014.

Winnicott, D.W. *Playing and Reality.* London: Tavistock, 1971.

Zilhaõ, Joaõ. "Personal Adornments and Symbolism among the Neanderthals," in S. Elias, ed., *Origins of Human Creativity and Innovation.* Amsterdam: Elsevier, 2012, pp. 35–49.

INDEX

For Product Safety Concerns and Information please contact our EU
representative GPSR@taylorandfrancis.com
Taylor & Francis Verlag GmbH, Kaufingerstraße 24, 80331 München, Germany

www.ingramcontent.com/pod-product-compliance
Lightning Source LLC
Chambersburg PA
CBHW070553270326
41926CB00013B/2293